Politics and Foreign Policy in Australia

To Ethel, Larry, and Gillian

Politics and Foreign Policy in Australia

The impact of Vietnam and conscription

Henry S. Albinski

Duke University Press *Durham, North Carolina* 1970

© 1970, Duke University Press
L.C.C. card no. 76–101128
I.S.B.N. 0–8223–0222–5

*Printed in the United States of
America by Heritage Printers, Inc.*

Table of Contents

Introduction

This book is, in part, a study of Australian external policy. More particularly, it could be understood as a study of Vietnam and conscription as dominant themes in recent foreign and defense policy. The main purpose of the book, however, is to adopt the Vietnam and conscription themes as vehicles for interpreting the interplay between external affairs and domestic politics in Australia. It is, therefore, a book about the Australian political process. Political culture characteristics, the traditions of public policy, the role of various socializing agents, parties, and political elites, manifestations of public sentiment, electoral reaction, and other features of the political process are tied together and related to the foreign policy dialogue. While there are many potential pitfalls that require such an undertaking to be couched in qualified terms, it is hoped that it will represent a contribution to the literature on Australian politics, especially with regard to linkages between foreign policy and domestic politics.

First will be noticed the degree to which and in what manner Australian political life may over time have generated a tradition of general public and elite interest in, and politically relevant response to, external questions. Attention will be paid to the contributions of political culture dimensions, foreign policy traditions, Australia's involvement in external affairs, the style and predispositions of political elites, and the weight of political institutions. The role of the media, the schools and universities, voluntary associations, and general alterations within Australian society itself will also be taken into account.

The appearance of sharp party discourse respecting Vietnam and conscription has offered Australia certain alternatives of public policy. Which parties have provided certain policy formulations will be examined, which requires an appraisal in terms of the continuity of Vietnam-conscription, as policy issues, with the principal concerns and directions of public and party thinking about external affairs. These contemporary issues are closely associated with established foreign policy legacies which have stressed nationalism and internationalism, realism and sentiment, identification of and response to external friends and foes, and the like. Furthermore, Vietnam and conscription will need to be pictured not simply according to their proffered policy options or their historic connection with substantive foreign policy traditions, but in terms of their urgency and intimacy for the Australian public.

The political process at various levels is affected not only by what the parties say, but by how and in what setting they say it. Distinctions in party leadership style, organization, and decision-making procedures carry their own importance. Different parties or factions within parties hold their own perceptions of where to draw the lines between principle and expediency, be it in interparty debate or in intraparty councils. What the Australian public knows or imagines about foreign policy issues and how it decides to cast its electoral allegiance are conditioned by images of political actors themselves as much as by the cogency or historical heritage of the debate over Vietnam and conscription. This requires a careful analysis of the style which has characterized the party dialogue on these questions, both among the parties and within them.

The dialogue over Vietnam-conscription has reached well beyond the arena of organized party politics. Interested sectors of the community have been caught up in these controversies, giving rise to protest activity and stimulating counteraction. Who and how many have become involved in organized public protest over Vietnam and conscription, and why? What do protesters hope to achieve, and how? How has protest activity affected the general, uninvolved public, and how has it looped back to recondition the content and style of the formal party debate? These are questions which will attract considerable attention in this book, because through their examination considerable insight can be gained into the nature of Australian society, both at large and in its various subcultural dimensions.

There will be an overview of the wider connotations of the Vietnam and conscription controversies for the Australian political process. What transformations have these controversies imposed upon the character and style of party life and political campaigns generally? Has the development of new avenues of political influence been measurably encouraged? What durable effects, if any, has the controversy had on the formulation and execution of significant areas of public policy, especially in external affairs and civil liberties? Have the Vietnam and conscription controversies served to increase public interest and sophistication in foreign policy generally? If so, which way has opinion moved, and with what consequences for electoral behavior and for the several competing parties? Hopefully, even tentative answers will illuminate the connective links between politics and foreign policy, and shed light on the character of the Australian political process more broadly.

This book has been prepared with the support and encouragement of the Department of Political Science, the Central Fund for Research, and the Institute for Humanistic Studies at the Pennsylvania State University. It was also made possible through the generous cooperation of many individuals and organizations in Australia. While the author wishes to express his genuine thanks to one and all, he would especially like to acknowledge the assistance of Mr. Roger C. Malot of the National Library of Australia, Canberra. Also, a special vote of thanks to the author's wife, Ethel, for her helpful editorial criticism, and to Mrs. Judy Wardle, for her expeditious and efficient typing of manuscript.

Henry S. Albinski

University Park, Pennsylvania
July 1968

Politics and Foreign Policy in Australia

Chapter 1. The Australian Public and the Salience of External Affairs: A Perspective

The Legacy of Political Culture

It is perhaps as difficult as it is important to identify and weigh those political culture characteristics which have helped to shape Australian public interest in and response to external subjects. In broad canvas, however, it is possible to mark off certain dominant strains in traditional Australian attitudes toward the political system and the style in which it has been managed. These strains, taken in bulk, have tended more to suppress than to inspire a vigorous and consistent popular concern with international affairs.

First in point is the manner in which Australian society developed and assumed its own personality. The main public issues in nineteenth-century colonial Australia were essentially social and economic, such as the prying of privilege from the hands of rural landholders and the installation of egalitarian norms in both town and country. There was no sharp and protracted battle to win popular and responsible self-government, no revolutionary struggle against the British colonial authority, no need to defend the shores from foreign invasion. In a way Australia achieved a sense of community before it gained formal statehood, which was accomplished by the conversion of the six colonies into states under the aegis of the Commonwealth of Australia in 1901. There had been no great patriotic movement, no clash with or undue reliance upon the state to mold the community into its natural shape. "Nationalism" became a social, not a governmentally or state-oriented phenomenon. In the last resort, these qualities of national unfolding encouraged an inward, rather than an outward-turning, frame of public mind.[1]

A related feature of this Australian syndrome has been a preoccupation with strengthening social and economic institutions, with populating and developing the country, and with keeping Australia racially homogeneous. A sense of pride was instilled from the building of a thriving community of Europeans domiciled halfway around the world from their ancestral place of origin. The very early appearance of a strong Labor party, a numerous and powerful trade union

3

movement among both city and country workers, and a mood among all parties generally favorable toward collectivist or at least state-involved socioeconomic policy gave momentum to a domestic orientation among the public. Australia came to prefer "the construction of a national paradise to exhaustion in international adventures."[2]

The Australians' reliance upon government probably in and of itself bred further retraction from foreign concerns. The rewarding hand of government, widely expected and accepted as a "given," promoted a feeling of letting government and politicians carry on the business of foreign affairs in their own way. This impulse of general disregard for the government's activities in external matters was reinforced by the facts of Australian geography and demography. The several colonial governments were established and thriving long before a nation or a national government or a national consciousness was created, and under a federal arrangement the states continue to attract as much if not more attention than the national government. Australians living in the island state of Tasmania, or in Western Australia or in Queensland, are physically separated from the center of national politics by great distances. This downgrades feelings of immediacy about the national political scene, where the business of foreign policy is transacted. Canberra, the national capital, is an artificial city, first occupied for official purposes as late as 1927 and still neither large (100,000) nor in the public mind a natural, magnetic, national center in the manner that Sydney and Melbourne are regarded.

The tone of public feelings about political questions at large also bears on the argument. In simplified form, it can be said that the Australian political mood is pragmatic rather than ideological, at least on domestic questions, which are considerably more salient and absorbing than foreign affairs. Though its temper is cutting, domestic political debate is mainly on details, not fundamentals. Practicality dominates over formulas, a leaning inherited from Britain and refurbished by the egalitarian tendencies peculiar to Australian settlement and the construction of social and economic institutions. "Australians do not readily join or support abstract movements, whether political or spiritual, and pragmatic slogans such as 'give him a fair go' or 'live and let live' are much more apt to be heard than 'Peace, Democracy, Liberty, and Communism.'"[3] If anything, this empiricism has engendered more skepticism than commitment toward external affairs, and reinforced other tendencies working to keep the public detached from outside concerns.[4] The primary Australian "outside" concern was for long the maintenance of racial homogeneity. This implied keeping at bay those Asian foreign powers or migrant groups which might encroach on Australia and spoil its racial symmetry and living standards. Relatedly, it also implied discouraging the presence of non-British European powers, such as France and Germany, in the Southwest Pacific. Their ambitions and rivalries, it was reasoned, could lead to conflict in the region, isolating and making Australia more vulnerable to some manner of intrusion by Asiatics. At bottom, it was a concern which was defensive, inward-turning, and attached to an intimate social value. In a word, it was parochial.

Interwar Traditions of External Policy

The traditions of Australian foreign policy and political party outlooks both, of course, result from and serve either to reinforce or to redirect established patterns of public outlook. For the time being we are concerned hardly at all with the substantive contributions of the foreign policy tradition. Rather, it is necessary to continue noticing the degree to which governmental and party approaches to external problems may have stimulated or depressed public interest.

Much of Australia's foreign and defense policy tradition, particularly up to but also exceeding the Second World War, was cast in terms which discouraged an active, perceptive public view of the outside world. One strand in this tradition has been dependence upon powerful but far-removed friends. Before 1941 this almost exclusively meant British power, symbolized by the Royal Navy and the great naval complex at Singapore. Australia is a severely underpopulated island continent. Between the turn of the century and 1968, its population nearly tripled, but the growth was only to a figure of twelve million people, living within an area virtually as large as the continental United States. Furthermore, Australia is located on the fringe of Asia, isolated from the centers of its Western heritage. Hence, it is quite understandable that many should have thought of external policy less in Australian-executed terms than in British, or Imperial, terms. This comfortable view of looking to Britain and the Empire was fortified by natural emotions of sentiment toward British institutions, the Crown, and the bonds of common population stock. It was a position which dictated that, while Australia insisted on consultation, a British, or Imperial, policy represented the realities of power, and perhaps of wisdom as well. "So long as we are under the protection of the British Empire and the noblest fleet that ever rode the ocean," the thinking ran, "we are secure; but once we get out of the Empire we are prey to any hawk that may dart from the sky."[5] Britain's trouble was Australia's trouble, even if by inference; therefore, British wars and crises required Australia's active support, and an adequate Australian military posture, including conscription, to meet such challenges.

These were the assumptions which pervaded official Australian thinking between the two world wars, when the non-Labor parties—the Nationalist (later the United Australia) and the Country party—virtually monopolized national office. This was not an approach to external affairs which inspired serious public interest. It implied that the playing out of international politics, even if they directly touched on Australia, was generally a game of great powers, and that Australian originality and initiative could not, and possibly should not, count for very much. Even William Morris Hughes's much-publicized maneuvers at Versailles to gain a security buffer by achieving Australian control over German New Guinea was preceded by his successful appeal to the Imperial War Cabinet in London.

The opposite side of the coin of Australian external tradition, epitomized by the Australian Labor party (ALP), was no more conducive to exciting public attention. As a labor party, the ALP assumed a special interest in fostering social and economic reform, which predisposed it toward a domestic orientation. But generally it failed to share in the wider, extranational orientation common to labor and social democratic parties elsewhere, or even to associate itself wholeheartedly with international socialist movements. It preferred to encourage a special Australian nationalism, of which an integral part was the prevention of non-European migration. As the champion of "White Australia," Labor made a signal contribution to "keeping Australia small, self-concerned, and without a programme for Asia."[6]

In 1908 a Labor government brought conscription to Australia, and it gladly brought Australian aid to Britain's side when war erupted in Europe in 1914. But the war of 1914–1918 stamped itself profoundly upon the party, provoking an inward-turning view of the world. As Labor prime minister during part of the First World War,

William Morris Hughes concluded that, despite conscription, the fact of *overseas service* being dependent on volunteering precluded a sufficient Australian contribution to the Allied war effort. He failed to persuade his party to endorse the imposition of conscription for overseas service. He staged two unsuccessful referendums in an attempt to collect public endorsement for such a step. He and his "conscriptionist" supporters left or were expelled from the Labor party, some gravitated to the opposition, and Hughes became prime minister of a non-Labor government.

Labor had subscribed to conscription for domestic service as much to build a self-reliant community and equitably to spread the burden of defense as to supply a ready fighting force for unspecified exigencies. The sanguinary, protracted war of 1914–1918 took its toll on Labor's willingness to contribute unlimited manpower and resources. As will be seen in a later context, the conscription controversy of 1916–1917 became confused by a large number of arguments that were both emotionally charged and internal-political in origin. The point being underscored here is that Labor emerged from the war a badly weakened and frustrated party. In summary

> it had at its centre of authority those who appealed to Australian nationalism in a way that tended towards isolation, who deprecated imperialism in a way that impeded cooperation within the British Empire, who criticised British capitalism in a way that would favour a division of classes rather than an alliance of states, who abhorred and condemned war in a way that made it hard for them to entertain the idea that war between states might come again, and for whom phrases like "compulsion" and "equality of sacrifice" were the triggers of emotion.[7]

Hence, the ALP fell under an isolationist spell. Conscription, even for domestic service, was abandoned during the 1929–1931 interlude of an interwar Labor government. Arms preparations were damned. The bugbears in Labor's roll of dishonor included international finance, munitions makers, British leadership in Imperial councils, and even League of Nations sanctions efforts.

Consequently, while one dimension in Australian foreign affairs pointed abroad to Britain and the Empire, the other, subscribed to by the ALP, represented a shutting out from international concerns. Neither tradition served to arouse the public to the relevance of for-

eign affairs, or to Australia's appropriate role as an independent
international actor.

New Initiatives in Foreign Policy: The Second World War and Onward

In a number of respects the Second World War was a real cathartic.
It shook the principal parties, and with them the public, out of the
inhibiting traditions of complacency, withdrawal, and overdependence on someone else's sheltering wing which had been dominant
earlier. First there were the shocks of war, war which for the first
time in Australia's experience threatened physically to engulf the
country. The British capital ships *Prince of Wales* and *Repulse* were
sunk in Far Eastern waters within days of the outbreak of the Japanese war. Malaya and the allegedly invincible Singapore were captured, together with thousands of Australians. The Japanese occupied
Indonesia and almost seized New Guinea—areas to Australia's immediate north. In New Guinea, Australian troops faced some of the
most bitter fighting of the Pacific war. Darwin and Townsville, towns
in metropolitan Australia, were bombed, and there was a submarine
appearance off Sydney. External affairs were no longer a remote subject, the protective shield of Britain was broken, and wars were no
longer altercations fought by Australians in esoteric, far-flung places
such as Gallipoli, Passchendaele, or Tobruk.

The ALP assumed office in late 1941 after the presiding United
Australia–Country party coalition government fell apart. It was returned in 1943 and again in 1946, remaining in power until late 1949.
Labor's wartime prime minister, John Curtin, and his minister for
external affairs, Dr. H. V. Evatt, found themselves and their party
prosecuting the war with vigor while preparing for the postwar future. The Labor government argued with Churchill to return Australian troops from the North African theater so that they could defend
Australia. It argued with America and other allies to prosecute the
Pacific war effort no less assiduously than was to be done in Europe.
It time and again demanded a strong Australian voice in collective
strategic planning. It joined New Zealand in the so-called ANZAC
Pact to arrange regional cooperation and a special Australian presence in the Southwest Pacific. At the United Nations organizational
conference at San Francisco in 1945, Evatt and the Australian delegation were exceedingly energetic, and measurably contributed to

the framing of various provisions of the charter. Regardless of the merit of particular actions, here was continuous, almost furious involvement in foreign affairs, generated by an Australian government.

The postwar period has seen no slackening of Australian involvement in foreign affairs, especially in Asia. Labor acquired a keen interest in the problems of decolonization, and was immersed in the diplomacy which eventuated in Indonesia's independence. Labor and then non-Labor (Liberal-Country party) governments sought collective security arrangements, and Australia became a member of ANZUS and SEATO. Australian forces have fought in Korea, in Malaya, in Malaysia during Indonesia's period of "confrontation," and of course in Vietnam. Australia was instrumental in founding the Colombo Plan and has donated economic and technical assistance to Asian countries under this and other auspices. It has undertaken lively diplomatic initiatives—sometimes public, at other times private—in such disputes as the framing of the Japanese Peace Treaty, the 1954 Indochinese crisis, the Chinese offshore island crises, Indonesia's quarrel with the Netherlands over Dutch New Guinea (West Irian), and the like.

Before the Second World War it could hardly be claimed that the organization of Australia's "foreign affairs" inspired any sense of urgency about learning of developments abroad, or in the representation of Australian interests overseas. The External Affairs Department was for years a government stepchild, being a division within the prime minister's office. Finally, in 1935, it was made administratively autonomous. Not until 1937 was a diplomatic officer posted to a foreign country—and he was attached to the British Embassy in Washington. By 1940, with Australia already at war, there were only five overseas diplomatic missions. In that year External Affairs had a total of fifteen diplomatic officers abroad, and fourteen in Canberra. Comparable nations such as Canada and South Africa had made their international presence known earlier and more conspicuously. But the miniscule External Affairs Department of 1940 has flowered into a major and widely spread enterprise. As of mid-1967, it had fifty-six diplomatic missions overseas, with special attention being placed on Asia and the Pacific.[8]

Some Cosmopolitan Tendencies in Australian Society

This hurried account of Australia's post-World War II external activity illustrates that prewar traditions of complacency, noninitia-

9

tive, overdependence, or abhorrence of involvement in international politics have, at least on the basis of overt behavior, been dispelled. It still remains to be seen if the Australian public has followed the lead of a more energetic foreign policy, and may have translated any such heightened awareness into politically relevant behavior. Any such conclusions which might be drawn, however, would be more than the reflections of broad Australian political culture characteristics and of old or new foreign policy traditions. They would also hinge on the nature and force of socialization processes which may or may not have been serving to inculcate a sense of foreign policy salience.

High on the list of influences pressing on the Australian public is the far more variegated and cosmopolitan atmosphere that pervades the society today than was true before the Second World War. The composition of Australia's population reflects this phenomenon most strikingly. Before the war Australia's population was almost entirely derived from British (including Irish) stock, and its growth was gradual. Since the war a concerted migration program by Labor and Liberal-Country party (L-CP) governments alike has affected the population both quantitatively and qualitatively. Since the Second World War about half of the better than four million increase in population has been attributable to migration. Furthermore, about half of these migrants have been European, not British. The significance for Australia has been far deeper than simply the infusion of foreign languages and specialty restaurants. The presence of Greeks, Italians, Poles, Yugoslavs, Hungarians, and others has fashioned a society with a mix of backgrounds, values, temperaments, and the like, and has challenged many of the traditional, self-oriented and satisfied, even smug, propensities of the past.

Additionally, Australia's contact with Asians has left its mark. Thousands of Asian students, under Colombo Plan sponsorship or otherwise, have come to Australia to study at its universities. While the ban on Asian migration has in principle been retained, it has been visibly relaxed, with the result that by 1968 about a thousand Asians were quietly being allowed to enter and settle in the country. Large numbers of persons from commercial, journalistic, and other foreign, and especially Asian, delegations visit Australia annually. Australians themselves, many in private capacities, have increasingly been visiting Asian countries, including mainland China. Trade with Asian countries is flourishing, and Japan has become Australia's most important export market, bypassing Britain. Foreign goods, ranging from Japanese automobiles to Chinese shoes, are readily available to the Australian buying public. Foreign investment in Australia, cultivated and provided with incentives by the government, is making its own contribution to the diversification and remolding of the Australian temper.

These are only highlights of the broadening, deparochializing tendencies which are abroad in contemporary Australia. Separately and collectively, they have stirred and sharpened public awareness of the world beyond the Australian island-continent, and of that world's pertinence to Australian interests.

The Press as Public Socializer

But how thoroughly do Australians become familiar with externally oriented issues, especially as such issues relate to Asia? Here some comments are in order about the socializing function of the media, the schools and universities, and private organizations. Finally, comment will be needed about the public impact of the setting and style in which party politics address themselves to issues of foreign and defense policy.

The press, despite the advent of radio and television, continues to enjoy the reading attention of over 80 per cent of the public. The question of adequacy of foreign news coverage and interpretation arises first. Historically, the Australian press has, by common consent, been disgracefully deficient in this area. Before the Second World War and for some time afterward, the press was conspicuously parochial, intermittent in its coverage of foreign news, and more apt to stress the European than the Asian dimensions of world politics. In a way the press was catering to and strengthening ingrained Australian attitudes which either looked inward or simply skipped over Asia while searching for news from or about Britain. Then, too, London was the source of most news. Australian foreign correspondents were nearly a nonexistent breed.[9] Writing in 1958, a former editor of the *Sydney Morning Herald* was hardly sympathetic:

> The majority of Australians are still astonishingly ignorant about the rest of the world. They neither know nor care what is happening in Europe or Asia or America. Even the best newspapers give ridiculously little space to foreign affairs, which at best are

reported in an arbitrary and spasmodic way that makes it virtually impossible to follow them intelligently. The popular papers ignore foreign news altogether, and always prefer a good local story to the best foreign one.[10]

Such criticism, even if mainly deserved into the 1950s, has begun to lose its relevance. The actual amount of space devoted to foreign news has been moving ahead over the years. By the close of the Second Summer School on Journalism conducted in Canberra early in 1966, one reviewer wrote, "'More Australian Foreign Correspondents' had become an article of faith, if not quite a battle cry."[11] This call, it should be noticed, was for more correspondents, with no implication that Australian correspondents were not already in some evidence in Asia. Australian newspaper correspondents were on special assignment in China as early as 1956. As of the latter part of 1965, two full-time Australian newspaper correspondents were employed in Singapore, one in Djakarta, and one in Tokyo. There were also some correspondents who occasionally visited Asia, and a group of resident representatives of the Australian Broadcasting Commission. By early 1968, in fact, resident ABC correspondents were stationed in Saigon, Djakarta, Singapore, Kuala Lumpur, Tokyo, and New Delhi, as well as in London, Washington, and New York. When the first Australian battalion arrived in Vietnam in 1965, special newspaper correspondents were dispatched there, but were withdrawn after the novelty of the Australian presence there had faded. Since then the status of Australian reporting from Vietnam has become more systematic, but as of early 1968 the press continued to rely on intermittent newspaper correspondents' representation or the pooled services of Australian Associated Press, an Australian agency responsible for collecting foreign news. The standard of reporting has also been improved over the past several years because of the External Affairs Department's increased concern with public relations, including its creation of a public information officer whose primary responsibility entails the provision of factual and background material for media representatives.

Australian papers are more than before inclined to publish analyses and background stories, an area in which the *Australian*, a paper founded in mid-1964 with the intention of attracting a nationwide readership, excels. Generally, however, much of the interpretative commentary on Vietnam, aside from editorials whose level of perception should be ranked about "fair," is contributed by non-Australian columnists or Australians who frequently neglect to relate Vietnamese developments to Australian problems and policies.[12]

By and large, Australians resemble other national reading publics in that their foremost interest in a newspaper does not lie in foreign news or commentaries. A survey conducted in 1954 among the readership of the Hobart *Mercury* revealed that only 23 per cent listed overseas news as one or more of their preferences, while only 3 per cent indicated a wish for enlarged overseas coverage. A 1960 Sydney survey found that 31 per cent of those polled believed that newspapers overemphasized overseas life.[13] In a nationwide survey conducted in 1966, 44 per cent mentioned world news as one type of material they *might* read about in the press; when asked to rate the quantitative adequacy of international news in the press, 56 per cent replied "right amount," 20 per cent "not enough," and only 7 per cent "too much."[14] A year earlier, however, a survey commissioned by the Melbourne *Age*, one of Australia's better papers, had actually shown a majority of its readership desiring more overseas news and/or commentary.

The above surveys are not particularly comparable. In broad terms, however, they do seem to suggest that, while interest in foreign affairs press material continues to be limited to a minority, that minority is growing. As press coverage continues to expand and becomes more sophisticated, the Australian public is becoming increasingly inducted into an interest and understanding of foreign affairs. It is a tendency which, since the late 1950s, has been reinforced by the appearance of semipopular periodicals which provide incisive commentary on international and other political topics. Among these the most prominent would be the refurbished weekly *Bulletin* and the fortnightly *Nation*, both published in Sydney but with national circulation.

Radio, Television, and Private Associations as Public Socializers

In Australia both radio and television, the latter introduced in 1956, include private and federal government (Australian Broadcasting Commission) ownership. Since the popularization of television, radio in Australia has not been a significant disseminator of programs which widely enhance awareness of foreign or public affairs generally. However, it does attract some audience for such programs as a series of lectures on "Ferment in Asia," the regular

"Guest of Honour" series, or the broadcast of parliamentary debates. As part of the 1966 survey cited above, respondents were asked which of the three—newspapers, television, or radio—they would be most likely to miss. Forty-one per cent named newspapers, 36 per cent named television, but only 19 per cent chose radio. On being asked which of these three media ranked highest in such categories as providing the most complete news, or presenting things most intelligently, or giving the clearest understanding of issues at the federal election, only 15, 11, and 10 per cent of the surveyed group ranked radio first on these three criteria, respectively.[15]

Special mention should be made of the ABC's broadcasting of federal parliamentary debates, which it has been required to do since 1946. Only selected portions of the debates are broadcast, both from the House of Representatives and the Senate. Here is the potential for easy public access to ministerial statements, debates, and questions on international relations. But the popularity of this ABC service never was widespread, and has dropped markedly since its advent. Australian Gallup Poll data revealed the parliamentary debate listening habits shown in Table 1 during the initial years of the service.[16]

Table 1. *People Listening to Parliamentary Debates (percentage)*

	1947	1950	1953
Listened more than twice a month	39	35	24
Listened one or two times a month	19	23	17
Never listened	42	42	59

A 1966 survey drew responses indicating that 3 per cent listened regularly, 19 per cent occasionally, 9 per cent hardly ever, and 53 per cent never.[17]

Television, however, is quite another story. The public affairs programs offered by both commercial and ABC stations constitute a distinct minority of programming time, though the ABC is the more active of the two in this regard. Not until the early 1960s did ABC television equip itself with polished, in-depth presentations of public affairs programs, including overseas subject matter.[18] Its popularity has, in turn, enjoyed a substantial climb. Between 1965 and 1967 the number of Sydney families who turned to the ABC during prime broadcasting hours rose from 74,000 to 90,000, and in Melbourne from 47,000 to 91,000. Much of this programming was not "educational," but public affairs subject matter was deliberately drawn in, to fall before or after popular presentations.[19] An ABC survey in Tasmania revealed that "current affairs programmes would retain large sections of the mainland audience at a highly competitive viewing time. Indeed, in several cases, the A.B.C. share of audience within these peak hours has exceeded that of other channels with exclusively entertainment programmes."[20]

Nor has commercial television been lacking in innovative, public-informational programming. In April 1966, for instance, the Australian Television Network and the University of Sydney collaborated in staging a debate on Vietnam and conscription between the minister for the army, J. M. Fraser, and the then deputy leader of the ALP opposition, E. G. Whitlam. Among the studio audience, which entered the discussion, were students, members of anti-Vietnam protest groups, churchmen, academics, and members of parliament. It was the first program of its kind on Australian television. Broadcast at peak time throughout most of Australia, it was estimated to have been watched by millions.[21]

At all events, since nearly 90 per cent of the adult population has television in the home and half of this number watches every night, television has become a pervasive medium. Its power to inform and to enlighten may be something else again, though 19 per cent of a survey population named current affairs and 9 per cent named documentary programs as enjoying their regular viewing.[22]

To this discussion of the media should be added a note about the special place occupied by nonpartisan organizations whose purpose lies in enlarging public interest in external subjects.

Writing of the Australian Institute of International Affairs (AIIA), of which he is director, Sir Alan Watt has observed that, while the institute's precise extent of influence is difficult to measure, "there is no doubt that, through the dissemination of different points of view, it has contributed significantly to the formation of a more informed and questioning public opinion."[23] The institute has, indeed, probably become the principal unofficial organization which discharges such a function. It dates back to 1933, but only since the Second World War has it had branches in all states and in Canberra. While a good part of its work—publication, lecture, and seminar sponsorship—has been contributed to and benefited from by professional academic, political, and journalistic figures, the more educated portions of the general public have increasingly become exposed and even involved. In recognition of its work, in 1963 the institute was awarded $75,000 (U.S.) by the Ford Foundation, and an additional $100,000 in 1968.

Other groups have also made contributions toward the general end of better informing and involving the public considerably beyond the scope of their formal membership. Among them are the Australian Association for the United Nations, the Australian-American Association, and the Australian Institute of Political Science, whose appearance preceded the AIIA by a year.[24] Some politicized groups such as the Australia-China Society and the Australia-Free China Association, which support Peking and Taipei, respectively, have also served to publicize international affairs in their own manner.

The Role of the Schools and Universities

A singularly important channel for conditioning serious public interest in the outside world is, of course, the educational system. Australian secondary schools have yet to make significant strides toward altering a pedagogical approach which has been heavily prescriptive, geared toward the passing of various stages of examinations, and deficient in substantial offerings in Asian-related subjects. Some progress, however, is certainly being manifested. One illustration was the 1967 ABC series "Getting to Know Our Asian Neighbours," which was beamed to schools across the nation. In the same year New South Wales introduced a program of secondary school Asian social studies which provided linkage with Australian history, society, and external affairs.[25] Progress in teaching Asian languages at the secondary level has been painful and slow, but at least there is mounting awareness of the kinds of difficulties that need to be overcome. In early 1968, among some 2,500 secondary schools in Australia, Indonesian was being taught in 31, Japanese in 17, Malay in 5, and Chinese in only 1.[26] The teaching of Japanese, Chinese, and Indonesian in New South Wales has suffered in part through the lateness in the secondary school child's career at which such study could be begun. Victoria reported in 1968 that only 9 of its 300 high schools offered Asian languages—8 taught Indonensian and 1 taught Japanese. At the same time, however, Queensland was reporting successful pilot Japanese language instruction in selected Brisbane, Townsville, and Toowoomba high schools.[27] Interestingly, adult study of Asian languages, especially among businessmen, is apparently impressive.[28]

More and longer secondary school attendance, assisted by legally defined increases in the school-leaving age and expanding financial inducements from state and federal governments, is creating a much better educated population. Between 1939 and 1963, while the population at large rose 60 per cent, total school population expanded by 250 per cent.

The growth of university enrollments has been particularly dramatic. In 1939 the universities enrolled only about 14,000 students. By 1963 the figure had moved to 70,000, and by 1968 to approximately 100,000. This rise in university enrollment has, for present purposes, contributed to two advances in the state of public awareness on international topics. For one, curricular changes are endowing Australian higher education with more intensive and sophisticated approaches to domestic and international studies, and with increased attention to Asia and the Pacific. It is something of an irony that the first three major books on Australian foreign policy written by single authors should have been written not by Australians, but by Americans.[29] Conditions of this sort are rapidly being remedied. The study of political science and international relations is quickly shedding its previously staid, institutional character. Asian studies are moving forward, particularly at the Australian National University (ANU), the only federally sponsored university in the country.[30] There, in the School of General Studies (basically undergraduate), the Faculty of Oriental Studies offers work in Asian civilization, South Asian and Buddhist studies, and Chinese, Japanese, and Indonesian languages and literature. At the ANU's Research School of Pacific Studies, Institute of Advanced Studies (Ph.D. program), are departments of anthropology and sociology, economics, geography, international relations, Far Eastern history, Pacific history, and a New Guinea Research Unit. Qualitative changes such as these at Australian universities have brought more and better-trained persons in international relations and Asian studies, who by virtue of their public as well as academic writing and appearances have stimulated wider Australian appreciation of these subjects.

Secondly, the sharing in higher education by increasing proportions of the population is forming a more alert and serious-minded public. The author of a book on the Australian press has surmised that "if there were to be a sharp shift upwards in our educational levels, it would no doubt in due course be reflected in the character of the press."[31] This upward shift is already, and conspicuously, in train. Available Australian data confirm the unsurprising fact that the higher the educational level of the population, the more sophisticated their media tastes will be. Surveys made in 1960 in Sydney and Melbourne disclosed that the highest incidence of readership of the best newspapers in the two cities—the *Sydney Morning Herald* and the *Age*, respectively—was among upper occupational/social class persons, while the lowest incidence was among unskilled/industrial class people.[32] A Canberra survey inquired about the most important sources of information relative to the 1963 electoral campaign. The greatest proportion of choices on behalf of televised campaign speeches came from persons of primary education only; the highest proportion of persons identifying newspaper and magazine articles were those who had completed tertiary education.[33] In other words, the best educated selected the medium which provided a daily and in-depth source of news and interpretation. Improvements in educational levels, reading tastes, and the actual quality of newspapers are paralleling and reinforcing one another, resulting in better information on the part of more people in the area of foreign affairs.

Public Perceptions of Politicians

An interested and reflective public approach to overseas developments is also affected by the nature and style of political actors, and by the system in which they operate. One such consideration relates to the apparently dominant Australian proclivity, as Prime Minister Holt himself confessed in a 1967 lecture, to support a grudging democracy in which politicians are held in low esteem.[34] This phenomenon has not been sufficiently explored and must be treated guardedly, but some interesting evidences of its existence can be inferred. A survey conducted among 127 Melbourne workers in 1950–1952 disclosed that only 15 felt politics to be important. Thirty-nine said they were uninterested in politics. Seventy-three "inclined to the view that politics in Australia are a self-contained field of doubtfully honest activity that bears no relation at all to the interests or purposes of the ordinary citizen, and of these 63 (or half of the whole group) expressed this view ('all politicians are crooks,' etc.) without any favourable qualification at all."[35]

In 1959 a group of University of Sydney political scientists analyzed letters to the press written on the occasion of a proposal to increase federal parliamentary salaries. The letters were overwhelmingly hostile toward the idea of a salary rise. Politicians tended to be portrayed as managers of the political shop, not as leaders. They were defined as performing work of no particularly high status, and as being interested in self-aggrandizement and the grabbing of spoils. They were different from ordinary people; the distinction between "them" and "us" was painfully clear.[36] In 1966, furthermore, among those who *did* listen to ABC broadcasts of parliamentary proceedings, only 11 per cent felt that their opinion of parliamentarians had been raised, as against 29 per cent who thought it lowered—nearly three times as many; 60 per cent thought that their opinions of politicians had not been affected.[37]

No comprehensive or confident explanation of this Australian trait can be attempted here. Some of it is probably traceable to the makeup of political culture—of casually expecting government to perform sizable socioeconomic functions, but failing to ascribe to government and its practitioners any inordinately favorable status. Despite expecting government to perform, Australians, in their particular sense of stubborn individualism and egalitarian castelessness, at one and the same time suspect those who, by placing themselves above ordinary people, might encroach on these tenets. Also, at least among ALP supporters, antipolitician feeling might be strengthened by the tested tradition that Labor politicians are more the servants than the masters of the allegedly mass-based party organization.[38]

The upshot of the tendency to disparage politicians would seem to affect the credibility of politicians' pronouncements. Given the historic public apathy toward external affairs, the importunings of politicians that the people become excited and committed in this area would, in Australia, seem to count for relatively less than in other, less politically skeptical societies.

Parliament and Parliamentarians

The character of Australia's national political institutions and their usage would, on balance, appear to compound public ignorance of and indifference toward foreign issues. Cabinet government in Australia is very much like its counterparts elsewhere. The government of the day is the preeminent decision-making agent. Parliament, consisting of a House of Representatives, to which the government is responsible, and a Senate, is essentially a ratifying, not an initiating body. Party discipline is strong, and governments normally hold their House of Representatives majorities and therefore survive. The parliamentary committee system is fragile, sustaining the government's unwillingness to share authority.

The Australian Parliament has been relatively ineffective as a forum for disseminating constructive ideas about foreign policy among the public. The mere opportunity to ventilate the subject is meager. Up to 1949 the *combined* membership of the House and the Senate was slightly over a hundred. Even though in that year the two chambers were nearly doubled, Australia continues to have small parliamentary membership. The House has just over 120 members, fewer than half the number in the Canadian House of Commons. After ministers have been drawn into the government, in absolute terms few parliamentarians with an interest and capability in foreign affairs remain to debate from the backbenches. Furthermore, the Australian Parliament is in session for relatively few days in the year. Elections for the House must fall at least triennially, and in election years the House will sit about fifty days. In other, nonelection years, it will be in session on the order of sixty-five to seventy-five days.[39] Therefore, there are relatively few parliamentarians, with relatively few opportunities to speak.

A related factor pertains to the composition of Australian parliamentarians. Up to and until shortly after the Second World War the number of university graduates in Parliament was pitifully small. In the House, following the 1922 and 1940 elections, 7 out of 75 and 10 of 74 members, respectively, were graduates. In the Senate, there was only 1 graduate out of 36 senators in each of these years. At the beginning of 1967 about a quarter of the House and a fifth of the Senate held university degrees—in relative terms, at least, a marked improvement over earlier decades. As might be expected, a disproportionate number of university-trained people are siphoned off to the ministry.[40] Since 1949 the vocational background of parliamentarians has undergone very little change. In the main, persons from professions most apt to supply informed, serious commentary on external affairs have been fairly scarce. In the House elected in 1963, there were almost twice as many persons from pastoral and primary producing backgrounds as lawyers; twice as many manual workers and trade union officials as teachers; more shopkeepers than journalists; a host of persons from commercial and white collar backgrounds.[41]

Parliament's lack of adequate foreign policy information has detracted from building the type of informed discussion which, from the public's vantage point, would be especially interesting and persuasive. Individual parliamentarians have traditionally suffered from insufficient research and staff facilities. A very large proportion of documents held by the External Affairs and Defense Departments is classified and unavailable to Parliament. The fifty-year rule on keeping archives locked was changed in 1966, but with the date for available materials being moved only to 1922. Australia did not follow the British lead, undertaken shortly thereafter, of instituting a straight thirty-year rule. For some years a small number of parliamentarians from both sides of the aisle have been able to attend and benefit from sessions of the United Nations General Assembly, and from international conferences such as those staged by the Inter-Parliamentary Union and the Commonwealth Parliamentary Association. Firsthand overseas exposure has, however, been broadened in recent years, notably since 1964, when the minister for external affairs began to organize periodic overseas investigative tours by fairly sizable interparty parliamentary delegations.

Information which might have come to Parliament from committee work has been negligible. A Joint Committee on Foreign Affairs was authorized in 1950, but its work has, in the main, been of secondary importance. For some time only ministers could refer subjects for the committee's consideration. Ministers carefully supervised the type of material brought before the committee, and were the judges of whether committee sessions should be closed or public. The committee has produced several reports, but they have been rare, brief, and generally unedifying. Until 1967 the committee's usefulness, either to parliamentarians themselves or to the public, was curtailed by the refusal of the ALP opposition to participate in its work. The reasons were both technical and partisan. The tame, officially controlled nature of the committee's activities was felt by the ALP to bring the committee to a state of near irrelevance. Also, Labor was much afraid that its participation could, given the required pledges of secrecy taken by committee members respecting aspects of the group's work, create an impression of ALP acquiescence in government foreign policy. The installation of the Democratic Labor party (DLP) on the committee also touched a raw Labor nerve, since the

DLP was regarded as a schismatic, unmitigatedly anti-ALP party. Labor's open deprecation of the committee lowered the body's standing as a place of serious foreign policy examination. As its own chairman wrote, "the Committee has been a useful study group but has done little to analyse the great issues of the day and to enlighten the Parliament and the people in the field of foreign relations. And this can be traced to the determination of the government to safeguard the security of External Affairs information and Ministerial responsibility for policy."[42]

This ministerial attitude toward the Foreign Affairs Committee has been symptomatic of the treatment accorded to Parliament at large. Over the years debates on external relations have on occasion been enlivening and helpful to all who might have cared to take notice, but this has not been the regular pattern. Traditionally, ministers have been concerned "with how to bring together enough innocuous material to satisfy parliamentary formalities. The result is that ministerial statements on foreign affairs and defence are not only infrequent, but are so bureaucratically processed as to exclude, wherever possible, invitation to critical and informative debate."[43]

Political Style and Foreign Policy Presentation to 1949

If Parliament itself has not shown itself to be a particularly effective vehicle for socializing the Australian public into a foreign affairs interest, can much the same indictment be made of the political dialogue in general, and of electoral campaigns more explicitly? For half a century external affairs did from time to time intrude into political campaigns, but it is questionable whether when they did intrude the electorate's vote was predicated on the available foreign policy options offered by the parties, or that such campaigns provided the basis for a less jejune, more permanent and penetrating public appreciation of external affairs.

The referendums of 1916 and 1917 and the parliamentary election of 1917 were directly concerned with conscription. They became suffused, however, with issues and considerations of an essentially domestic nature. The split in the ALP created envenomed exchanges between personalities and within the party organization, which transcended the conscription issue per se. Dr. Daniel Mannix, the Roman Catholic coadjutor archbishop of Melbourne, prominently inserted himself on the side of the anticonscriptionists, in part to support the Australian Irish population's resentment against the British for their behavior in the Irish Easter Rebellion and its aftermath. This was an emotional question for the Irish, but one which had little to do with the intrinsic merits of conscription. The pressures of war created austerity conditions in Australia. Portions of the labor movement began to wonder if wartime windfall earnings by some privileged Australians were not a travesty. Farmers became irritated over worker shortages. The government's imposition of fierce censorship controls, executed in an amateurish and imperious fashion, rankled deeply. Work stoppages during the war derived from a potpourri of economic, sentimental, and factional motives, not simply a reasoned objection to overseas conscription. Thus, "conscription" and external affairs questions of interest to Australia were blurred and considerably swallowed up by extraneous considerations.

The climate of opinion on external affairs after the war contained something of a paradox. By one measure, the fierceness of the wartime battles over conscription should have raised the level of political and public tension over foreign policy. In a way this was true. But the resulting dichotomy in postwar politics was between isolationism and withdrawal on the one hand and beguiled faith in British and Imperial policy and protection on the other. Neither outlook, as has been seen, was at all conducive to stimulating rational debate about the world at large, or Australia's self-developed reactions toward it.

The 1937 election was heavily oriented toward foreign and defense policy. However, despite some weakening of established isolationist and British-reliance attachments on the Labor and non-Labor sides, respectively, the old images stuck, and were the basis of partisan charges and countercharges. Therefore, so far as the public was concerned, the old external policy desiderata were still in place.[44] The campaigns of 1940 and 1943 should likewise be discounted as having contributed much to a sharpening and cosmopolitanization of public views on external matters, despite being wartime elections. The war was treated by the parties more in terms of efficiency of execution, both domestically and abroad, rather than in terms of broad policy. At all events, when in 1943 Labor was elected to office in its own right, the non-Labor forces were in a state of internal turmoil and not capable of mounting a concerted, credible campaign.

In the postwar period it is probably necessary to wait until 1963 before encountering a prominent foreign and defense policy focus in electoral campaigns. In the late 1940s, with Labor still governing, the opposition Liberal and Country parties did take shots at the ALP's energetic concern for emerging nations and ostensible contribution to the weakening of British and Old Imperial ties. But what filtered down to the public was as much impressions about a man as about issues. Evatt as external affairs minister overshadowed everyone else in the Labor government, including the prime minister, in his demonstrative conduct of Australia's foreign policy, and the opposition's criticism was directed as much at him and his methods as at the actual policies he pursued. In all likelihood Evatt's extraordinary personal identification with the foreign policy movements of the time, as well as the barrage of criticism he personally received, dulled the public's understanding of what the substance and merit of prevailing foreign policy were.

After the war there was a sense of exhaustion and a natural turning to domestic concerns after six years of overseas sacrifice and internal austerity and restrictions. The Labor government, even before the war was done, began to present ambitious plans for social and economic reform and reconstruction. Public constitutional referenda designed to increase Commonwealth authority in these areas were held, controversial legislation was introduced, landmark judicial decisions by the High Court of Australia were handed down, debate burned over residual wartime economic controls, and the net result was to pull attention away from what was transpiring in foreign policy. The issue of domestic Communism became a lively, partisan topic. Communist influence in trade unions, Communist responsibility for strikes and other work stoppages, and alleged Communist intentions to subvert Australia were trumpeted about, including in the 1949 election, when Labor was evicted from office. While the Liberal and Country party complaints against Communism included reference to the threat of Communism abroad, such problems as the appearance of a Communist regime in China were strictly subordinated in the public mind to variations which were played on the theme of Communism within the country.[45]

Political Style and Foreign Policy Presentation in the Age of Menzies

During the period of Liberal-Country party government under Sir Robert Gordon Menzies (1949–1966), the public's awareness of and interest in external affairs was aided by the visibly energetic foreign policy which was being conducted. There were, however, offsetting political constraints operating in Australian political life. Menzies' domination over his ministers, his party, and Parliament probably created an overpersonalized image of Australian foreign policy, similar to though less prominent than that which had occurred under Evatt. Sir Percy Spender, Richard (later Lord) Casey, Sir Garfield Barwick, and Paul Hasluck, Menzies' external affairs ministers, were able men, and Casey especially, after holding the external affairs portfolio for nine years, left a lasting contribution in terms of better and stronger relations with Asian states. However, Menzies' over-bearing personality most likely muddied public impressions of the policies which were undertaken. Menzies was a most untypical Australian politician, a patrician to his fingertips. He was polished, courtly, eloquent, and brilliant; he was also acerbic, arrogant, domineering, and, in sentiment, an unreconstructed disciple of Crown and (Old) Commonwealth, a predisposition he made no effort to conceal.

While the Menzies government's foreign policy amplified the country's involvement at large, made connections with Asia, and reached for security bonds with America, Menzies maintained a personal coolness toward Asia and its political elites. It was an emotional problem of some proportion for him to adjust to the notion of a loosely strung, multiracial Commonwealth. On several occasions he delivered himself of virtuoso (and unsuccessful) performances in international politics, rather to the embarrassment of his own colleagues, as during the Suez crisis of 1956, at the United Nations in the aftermath of the 1960 U-2 incident, and in the 1960 and 1961 South African–Commonwealth crises, during which his was the strongest white Commonwealth voice raised against the ventilation of South Africa's racial policies. While Australian foreign policy was independently constructed, concerned with Asia, and American-reliant in content, some of its style left a contrasting image, perhaps encouraging some popular feelings of cynicism and confusion.

The actual conduct of campaigns by the L-CP during Menzies' tenure probably abetted public failure to come to grips with external problems in clearer, more reflective terms. Most elections under Menzies lacked the bite of incisive debate over external issues. When the debate did arise, it was obfuscated by ancillary issues, usually referring to Communism in general or to the trustworthiness and responsibility of the Labor party and of its leadership. In the 1951 campaign, at the peak of the Korean War, the overhanging issue was the government's wish to outlaw the Communist party, an issue on which Labor had evinced equivocation and which offered the L-CP opportunity to serve up an undifferentiated plate of external Communism, domestic Communism, and Labor's incapacity to be trusted in office. In 1954, at the height of the Indochinese crisis, neither party group so much as mentioned foreign policy problems in its policy speech, and in fact the entire campaign was almost equally devoid of any external affairs guidance to the electorate.

In 1954–1955 the Labor party split. A new, fiercely anti-Communist and largely Catholic-supported group, briefly known as the Anti-Communist Labor party and thereafter the Democratic Labor party, appeared. At its 1955 federal conference in Hobart, the ALP swung to the left respecting the commitment of Australian forces overseas, the seating of Peking at the United Nations, and the Southeast Asia Treaty Organization. The presence of the DLP in the electoral field from 1955 onward did in its fashion invigorate the foreign policy discourse, since the party served the tendentious cause of exposing the dangers of international Communism to Australia, and bruited the notion that the parent ALP had to be denied office almost at any cost, since it had made itself the unwitting protagonist of an appeasing foreign policy.

The 1955, 1958, and 1961 campaigns on the government and Labor sides were not distinguished by basic collisions or even serious dialogue over foreign policy. When external affairs were broached by Labor, it was largely in niggling terms, such as huffing at the government's inconsistency in countenancing trade with China while failing to recognize it diplomatically. In 1961, with the country caught in an economic squeeze, Labor's attack was almost exclusively domestic. Although the DLP was unrelenting in its diatribes against Labor's foreign policy, the government's campaign tended to be short on foreign policy specifics. Both the DLP and the government parties, however, when introducing external affairs into campaigns, did so with the purpose of besmirching Labor's image. The assaults against Evatt in 1955 and 1958, while he was ALP Leader and therefore an aspirant to the prime ministership, were intensely personal. The ALP was impeached on grounds of being locked in the deadly embrace of a small, pernicious clique of men in the party organization, who were themselves indifferent to insidious Communist influences upon the party, and whose signals were obeyed by the parliamentary party and its leadership. The question of validity or nonvalidity in ALP foreign policy, for whatever attention Labor paid it in campaigns, was therefore somewhat dissipated in the din of allegations about cranks, fanatics, subversives, and innocents running about the party.

The 1963 House of Representatives election was the last before first conscription for overseas service, and then conscription and Vietnam, became public controversies. In that campaign all parties gave unmistakable emphasis to foreign and defense questions. At particular issue were the status of Australian troops dispatched to protect Malaysia against Indonesian confrontation, the terms on which an American naval signal station on Australian territory had been authorized, Labor's proposal for a nuclear-free zone in the Southern Hemisphere, Australia's military preparedness, SEATO, and the American alliance generally. But as a campaign it was burdened more than any since the Labor split by assaults against the ALP's credibility as an alternative government. Labor had just passed through a number of internal hassles over overseas troop commitments, the signal station, and the nuclear-free zone proposal. In domestic affairs, the parliamentary leadership, the federal conference, the federal executive, and the Labor government in New South Wales had just been entangled in a raucous, confusing, and demeaning tug of war over aid to parochial schools. Enormous political currency was extracted by Labor's opponents from these essentially internal Labor problems, with the result that the 1963 campaign, while punctuated by foreign and defense policy exchanges, seemed to make Labor's fitness to govern the salient issue.

The Public and Foreign Policy Salience: Some Evidences

The thrust of the foregoing discussion has been that, while external issues have on occasion figured prominently in elections, for a variety of reasons the public has not been subjected to a reasonably sharp, uncluttered dialogue on this subject. So far as assessment is possible, the available data would seem to confirm that Australians traditionally have not perceived external questions in campaigns as being salient, and have not made electoral judgments which have had much to do with preferences of one party-recommended line of foreign policy over another.

Prior to the 1951 election, a Gallup Poll survey inquired what one thing was most apt to decide the respondent's vote. Two per cent of L-CP voters opted for "good defense policy," 1 per cent of Labor voters claimed foreign policy, and all other responses were domestically inclined.[46] Before the 1954 election, another Gallup survey asked government and ALP supporters what the best campaign arguments of their respective parties were. Two per cent of L-CP voters elected foreign policy. Although 2 per cent of Labor voters chose "against Japanese," the survey recorded a blank for ALP followers under the "foreign policy" category.[47] It should be recalled that the 1954 campaign was conducted in the heat of the Indochinese crisis. Another survey shortly thereafter asked, "If the French are driven out of Indo-China, do you think Australia will be greatly affected?" To this query, 37 per cent replied "greatly affected," 17 per cent "affected a little," 16 per cent "won't be affected," and 30 per cent had no opinion.[48]

The early 1960s apparently did not speed up public enthusiasm for external issues in electoral campaigns. After the 1961 election, a Gallup survey directed its attention to why the public felt the Menzies government had nearly been evicted. No foreign or defense topic, or foreign or defense policy at large, was among the nine responses given by 99 per cent of the interviewed sample.[49] A passage from a study which analyzed the LaTrobe (Victoria) federal by-election in 1960 is worth quoting in this respect. External questions had not seriously entered into the campaign, but Menzies' highly controversial and publicized handling of the 1960 South African–Commonwealth crisis, in the aftermath of Sharpeville, did intrude in the midst of the campaign:

> The issue broke during the campaign. Of those interviewed after it came alive, 6 per cent mentioned South Africa. An equal number of Labor voters and Liberals quoted it as evidence of their party's greater ability in handling foreign affairs. In one case only—a part-time accountant, retired, who had voted Liberal until the by-election—did it seem to be a matter which actually had influenced the respondent's vote.[50]

For the 1963 election, celebrated for its stress on foreign policy, once again the underrelevance of this theme for the electorate seems to have been confirmed. A sample of Canberra voters, somewhat *higher* in education and socioeconomic status than the general population, was tested. After nearly year-long public discussion, following the ALP's formal campaign policy address but just before the Prime Minister had delivered his, the group was asked to react to Labor's insistence on a treaty to govern Australia's troop commitment in Malaysia. Of the sample, 31 per cent saw it as a nonpartisan item, and another 20 per cent identified it as a Liberal, not a Labor, point of view. In other words, 51 per cent of the group was absolutely wrong simply in judging which party stood where on this key issue.[51]

The Canberra survey also was interested to learn what elements of ALP leader Arthur Calwell's policy speech were recalled after less than a week following its delivery. The authors of the survey concluded that "the tendency to recall items of domestic policy rather than defence and foreign policy is quite striking, and makes one somewhat suspicious of the proposition that the 1963 election was about defence and foreign policy—unless it is the case that the expectation that a Labor leader talks about domestic policies rather than external ones is strong enough to affect recall markedly."[52]

Data such as these may require some qualification. When a voter has marked his ballot or replied to a survey research question that he was influenced by some issue such as "Communism" or "the best party for the job," the campaign treatment of external policies probably has contributed to such general judgment, consciously or not. Most people, furthermore, habitually vote for a particular party. Their vote would not be influenced by what was said about foreign policy, or how it was said. Their selection of strategic issues in response to a survey interview, before an election or retrospectively, would probably have little bearing on the conduct and programmatic nuance of the election.

It is, nevertheless, difficult to escape the conclusion that, prior to the entry of conscription and Vietnam into political controversy, the public was not much interested in or affected by electoral presentations of foreign policy, and therefore that elections were seldom if ever decided, or even the magnitude of swings perceptibly influenced, by external considerations. This tendency was buttressed by established political culture traits, by prewar traditions of party views on foreign and defense policy, by the unsympathetic image of Australian politicians, by the shortcomings of Parliament as a communicator, and by the style of political warfare. By the 1950s and 1960s, however, some countervailing tendencies were developing in the system. Among them were quantitative and qualitative educational developments, population changes and fresh exposures to Asia, improvements in the projection of foreign affairs material by the various media, and the energy of Australian foreign policy activity from the Second World War onward. It is against this background of public exposure to, interest in, and electoral response to external subjects that the appearance of the Vietnam-conscription controversy may now be examined in some detail.

Chapter 2. The Clash of Party Positions on Vietnam-Conscription

The preceding discussion has described the role in which Australian political culture, foreign policy traditions, style of politics, political structures, and communications and associational agencies have served in sensitizing the public to an interest in external affairs. It was seen that traditionally these coalescing constraints neither measurably raised the level of public interest nor disposed the public to respond to external issues with much politically relevant behavior. In recent years, however, there have been both qualitative and quantitative changes in the potentially socializing agents, suggesting increased public disposition to assign salience to foreign and defense policy questions.

It is now necessary to turn to the Vietnam and conscription controversies per se. The concern hereafter is to notice and evaluate this controversy's influence upon Australian political life at large, in terms of how it came to pervade Australian political dialogue, to animate response among both organized political and public sectors, and ultimately to reinforce or reshape prevailing patterns of the political system's process.

The Weight of Vietnam and Conscription as Public Issues

The present chapter gives attention to the manner in which Vietnam and conscription have, as substantive, public policy issues, become embedded in the organized political party dialogue. They have engendered powerful commotion in party debate, and have become dominant themes in national and even by-elections. Furthermore, Vietnam and conscription have preoccupied parties other than those representing the government or the official opposition. The Democratic Labor party, with its traditional focus on external affairs, has found Vietnam-conscription to be a natural subject for vigorous declamation. A completely new party, the Liberal Reform Group (later renamed the Australian Reform Movement), was founded in 1966 and ran candidates in New South Wales and Victoria in the House election of that year, and in the Senate election of 1967. It had little quarrel with Liberal party domestic policy, but took fundamental exception to L-CP foreign policy, and to Vietnamese policy in particular. Vietnam, according to the party's founder, Gordon Barton, was to him and his associates "the most important issue that this country has had to think about since it came into being."[1]

Vietnam and conscription have become quite special because of their direct, even intimate impact upon the society. The troop commitment has become the largest for Australia since the Second World War. For the first time in Australian experience, conscription for unrestricted overseas service has been adopted. Conscripts have been shipped to Vietnam in considerable numbers. In June 1966 they represented 24 per cent of the men in the army units serving in Vietnam. A year later the figure had risen to 41 per cent, and by March 1968 it stood at 44 per cent.[2] Conscripts and regular service personnel alike have been killed and wounded in action. The armed forces have been considerably augmented and the defense budget has risen sharply. In other words, the public itself has been exposed to compulsion for military service, to service in an active overseas theater of war, to the fact of casualties, and, to a degree, to a reorientation of governmental priorities and heightened taxation and expenditures for defense purposes.

Another reason why Vietnam and conscription have become centerpieces of party-political concern relates to the nature of the Vietnamese conflict itself. The Australian government has made serious military and diplomatic commitments in a conflict whose very character is uniquely controversial. The war lacks precision—is it a war between opposing powers, or a civil conflict, or a combination thereof? Can "blame" or "culpability" for starting or continuing the struggle be exactly ascribed, be it to the Viet Cong, or North Vietnam, or the South Vietnamese regime, or the major Communist powers, or to the United States? What are the goals of Australia, America, and others, either on the battlefield or respecting an eventual political settlement? Furthermore, the conflict in Vietnam lacks international auspices. Unlike Korea, it is not a United Nations operation. Unlike the Malayan emergency or Indonesia's confrontation of Malaysia, it lacks concerted British–Australian–New Zealand response. Nor, for that matter, is Vietnam being fought as a joint SEATO, collective security effort. Indeed, some of Australia's closest friends, such as Britain, have made no material contribution to the Vietnamese war effort. A great many governments, including Western, have in various degrees been critical of the war. Even within those nations involved in Vietnam, notably the United States, there has been considerable and vocal dissent.

Finally, Australia's entanglement in Vietnam, conscript troops and all, has called attention to some of the key considerations which govern the country's external affairs. These include the appropriateness of a "forward" defense-in-depth strategy, perceptions of and reactions toward China, Australia's relationship with Asia at large, the regional alliance system, and the privileged ties with and dependence upon the United States. In this sense, Vietnam encapsulates the cardinal elements which enter into the formulation of Australian foreign policy, and the alternatives submitted by critics.

The special features of Vietnam and conscription in Australia have therefore provided particularly abundant fuel for dialogue within the framework of organized politics. The tone of this dialogue, primarily but not exclusively as shaped by the two major party groups, will be examined under such rubrics as evaluations of the nature of the Vietnamese conflict itself, the wisdom of the Australian military commitment, appropriate steps toward conflict resolution, and the bearing of Australia's role in Vietnam on the American alliance.

Party Traditions in Recent Foreign Policy Experience

Before moving to the details of the party debate over Vietnam and conscription, it is useful to set these issues in their societal and party perspectives. It is well to remember that the general absence of ideological overtones in Australian domestic politics has not as a rule been duplicated in foreign policy. The nonideological bent in internal matters has a varied base. There is the essentially egalitarian, nonaristocratic, and nonelitist proclivity within the nation at large. Australia is a nation which "did not emerge out of a vanquished democratic revolution, and has no history of defeated nineteenth-century reformist movements. If anything, the reverse is true: the 'left' played the major role in defining political and social institutions in the periods in which national identity was established."[3] Neither Labor nor non-Labor ministries have been reluctant to use government—federal and state alike—for economic intervention and the creation of a quasi-welfare state. Both main party groups have accepted the place of a strong trade union movement. Many of the ALP's own socialist ambitions have for some time been a dead letter because of adverse constitutional rulings by the High Court. Attempts at enlarging federal power in the socioeconomic province through constitutional amendment referendums have at times been advocated by both party groups, but in general have been vetoed by the electorate. A number of institutionalized "buffer" structures, such as nonpartisan wage fixing apparatuses, have kept potentially sensitive issues out of the open political forum, while federalism itself has served to disperse controversy.[4]

Foreign policy, however, has been something rather different. It certainly has not represented a 180-degree difference between the main parties, but it has been substantial. Between the First World War and the present, only two interludes of relative "bipartisanship" can be identified; once during the Second World War, and again during the early fifties, before the Labor split. According to the Liberal party federal president, "Nowhere does the conflict of political thinking—of ideological attitude—stand out more clearly than in the area of external security and on the part Australia is to play in this changing area of the world,"[5] while a Labor spokesman wrote in 1967 that "the clear alternative is between the Australian Labor Party on the Left and the Liberal Party on the Right. The two parties have nothing in common. They represent two different outlooks, two starkly divergent ways of life."[6] Even when allowance is made in such assertions for overstatement and oversimplification, a tradition of high major party disagreement over external policy during the past half-century remains. Still, the traditional *disuse* of external issues in electoral campaigns, or their blurring with extraneous issues, combined with a public both ethnocentric and indifferent toward foreign affairs, has helped to prevent the political process at large from becoming more ideologically clogged.

The Liberal-Country party group gradually and rather reluctantly came to terms with the "new" Commonwealth and with the decolonization of European territories in Asia. These parties have looked with particular alarm at Communism and Communism's hand in fomenting dislocation in Asia. They are "anti-Communist for basic reasons of belief, sentiment and social condition. They would be anti-Communist if the Australian Communist Party was the only one in the world. The fact that Communism is a world movement hostile to the kind of institutions we have in Australia and to the countries with whom our associations are closest fortifies their natural inclinations and gives them strong reason for supporting Britain and the United States in major matters."[7]

Labor, on its part, has been less intrinsically suspicious of an international Communist conspiracy, less impressed by military solutions than the Liberals, and more impressed by the power of economic uplifting, of negotiation efforts, and of internationally sponsored suasion as through the United Nations. It has had more confidence than the Liberals that China could be placated and made more responsible, and it has been somewhat less convinced that the United States is the *sine qua non* of Australia's security. Some of this is derived from a socialist background. Part of it stems from the great interwar cleavage which divided Labor from non-Labor parties. Part of it comes from the restlessness stimulated by a continuous deprivation of federal office since 1949. Part of it comes from the Labor split, which not only released some of the more conservative elements from the party, but endowed many ALP elites with a fierce, almost reflexive sense of resentment against the new, "schismatic" DLP—and against almost anything the DLP represented. Part of Labor's feeling results from the recurrent clashes of principle and expediency in the context of party decision-making.

Since 1955 there have been numerous instances of an apparent divergence between the L-CP government and Labor on foreign policy—certainly more so than during the same period in the U.S., Britain, Canada, or in neighboring New Zealand, the other principal English-speaking systems. Thus we find that between 1955 and 1963 Labor was officially opposed to the L-CP-sponsored troop commitment in Malaya. In 1963 the ALP accepted the possibility of overseas stationing for Australian forces, but only if a satisfactory treaty governing the status and use of such troops were concluded with the host country—and no such treaty was forthcoming between Australia and Malaya and later Malaysia. Technically, Labor was pledged to return such troops home at the earliest moment; only glosses on the party decision by the ALP parliamentary leadership mitigated the impact of this declaration.

In 1957, the ALP federal conference declared that SEATO "has failed to perform its basic [security] functions, that it is fast becoming an instrument for bolstering reactionary regimes such as in Thailand, and that the Liberal-Country Party Coalition Government has contributed to S.E.A.T.O's ineffectiveness."[8] Two years later, the party added that SEATO should be reorganized on a cultural, educational, medical, and technical basis rather than retain its discredited military emphasis, and should include all the peoples of Southeast

35

Asia. By 1963, a clause was appended which suggested that Australia need not withdraw from SEATO while the organization was being reshaped—though the previous strictures remained.

The foregoing are only examples of Labor's tendency to evolve a hodgepodge of notions and platform planks which have scolded military arrangements abroad, denounced reactionary regimes, heralded the power of socioeconomic reform to counter almost any emergency, and idealized the universality of Asian membership in regional organizations. It was reasonably clear, however, that the ALP leadership, if raised to office, would not, for instance, have dismantled SEATO or forced impossible amendments to the Manila Treaty upon other signatory governments. But the official ALP SEATO position had been sincerely believed in throughout various party quarters, and was briskly defended as a canon of Labor's repugnance of militarism and political reaction. As has rightly been observed, "The first thing to note about Labour Party foreign policy, and indeed about any aspect of the Party's policy, is that it is an endless, open debate."[9]

Basic Government and Labor Assessments of the Vietnamese Conflict

Vietnam and conscription have crystallized many of the recurrent government and Labor perspectives on world affairs and foreign policy. The government parties have perceived Vietnam neither as an isolated conflict, nor as an essentially indigenous conflict, nor as a conflict which interests Australia only academically or peripherally. The government parties have long felt that, regardless of the imperfections of successive South Vietnamese regimes, the basis of strife there has been Communist in inspiration, which could be traced from the Viet Cong to Hanoi and then to Peking. Its design has been to overthrow the constituted authority in South Vietnam and to impose a Communist administration, even if some allowance is made for nuances which separate the National Liberation Front, Hanoi, and Peking.

This is a calculated, aggressive war, for which "war of liberation" and "people's war" are misleading and dangerous euphemisms, invoked by the Communists as a masquerade. It is a gambit which requires checking for reasons other than denying Communist primacy over millions of unwilling South Vietnamese. Australian interests demand tranquil conditions in Asia. The superimposition of Communism upon a small and relatively defenseless country only increases the Communist, and especially Chinese Communist, appetite to expand and thereby create more friction and disorder, the opposites of desired conditions. It also demoralizes, compromises, outflanks, and otherwise makes vulnerable other states in the region. It constricts the strategic elasticity of anti-Communist forces in any future conflicts, and in particular denigrates the credibility of America's security shield, the single most important source of deterrence in the region, of which Australia is a part. Hence, as the late Prime Minister Harold Holt summarized it, "Vietnam itself means so much to the kind of world in which Australia is to live, to co-operate and trade. We are fighting to resist aggression against a small country. But the issues are very much larger for us even than that. We are fighting to preserve the security of South-East Asia as a whole."[10] Similarly, according to John Gorton, Holt's successor, the United States was wise to have resisted aggression in Vietnam,

> not because it was Communist aggression but because it was aggression, and such aggression, whatever the reason, was a threat to the ultimate peace of the world. If it is successful, it is likely to be repeated again and again, until, as we have seen in our lifetime, it eventually must be stopped at a cost of pain and blood and treasure infinitely greater than if it were stopped at the beginning.[11]

Labor's analysis admits that Vietnamese developments are central to Australia's well-being, but the reasoning is different from that of the L-CP. Most Laborites would stop short of Victorian Senator Albion Hendrickson's evaluation that, in a conflict which had become patently immoral and unjust, "the preponderance of evil in the war is clearly on the American side."[12] Most would feel, however, that the origin and development of the conflict were something other than a meticulously prepared, externally directed set-piece of Communist aggression. The government's obsession with Chinese mischiefmaking only obfuscates an appreciation of the conflict. China cannot ordinarily hope to direct the course of social protest and nationalism in an area as complex as Southeast Asia generally or South Vietnam more specifically. China may be an interested and even supportive party for the Viet Cong and North Vietnamese efforts, but the Chinese presence has been enlarged only as South Vietnam's friends have, in a frenzy of misplaced alarm, poured in men and arms to wage what they have construed to be a confrontation of international powers.

Mistaken assumptions have led to mistaken methods. They have become ironically and tragically counterproductive, since China has become the beneficiary of the failures of Western policy in the area. Legacies of more and more warfare, of the retardation of any genuine reconstruction in South Vietnam, of foreign intervention in other people's affairs, enable China to develop a grip of influence which it otherwise would have lacked.[13]

Indeed, according to dominant Labor opinion, Communism's cause within South Vietnam itself, though always enjoying some following there, has risen as the "unwinnable war" has driven local conditions into a shambles. The Australian government has misunderstood the strength of Asia's yearning for evolving its own institutional patterns and socioeconomic style; it has substituted specious simplicities and evasive generalities for reality. At the core of the Vietnamese situation has always been an indigenous impulse for nationalist expression and social reform, with which the American-supported authorities in Saigon have been hopelessly out of touch. "Vietnam is not the battleground of freedom, as alleged by some. Everyone knows that the nine military dictatorships that we have so far supported in South Vietnam have been tyrannical, corrupt and unrepresentative of the people of South Vietnam. Every one of the nine has been an enemy of freedom, and therefore not worth defending," Calwell insisted.[14] E. G. Whitlam, Calwell's deputy and from 1967 himself parliamentary leader, reflected the party's general disposition with the following embellishment of this theme:

> The only ideological counter to Communism in Asia is nationalism. The West has too often frustrated nationalism and forced it into the hands of China and the Communists. Is this not what has happened in Vietnam [?] Genuine nationalists have often been faced with the choice of joining the Communists or going into exile or going to prison. A real nationalism will be neither pro nor anti western; it will be concerned with its own nationals. Events have shown that a country on the border of China which is aligned with the West is courting subversion.[15]

In their appreciation of Vietnam, therefore, both principal party groups have dramatized the conflict as carrying great importance.

Both have felt that Australia's interests in Asia are at stake. Both have believed that the war is somehow tied to the factor of China. But while the L-CP has argued that the allied investment has represented an invaluable counter to a carefully orchestrated, international Communist conspiracy, to the ALP this investment has been something considerably different. It has spurred a war against a not really imagined, though surely secondary, enemy—since the root of the problem in South Vietnam lies not in a Communist conspiracy but in the social and political fabric of the society itself. It has also been a conflict which, unlike the Liberals' metaphor of applying a tourniquet to the spread of Communism, has only succeeded in widening Communist appeal in Vietnam, committing Hanoi to new levels of intractability, and allowing the Chinese a windfall of influence throughout the region.

Australia's Military Commitment in Vietnam: Justification and Criticism

The war in Vietnam has embroiled Australia and Australians in a direct and personal manner, and has opened a pronounced party debate over the entire range of instruments appropriate for handling it, be they military, economic, or diplomatic.

An Australian military presence had been established in Vietnam almost three years before combat troops were committed in 1965. By gradual steps, military advisors were assigned to the South Vietnamese army, and in July 1964 a transport flight was dispatched. These steps did not, however, arouse much notice. Prior to 1965 Australian service personnel in Vietnam numbered only about two hundred. They were all members of the regular forces, not conscripts. They were not actually combat personnel. They were involved in a situation which, at that point, had not assumed grave overtones.

But by the close of 1964 the Menzies government brought down legislation to conscript men for unlimited overseas service. This measure envenomed party politics and led to the broader debate over Australia's military role in Vietnam. Menzies reiterated his long-established view that Southeast Asia was a buffer, and it was there that Australia and its allies needed to take a stand. The control of small conflicts was one method by which to avert large conflagrations, and their containment would bring Australia relative immunity from facing potential enemies at its doorstep. Indonesia was continuing its unreasoned confrontation of Malaysia, the Gulf of Tonkin incidents had appeared, Vietnam was generally growing more agitated, and the situation in the area was otherwise seriously unsettled. To render its proper contribution and to support its allies and the spirit of collective defense obligations, Australia needed to strengthen its armed forces. Since voluntary enlistment had shown itself inadequate for raising an army of sufficient strength, conscription had now become the only recourse.[16]

Labor's response was instantly critical. Conscription was a red flag before the party's eyes, especially because of its unlimited overseas service feature. A non-Labor government had reintroduced conscription for domestic service in 1939, after Labor had removed it a decade earlier. During the Second World War, in the face of the Japanese threat, Labor Prime Minister John Curtin had been able to receive party approval to send conscripts beyond Australia and its possessions. But the party allowed conscripts to be sent only within a carefully defined area of the Pacific and Indian Oceans, south of the Equator. Even that concession had been grudgingly given, with the party divided.[17] After the war, Labor promptly removed all forms of conscription. Then the L-CP revived conscription for domestic duty in 1951, but abandoned it nine years later because the system proved inefficient. Labor's position in 1964 was that conscription for unrestricted overseas service, never before imposed, was a challenge to all of Australia's traditions. Its lottery-system approach was dubbed a "lottery of death"—an arbitrary method of pulling young men out of civilian pursuits to serve on behalf of purposes which the government had failed to justify. The government parties had for years been crying "wolf" regarding threats to Australian security. The public had been egregiously misled about Australia's state of preparedness. The present conscription move was a political stunt and an appalling admission that the government had been unable—or unwilling—to organize a defense establishment requisite for the country's needs.[18]

Hence, even before it was known where and for what purpose and in what numbers conscripts would be employed abroad, the government and the ALP opposition had fundamentally clashed. For the government, conscription was the necessary adjunct of a forward defense in an increasingly troubled Asia. For Labor, it was unnecessary, impractical, politically inspired, and ideologically repugnant.

In February of 1965 decision was taken to shift a battalion from Malaya proper to Malaysian Borneo, where Indonesian confrontation was in progress. In April 1965 a battalion was authorized for combat service in Vietnam. Eventually, as the Vietnamese conflict mushroomed and the Australian commitment there rose, Australian conscript troops were shipped there. They began to fight and to die in a war which has been assigned very different interpretations by the Liberals and by the Labor party.

The L-CP government, be it under Robert Gordon Menzies, Harold Holt, or John Gorton, has taken the Vietnamese war very seriously. Longstanding neglect of the military establishment has been considerably remedied—not only by nearly doubling and reequipping the armed forces from a 1964 starting point, but by making a substantial financial investment in defense, which from 1964 to 1968 increased by an annual rate of over 20 per cent. By 1968, as has been seen, over eight thousand troops were serving in Vietnam—nearly half of them conscripts—as well as air and naval elements. Shortly after assuming office, Gorton suggested that the Australian military commitment in Vietnam had reached its limit; but he later qualified these remarks and did not foreclose the possibility of reinforcements.[19]

Vietnam had become a major test of the anti-Communist will, according to the government. The conflict bore all the unmistakable marks of a coordinated, foreign-inspired, Communist effort not just to overrun Vietnam, but to set the dominoes in Southeast Asia tumbling. Should this adventure succeed, Australia itself would face encirclement and isolation. Vietnam is also regarded as a conflict arranged by the Communists, especially Chinese, to frustrate America's willingness to stand and fight in Asia, and to expose the noncredibility of anti-Communist professions of solidarity and courage of conviction. The Australian military commitment in Vietnam, necessarily supplemented by conscript soldiers and heavy defense expenditures, is therefore serving a distinct Australian national purpose. It is a material contribution to galvanizing the will of others to fight and sacrifice, and a sign to America that it does not stand alone and must not falter in doing what is needed with whatever instruments are required to deter or defeat aggression.

Spokesmen for the L-CP have strenuously denied that theirs is a warmongering policy, unmindful of the value of Australian lives. Rather, a "peace through strength" outlook serves to protect Australian people and institutions. Labor's "craven sentiments" on Australia's military role in Vietnam made Harold Holt feel "sick inside."[20] A 1966 Liberal party electoral advertisement asked rhetorically, "If Vietnam Goes, Who's Next?" The answer given was that other Southeast Asian states and perhaps even Australia would go under "unless communist aggression is stopped while it is still controllable and far from our own shores . . . To disregard the threat—to isolate Australia—to be anti-American—is *suicidal* . . . and is Labor Party policy . . . *suicidal!*"[21] The conviction that the Australian military presence in Vietnam was designed to provide tangible support for the American effort, and therefore confirm and protect the Austral-American alliance, became even more dominant for Gorton than it had been for his predecessors, Menzies and Holt. If the Americans stayed, Australia would stay. If they departed from Vietnam, Australia would follow.[22]

This allegedly "suicidal" Labor policy has shifted in detail over time, but at bottom has entailed resistance to the dispatch of troops, conscript or otherwise, and has also dwelled on the terms allied policy in Vietnam would need to observe if the present troop consignment were not to be pulled back and returned home. In May 1966 the federal parliamentary Labor party formalized the view that an ALP government would immediately return conscripts from Vietnam and after consultation with allies would return the balance of the force.[23] As the year 1966 progressed and a federal election grew nearer, ALP leader Calwell construed "consultation" about withdrawing the balance of the troops to be a formality, and that Labor would not feel bound to receive the consent of the United States or other Vietnamese military partners. Whitlam, Calwell's deputy, did not dissent from the principle of removing conscripts, but assumed a more cautious, indefinite position about the timing and circumstances of removing the other troops.[24] Early in 1967, after replacing Calwell as parliamentary leader, Whitlam intimated that he did not at that juncture favor the return of all Australian forces; their wholesale repatriation should be dependent on a Vietnamese armistice or settlement.[25]

The ALP's federal conference, held in Adelaide in August of 1967, declared that conscription for overseas service was unwarranted except in time of declared war. Conscription without compulsory overseas service obligation was justified only in instances of a threatened attack upon Australia or its external territories. The current troop commitment in Vietnam could be retained only if Australia's allies in the conflict agreed to cease the bombing of North Vietnam, recognized the NLF as a principal party to negotiations, and transformed the conflict in the South into a holding operation. The Australian military presence could be maintained for a longer period as part of an internationally regulated peacekeeping operation.[26] Hence, *categorical* opposition to conscription for either domestic or foreign service was officially ended, as was the injunction to remove all troops from Vietnam. But conscription was still outlawed except under extraordinary circumstances, and the retention of troops in Vietnam became conditional upon a vast reconstruction of prevailing allied policy.

Whitlam proceeded to tone down the Adelaide platform by stressing efforts to bring hostilities to a close, rather than the strict terms under which a Labor government would accede to retaining troops in Vietnam. He acknowledged that if all efforts at moderating the war failed, Australia's forces would be pulled out—but, in effect, not until a Labor government felt it had exhausted all of its leverage opposite the United States[27]—a circumstance both vague in its formulation and unlikely in occurrence.

Labor's reluctance to countenance the presence of Australian troops in Vietnam, whether expressed categorically or guardedly, has derived from idealistic, humanitarian, and pragmatic considerations. The combination of a conscript army being sent to fight and suffer in a war so tangled in its origins and pernicious in its consequences has been especially offensive to Labor. Calwell did not regard Vietnam as the "battleground of freedom." He did not care to commit himself to a "peace at any price" philosophy, but "I don't want Australia involved in foreign wars which the Labor party believes we should never have been involved in."[28] Twenty-year old, voteless Australian youths were being sent away not to defend Australia, "but to fight and die in a cruel, filthy, brutal, unwinnable war in Vietnam mangrove swamps."[29]

The war in Vietnam had become increasingly pointless, if not dysfunctional. Massive warfare had created dislocation on an unimaginably high scale, thereby retarding rather than promoting the cause of genuine self-determination and economic consolidation—objectives for which the Australian government was purportedly fighting. The legacy of an armed Australian intervention in a conflict of this nature was cancelling whatever good will and influence Australia might in past have earned in Asia. At home, rising military expenditures to support the effort in Vietnam were beginning to take their toll on Australian taxpayers. They were eroding necessary investments in welfare programs, generating inflationary pressures, and encroaching on the development of a prosperous Australian economy. Potential migrants, who were subject to compulsory military training and Vietnamese service, were being frightened off. Vietnam was not only wrong foreign policy, but wrong for the people and aspirations of Australia itself.[30]

The emphasis on force of arms in Vietnam has also prompted the ALP to complain that requisite socioeconomic assistance for Vietnam is being shunted off to a secondary, war-casualty status. In the government's 1967–1968 budget, nonmilitary assistance was scheduled to rise to $3,000,000 annually, a 50 per cent increase over 1966–1967. Still, at the beginning of 1968, only about one-twentieth of Australia's Vietnamese expenditure was civil-aid directed. Moreover, the 1967–1968 figure of $3,000,000 for Vietnam represented a barely visible fraction of overseas aid funds allocated for that period. The total figure was $142,000,000, of which $92,000,000 was directed toward Australian Papua and New Guinea.[31]

For Labor, if poverty and unrest, and therefore Communism, are ultimately to be defeated in Vietnam, the battleground will have to be as much if not more social than military. Some of this will be the Vietnamese' own responsibility, but much responsibility will fall on Australia, America, and other sympathetic nations. It is an effort which must both precede and follow the suspension of armed hostilities. The Australian stress on military solutions only detracts from its willingness to enlarge economic aid, encourages the United States to behave likewise, and most importantly delays the time when a massive, postarmistice economic program could be launched. As a variation on the theme of Labor's willingness to maintain any troop commitment in Vietnam, Whitlam told Vietnamese leaders early in 1968 that his party would consider any continuing Australian military presence only if drastic internal reforms were undertaken.[32]

Finally, Labor's thesis has been that an uncomplaining Australian military commitment in Vietnam has acted as a brake on allied and particularly American incentive to search for a more accommodating policy orientation—in itself a desirable objective—and has only enlarged the chances of American failure and therefore future disengagement from the region. American help could not automatically be expected in future, since America, like every other nation, helps others so as to help itself. But there is an Australian interest to be met if America, unless thrust by frustration into a fresh isolationism, does retain its presence in Asia. A hawkish, sycophant, Australian Liberal government had therefore assumed an awful burden of conscience. Pretending that a military commitment in Vietnam would quicken victory and satisfy America, it was courting disaster: "The true friends of America will not encourage her to adopt a course which must lead either to the disaster of a humiliating withdrawal from Asia or the even greater disaster of a nuclear holocaust."[33]

On Negotiations and the American Alliance: 1

The party argument has boiled down to how the war can be brought to a rapid and acceptable conclusion. While it would be misleading to characterize the government and Labor positions as diametrically opposed, they have precipitated some of the bluntest clashes between the parties. The public has in this sense been given a real choice of options, themselves reflecting traditionally different L-CP and Labor approaches to the handling of international disputes.

Persisting in military operations has been defended by the Australian government as necessary to secure South Vietnam from Communist absorption. But it has also been defined as a way to persuade the enemy that his war costs were prohibitive, he could not win on the battlefield, and he therefore should consent to serious negotiations.

> On our side we have done what we can to bring Hanoi to the conference table. We would prefer to talk than to fight. But if we are to make real progress towards a peaceful solution, our policies for peace must be conducted with great care and realism and an unfaltering firmness of purpose. This has been the lesson in all the efforts to negotiate with the Communists in the successive post-war crises.[34]

On the very eve of President Johnson's 1968 announcement of an unconditional reduction of bombing in the North and a call for negotiations, Gorton exclaimed that "we are not interested in things that are called peace talks but in fact are surrender talks."[35]

For months and then years, the government insisted that no basis

45

for negotiation existed, although by the close of 1967 it claimed to have supported over fifty United States initiatives to end the war.[36] The Communists, both in the North and the South, had been unwilling to de-escalate their own efforts unless America and its allies yielded to terms so unacceptable as to vitiate the entire purpose of their Vietnamese presence. Hence, to protect allied forces, to enhance the military effort generally, to maintain pressure on the Communists so that the allied commitment would not lose credibility, and so that in proper time realistic rather than "surrender" talks could be placed in train, the bombing of the North and the maintenance of military momentum in the South had to continue.

If there were a reduction in the allied military effort, it would need to be reciprocated by the enemy—the essence of Lyndon Johnson's September 1967 "San Antonio formula." But when incoming United States Secretary of Defense Clark Clifford suggested that if America de-escalated he did not expect the enemy to lower its military activities or to curtail resupply efforts in the South until a ceasefire had been agreed to, the Australian government did not correspondingly adjust its own position.[37] Johnson's announcement of the unconditional bombing reduction and invitation for talks was made without consultation with Australia, and only with the briefest possible advance notice. Gorton's reaction was that "this gesture by the U.S., giving up . . . a military advantage, is the most significant and generous gesture yet made in the hope of starting such negotiations." He strongly implied that there were military risks in such unilateral concessions, but now that the President had "gone the second mile," here would be the acid test of Hanoi's professions of desiring an honorable settlement.[38] A month later, shortly before the Paris talks, Defense Minister Allen Fairhall said much the same thing. Even a further reduction of American bombing in the North would be acceptable, but should be tied to de-escalation by the enemy; bombing was therefore continuing to receive Australian support.[39] In short, Canberra accepted the President's initiative with misgivings. It had been caught unprepared by an American initiative more conciliatory in tone and content than Canberra had itself been willing to countenance.

Labor's persistent rejoinder over the years became that the government was displaying an excessively timid, uncritical, even stagnant attitude toward the prevailing allied doctrine, and failing to assume the initiative to break out of the stalemated situation in

Vietnam. In light of continuing allied failure to establish rapport with the enemy on de-escalation and negotiations, it had drastically misread the tenor of American politics and of Australia's ability to render a signal contribution to the conflict's resolution. In sum, said Whitlam,

> What must now disturb Australians most is the apparent supine-
> ness of our Government. It is a truly defeatist government, for
> it offers nothing more than a continuation of policies that have
> failed. . . . The true destroyers of morale are those who offer
> nothing but failure, and maintain that failure must be sup-
> ported because there is no alternative. This is truly a counsel
> of despair—and it is the only course offered by the Government
> of Australia.[40]

In other words, Labor long disapproved of America's lack of imagination in the search for peace openings in Vietnam, and it simultaneously berated the Australian government for being at mini-mum an imitator of American policy, and worse still an obstruction-ist to the evolution of a more plastic American policy. Labor has subscribed to the *Australian*'s editorial observation that "so unorig-inal are our own attitudes to the Vietnam question and so quick are we to follow the example of the U.S., [that] when the Americans reconsider their policies, ipso facto they reconsider ours. . . . Our dogged support for the U.S. position through thick and thin must be remarked upon as much in uncommitted Asia as it is here in Australia."[41] Labor has been quick to point to highly placed Aus-tralian expressions which have intimated stubbornness or slavish-ness or both. These included Menzies' assertion that the idea that America should negotiate instead of fighting was fantasy, "and if I am the only Prime Minister left to denounce it, I denounce it,"[42] and Holt's remark that Australia would be "all the way with L.B.J.," and Treasurer William McMahon's promise that "where you go, we go." Such unadulterated sycophancy not only failed to contribute anything to American re-evaluations of Vietnamese policy, but was harmful, according to Labor. Canberra, for instance, seemed less interested in terminating bombing pauses than Washington itself, and disregarded and even discouraged American initiatives to in-clude the Viet Cong as a party to negotiations.[43]

The Australian government's judgment to tag along with American policy—and sometimes even to dampen down promising American proposals—has, for Labor, exposed the bankruptcy of official thinking in Canberra. The ALP has insisted that not only has Australia needed to be more forcefully critical of the harsher aspects of American policy, but that it has also been deficient in evolving initiatives and alternatives of its own. The government has seemed to look to today, not to the future. It has seemed to have become mesmerized by kill ratios and statistics about who controls what proportion of Vietnamese real estate. What it has failed to recognize is that the war's intensification has misjudged what arms alone could achieve and what, in the Vietnamese context, could reasonably be defined as "victory." In Labor's interpretation, the government parties have fastened on the illusion that only two polar options have been available in Vietnam—to scuttle or to escalate, i.e., wholesale retreat and capitulation, which the government abhors, or a military solution, which it has selected. Thus the government "ignores the central need to find a political solution and to use whatever influence it has to pursue a political solution through diplomatic means."[44]

It is here, in the area of fresh and constructive political solutions, that the ALP has claimed to be far ahead of the government parties. When the Johnson announcement came in 1968, Labor bluntly described the government's Vietnamese policy as being in ruins. For the ALP, the necessary changes in orientation have consistently entailed a shift from attacking the North to securing the South, and to fashioning a climate in which discussions, an armistice, and some form of compromise settlement could be effected. Hence, the party has looked with alarm at the bombing of the North, the mounting buildup in the South, and the refusal of the Australians to foster a holding-operation military posture. If the Viet Cong and North Vietnam could be persuaded that the allies were sincere about negotiating, then all available routes for communicating with them should be sought out, e.g., the United Nations or the Geneva Conference structure. If possible, a United Nations peacekeeping presence should eventually be created to supervise the truce and whatever political settlement might be arranged. At one time, Calwell went so far as to propose an Australian peacemaking mission to North Vietnam, to sound out Hanoi on its terms and feelings, to advise it of the limits within which America could logically be expected to offer concessions, and generally to induce a climate of improved understanding.[45] This particular Labor recommendation died out, but de-escalation and a vigorous search for a political solution remained and remain as hallmarks of party policy. It is a policy which the ALP insists the Australian government, of whatever political composition, should urge upon Washington.

But of what value could Australia's advice to Washington be? Does it carry any hope of being accepted? Is there a serious chance that Australia's departure from a follower's to a prompter's role would create reverberations which could adversely affect both the situation in Vietnam and the Austral-American alliance? Labor has not been unmindful of such questions, in part because it has appreciated their intrinsic relevance, and because it has been compelled to defend its Vietnamese policy against allegations of utopianism and anti-Americanism, especially as such charges have been raised in political-electoral contexts. Once again it should be made plain that the party has, on these questions as on others, not been at one. Arthur Calwell, for instance, became increasingly obsessed by the wrongness of the Vietnamese war and by Australia's unpardonable acquiescence in and even prolongation of it. After he resigned the parliamentary leadership following the 1966 electoral campaign, his views stiffened to the point where he could say that because truth was more important than ephemeral military or economic alliances, he would not be interested in the impact on the Austral-American relationship that a refreshing, peace-seeking Australian initiative on Vietnam might produce.[46] Gough Whitlam, on the contrary, despite deep personal disquiet over Vietnam, has on grounds of conviction and political expedience acclaimed himself a defender of the American alliance; so much so, in fact, that as ALP leader "the greatest obligation I have on the party platform in foreign affairs is to preserve the U.S. alliance, to make it enduring and fruitful."[47] This ambivalence in Labor's ranks respecting America and the Austral-American connection is not novel. As will be shown in another context, it has profoundly affected the dialogue within the party, and the style of politics in the country generally.

According to widespread Labor opinion, if the Vietnamese conflict is to be brought under control and all the tragic consequences of protracted and escalated war are to be averted, then it is preeminently the United States among the Vietnamese allies that must become a convert to an accommodationist viewpoint. Australia has been placed in an especially strategic position to plead and induce such a viewpoint, since it has long been regarded in Washington as a steadfast and reliable ally, in Vietnam and otherwise. Therefore

Australia's voice would be received with special sympathy, not dismissed as the pleading of a fair-weather friend or spectator to the conflict.[48] Within the United States, an intensifying debate developed over both the details and the assumptions of the war, with prominent figures of both major parties questioning the prevailing line and urging some form of de-escalation. Moreover, many respected world figures, such as the Pope and the Secretary-General of the United Nations, publicly appealed for some swallowing of pride and an acceleration of efforts toward peace. Even some of America's closest friends, such as Great Britain and Canada, urged restraint and experimentation at getting negotiations in motion. Therefore, Labor explained, an Australian peace initiative would not only emanate from a respected source; it would not stand in isolation, but as part of a growing, distinguished community of critics.

Indeed, by mid–1968, Washington was seen by Labor as evincing at least a few signs of moderation, as for instance in loosening its attitude toward Viet Cong participation in eventual negotiations and adopting the Clifford gloss on the San Antonio formula. Labor clutched at such straws and even made invidious comparisons with the Australian government's own reluctance to endorse such steps, alleging that if there was a major Australian party which understood the United States government's striving to disentangle itself, it was Labor itself, not the L-CP. The L-CP's intransigence only served to embarrass America and to hold it back from investigating promising, conciliatory initiatives.[49]

The Australian government's hawkish line was being used in America by the President's hard-line advisers to buttress their arguments, and "President Johnson's understandable reluctance to disown a friend increases the difficulties of his position." With the stakes in Vietnam for world peace being so high, Australia bore a heavy responsibility, for "the true friends of America, those who wish her well but are not content just to cheer from the sidelines, are urging negotiation—negotiation from strength, negotiation now while she has, in Asia, the strength to negotiate."[50] In other words, Australian Labor has felt that new initiatives in Vietnam have been imperative for everyone's sake, that the American administration might be responsive to responsible cautionary counsel, and that Australia has been peculiarly well equipped to discharge such a function. When the American bombing suspension was announced in 1968, here was ample evidence for Labor that its own commitment to a conciliatory policy had been right. It was also glaring evidence that the Australian government had misjudged the temper of the United States administration, had bungled opportunities to influence an even swifter American offer, and had discredited, not enhanced, Australia's standing in Washington.[51]

On Negotiations and the American Alliance: 2

Over time and in principle, the L-CP government has agreed with the opposition that arms alone would not "solve" Vietnam, and that probes for negotiations and an eventual settlement should be kept alive. But beyond these surface resemblances, the government parties have produced a different interpretation of what Australia's interests demand. For the government, if the ALP's position on troop removal, on confining the war to a holding action, and on bold new peace overtures were adopted, the result would be unqualified disaster.

Labor's policy would create intolerable dangers for the Australian fighting men themselves. Since regular and conscript troops are integrated into military units down to the lowest levels, Labor's once-emphasized proposal to return conscripts first and regular troops later would have grievously dislocated the entire Australian military operation. It would not only have deprived the effort of efficiency, but would have positively endangered the lives of men. The recommended bombing suspension of the North and the adoption of an "enclave" or holding operation in the South would do little better for Australian servicemen in combat zones. The enemy would only be handed an open invitation to infiltrate unlimited quantities of troops and military stores. The enemy would welcome such an opportunity to enjoy the tactical advantage accorded by a stand-still posture in the South, and the killing of Australian troops would be simplified for him. "Do you squat like a lot of sitting ducks in an area waiting to be picked off or harassed?" Holt was impelled to inquire rhetorically.[52] Such, to him, would have been the consequences for Australian and other allied soldiers in Vietnam if Labor's plan were to be adopted—to say nothing of weakening South Vietnamese army morale, delivering countless South Vietnamese civilians into Communist hands, debilitating the allies' bargaining position, and prolonging the war itself.

Furthermore, Labor's Vietnamese proposals have consistently been derided as sapping the determination of those who, opposed to the insinuation of Communism into the Vietnamese area, wish to stand and hold until the objective of denying the Communists a military and/or diplomatic victory is met. The ALP has long claimed that a bold Australian initiative might tip the balance in Washington by opening the door to a more sensible and progressive policy. The government parties have agreed that, as a firm and honored ally and one with a sizable military force in Vietnam, Australia would indeed have an effect on American thinking should Canberra choose to reverse its standing policy. But the result would be pernicious, not desirable. The consternation in Washington, as well as in other allied capitals, might well trigger feelings of isolation and abandonment, eroding the resolve to persevere and making a mockery of the sacrifices being endured in Vietnam.

Here has been the centerpiece of official Australian reasoning, and it deserves reinforcement. Communism in Asia is dangerous and must be deterred or defeated whenever possible. America is by far the best guarantor that this will be done. Vietnam is a pivotal test for such resistance, but the conflict itself has brought burdens of frustration and impatience to American political life. Hence Australia must sustain America's resolve both by moral and material support. It must understand and help to alleviate the "loneliness of a great Power"[53] which could stir American second thoughts about entanglement in Vietnam today, or in some other Asian emergency in the future.

The removal of Australian forces from Vietnam would consequently have much greater impact than could be measured by the simple number of men being withdrawn from the war effort. Under Calwell's leadership, Labor was accused of having entered into a "shameful course"—the first instance in Australian history of a political leader having committed his party to the desertion of Australia's allies as a national policy.[54] Following Whitlam's elevation to the leadership and the passage of the 1967 ALP conference resolutions, the ALP was in substance regarded as not much less dishonorable and mistaken on Vietnam. Its tone was pious, its recommendations were tantamount to an ultimatum to America, and it utterly miscalculated the value of the American security shield to Australia; the shield would be thrown into disrepair if not broken if Labor thinking became official policy. Speaking during the 1967 Senate election campaign, less than two months before he succeeded to the prime ministership, Senator John Gorton summarized it this way:

> Wriggle and slither how he may, Mr. Whitlam cannot disguise the fact that Labor's policy is to say to the Vietnamese and the United States: "You must stop fighting the invaders, you must stop bombing the communications, even though this makes it easier for them to kill our own troops. You must do this or we Australians will pull out and leave you in the lurch." Our foreign policy would be at risk . . . . It would not only be the United States that would not be sure that those policies would continue . . . . [so would certain Southeast Asian countries] that don't glibly dismiss the domino theory as do our Labor strategists.[55]

That, of course, was before the President's 1968 announcement. The American move toward talks was not accompanied either by a total cessation of bombing in the North or by any lessened vigor in the prosecution of the war in the South. The failure of attempts to effect an armistice and subsequently a satisfactory political settlement could prolong and even intensify the war, presumably confirming *post hoc* the appropriateness of the Australian government's tough line and imputations of error to the ALP. In the meantime, however, such imputations, routine over the years, have been rendered less credible.

The Democratic Labor Party and the Australian Reform Movement

The mood of the major party debate over Vietnam has therefore been one of fairly wide divergence over premises on the nature of the war, the principal direction to be followed in seeking its resolution, and the appropriate methods for Australia itself to apply or to counsel upon others. This debate has become steady—almost ubiquitous—in Australian politics. Its pervasiveness and sharpness have, however, been contributed to by smaller yet highly vocal parties, to whom their respective positions on Vietnam-conscription have become near articles of faith.

The Democratic Labor party has consistently followed an uncompromisingly anti-Communist position, both at home and abroad. Its interpretation of Chinese designs on the non-Communist nations in

53

the region borders on the apocalyptic. It has steadfastly maintained a defense and foreign policy emphasis in national elections, which it has contested in every Australian state, and its small contingent in the Senate has made disproportionately emphatic contributions to debates on these subjects.[56]

It has agreed with the government's evaluation of Vietnam as a case of an imperialist Communist conspiracy, and has likewise agreed that Australia, America, and others must assume a firm stance there and persevere despite temptations to the contrary. Unless Australia helps to combat the Chinese and their confederates in Vietnam, it would surely have to fight them nearer to or within its own boundaries. But the DLP has not simply been a government echo. It has long insisted that the L-CP, despite its public pronouncements, has taken the Communist threat too casually. While the ALP would "leave the defence of this country to the boy scouts and brownies,"[57] the government has continued to misread the necessity for a truly powerful defense establishment. National security demands a large standing army, including the replacement of the present *selective* service with a system of *universal* military service for every young man. The DLP has also recommended the acquisition of an Australian nuclear capability, something the government itself has consistently rejected.

The DLP's insistence on such heavy military preparation has not been predicated exclusively on the belief that Australia should be fully equipped to assist America and other allies in waging localized wars such as Vietnam. It has reasoned that as Britain disengaged militarily from the region and the Chinese nuclear capability becomes ominously real, there does not remain the certainty of an automatic, unlimited American riposte to any events which might endanger Australia's safety. Therefore, in preparing itself for a possibly inescapable self-reliance, Australia must arm itself well, and must include in its arsenal nuclear weapons.[58]

The Liberal Reform Group–Australian Reform Movement (ARM) is a more recent and less politically ambitious phenomenon than the DLP. Its federal candidates have stood only since the 1966 House election, and then competed in the 1967 Senate election. In both instances, ARM candidates were present only in New South Wales and in Victoria. Moreover, no ARM candidate has ever been elected. The ARM is, however, a party of very special interest in the present context, since its creation resulted from the explicit dissatisfaction over Vietnam of a number of middle-class, mainly Liberal-voting individuals.

While the Movement's domestic policy is quite conservative and therefore bears little resemblance to Labor's, the foreign policies of the two parties, despite different socioeconomic clienteles, are remarkably harmonious. The ARM's analysis of the war in Vietnam has been that the conflict has become dirty and inhuman. The early, lofty objectives of protecting the indigenous population have long been buried beneath the rubble of war. Compounding the problem in the Vietnamese situation have been confusion over ends, and a gross inflation of China's alleged perversity and ability to knock over the Southeast Asian domino blocks one by one. The ARM concluded that what Australia needed to do in Vietnam was to remove its troops, encourage the cessation of interdiction against North Vietnam, and to do all in its power to reorganize the military effort in South Vietnam on a holding basis while meaningful negotiations with all interested parties were sought. Both now and after a settlement, Australia would need to sink a heavy investment into economic and technical assistance programs in Vietnam. Finally, the ARM asserts that Vietnam has made of Australia a caricature of an ally— servile, dependent on American favor, paranoid about Communism, ludicrously bombastic, and addicted to a worthless gunboat diplomacy.

The Movement does not disparage friendship and even security connections with the United States, but insists that Australia's prosperity and security are linked to Asia, and thereby require a more independent and flexible foreign policy than the L-CP has pursued heretofore. Something on the order of a Sweden or a Switzerland is envisaged for Australia by the ARM. Rather than being tangled in a maze of treaty obligations and overseas commitments, Australia should build up its own defenses substantially—perhaps to 100,000 men—and with nuclear weapons possibly being included in its armory. There should not, however, be conscription for overseas service without a formal declaration of war, or except in instances of extreme and immediate national emergency, or except to sustain obligations transacted under the aegis of the United Nations. The Australian military establishment would be powerful, but its application would be defensive or internationally collective. In the meantime, Australia's diplomacy would be accommodationist, seeking a diplomatic and United Nations *rapprochement* with China, utilizing the United

Nations in maximum degree to settle disputes, investing generously in the socioeconomic reconstruction of Asia, and refusing to condemn or overthrow Asian regimes regardless of their economic or political organization.[59]

More will need to be said of the DLP and the ARM in later connections. For now, it is sufficient to notice that their electoral presence and special emphasis on Vietnam and related foreign and defense policy subjects have added to the volume, variety, and interest of the Australian party dialogue. It is a dialogue which has borrowed from established party orientations on external affairs, but has acquired a relevance and pungency of its own. It has exposed all the really significant assumptions and strategies governing Australia's foreign and defense policies. It has been a stimulating exercise in drawing connections between the ordinarily remote theme of foreign affairs and personal ideals and interests. Its socializing effect has, in this sense, been substantial.

Chapter 3. Stylistic Characteristics of the Party Dialogue over Vietnam and Conscription

The debate over Vietnam and conscription has revealed a number of fundamental substantive differences between the political parties. It has involved all principal party groups, and has given birth to a new one. It has exposed to reexamination the tenets on which Australia's national interests are presumed to hinge, and the foreign and defense measures which could be judged as appropriate for securing those interests. It has been a debate heightened by the personal relevance of conscription and the Vietnamese commitment for members of the community. In this sense, Vietnam and conscription have become a distinctive and pressing feature of Australian political life.

But the influence of Vietnam and conscription upon organized political activity, and ultimately upon public attitudes and behavior, must be evaluated on grounds other than the substance of the arguments and counterarguments which have been advanced. It not only matters what parties and politicians say, but how and when and where they say it. In other words, the Australian debate has been colored as much by its vigor and style as by its content. It is with this added dimension of the party dialogue that this and the following chapter are concerned.

The Climate and Intensity of the Political Dialogue

During the time that Vietnam and conscription were becoming contentious public issues, the Australian government's demeanor toward Asia generally underwent a qualitative change. Much of this was attributable to the transfer of Liberal leadership early in 1966 from Menzies to Holt. While Menzies was an uncommonly shrewd politician, his intellectualism and aloofness lowered the scale at which the government might have dramatized the whole complex of reasons which underlay its concern about Vietnam, as well as the attendant expenditures on defense, conscription for unlimited overseas service, and the assignment of combat forces to Vietnam. Harold Holt's temperament was quite different. He was open and direct, more human and passionate than Menzies, more intensely and personally involved than his predecessor had been. Although Holt's background in external affairs had been modest, he very quickly assumed inordinate personal responsibility for foreign policy. He paid a visit to Vietnam shortly after his installation as prime minister—a trip Menzies had never bothered to undertake—and while there mixed with the troops as well as conducting official talks. During his less than two years in office he became a veritable peripatetic, both in Asian as well as Western capitals. He exuded a genuine concern for the problems of Asia, thus making more credible than before, both by word and deed, the official view that the Asian social and economic environment could not be expected to remain static, or to model itself on Western lines. Under Holt defense spending and the number of Australian troops in Vietnam continued to climb but so did Australia's overseas aid expenditures, whatever doubts Labor may have expressed about their sufficiency. The restrictive migration policy was not in theory disturbed, but annual permanent entry visas to non-Europeans reached about 1,000 during Holt's prime ministership, and visas were granted to orphaned Vietnamese children who had been approved for adoption by welfare agencies in the several Australian states.[1]

There was criticism of some of Holt's rather impulsive remarks overseas, such as the "all the way with L.B.J." slogan, and his public scolding of Britain and other European powers for their failure to contribute to the military effort in Vietnam. In Parliament, Holt lacked Menzies' cultivated grace and style. But he plunged into foreign policy with both feet, in and out of the country, in and out of Parliament, to the point of overshadowing his own external affairs minister in this field. While Evatt and Menzies in their own ways had tended to personalize foreign policy, Holt's personalization was more exciting, more humanly dramatic, more understandable, and in the last resort more publicly credible, both because of the nature of the man and the intensity of the contentious issues with which he was dealing.[2]

When Holt died, it was not coincidental that his memorial service drew an impressive assembly of dignitaries from Western and Asian nations alike, and that the political obituaries stressed his special, personal contribution to Australian external affairs. Holt's almost overwhelming concentration on the outside world, his attempt to symbolize Australia's place in Asia, had left their mark.

In two years, Harold Holt cheerfully disrupted Australian politics. He did it by making an abrupt change from the authoritative style of Sir Robert Menzies. He did it by chancing his arm on personal diplomacy in Asia . . . . He did it by making loyalty to the alliance with the United States the crux of our own attitude to the world . . . . More by temperament and political instinct than by calculation, he was a catalyst of the major forces at work on Australia's destiny in this century.[3]

So did Holt catch the imagination of Australians, that "any man who accepts the Prime Ministership without a readiness to continue this part of Mr. Holt's work," another commentator wrote, "will not only be doing his country a disservice: he may be finishing himself off as a political leader and the Liberal Party as a political force."[4]

To repeat: By his dramatic, personal style, Holt imbued Australian foreign policy in general and the immediate, contentious issues of Vietnam and conscription with special meaning—not only for the conduct of the organized party debate, but also for the public at large.

Whether before, during, or after Holt's incumbency, Australian party politics were vastly enlivened by the voluminous and often acrimonious exchanges over Vietnam and conscription. This phenomenon obtained both in and out of Parliament, and both during and between electoral campaigns. One measure of this became the attention which was given to foreign policy in Parliament in 1965 and 1966, the years when the government's Vietnamese position was taking shape and the combat commitment was first made and then augmented, including with conscript troops. The seven-year period 1958–1964 can usefully be compared with 1965 and 1966 on the basis of a content analysis of the number of *Hansard* pages devoted to explicit foreign policy ministerial statements and debates in the House of Representatives. Between 1958 and 1964, the median annual percentage of total House pages devoted to foreign affairs debates was 3.7. For the same period, the mean was 3.2 per cent. For 1965 and 1966, however, when Vietnam was the axial external issue, the mean for foreign affairs was 6.7 per cent—more than twice the mean for 1958–1964. In 1966 alone, the percentage of total House of Representatives *Hansard* pages was 7.7. These figures were computed without including "defense" topics, even defense topics closly touching on Vietnam, e.g., conscription and rearmament.

Australian electoral campaigns have become generously laced with clashes over Vietnam and conscription, and both major party groups have, for their separate reasons, generally welcomed the opportunity to present their cases and to embarrass the other side. These clashes have not been tame affairs by any stretch of the imagination. One index of their intensity can be found in the public reception party speakers have been accorded. Australian poltical meetings are not generally reputed to be soporific. Opponents as well as supporters of the headline speaker or his party tend to intermingle in the audience. The barbed, hostile question is expected, and so is the cutting riposte. But since Vietnam and conscription have arrived as outstanding issues in public controversy, electoral meetings have been among the most disorderly in memory, and have elicited some of the most disparaging if not cruel exchanges ever uttered. Each party group, moreover, has been quick to impute tastelessness if not outrageousness to the other.

The government parties have complained the most. During electoral meetings in 1966 and 1967, Holt in particular was confronted with placards and jeered mercilessly, sometimes to the point where he could not be heard over the uproar. Cries of "murderer" and "fascist" and "only political prostitutes go all the way" were common at his mention of Vietnam or the wisdom of employing conscript troops there. At a Sydney rally in November 1966, Holt was mobbed and punched, and had his car bounced and pommeled. Holt and his colleagues quickly responded by attributing nearly all instances of electoral meeting misbehavior to a rabid, mischievous ALP. Sometimes the government parties' response was one of icy indignation. In March 1966, during the Kooyong federal by-election campaign in Victoria, the Liberal candidate made much display of Labor's "emotional" and "lurid" propaganda, which depicted horribly disfigured civilian Vietnamese war victims.[5] At other times, the Liberals' reaction was an unvarnished blast at Labor, whose leadership was accused of having incited the stormy atmosphere. It was asserted to have joined forces with Communists and other fringe groups to promote disorder. It was charged with resorting to desperation tactics, since it was alleged to possess no constructive and electorally viable programs of its own.[6]

There is no question that ALP supporters were among the unruly elements at Liberal meetings. But others were there as well, ranging from Communists to Liberal demonstrators who tried to reply in kind to the antigovernment hecklers. There is no conclusive evidence that the Liberal meetings were disrupted at the behest of the ALP high (or even intermediate) command, and all such imputations were denied by Labor spokesmen. If anything, Liberal allegations of a Labor conspiracy to upset rallies only lifted the fervor with which Labor conducted its own meetings and railed at presumed government calumnies in respect to Vietnam and conscription. If the Liberals could claim that their leader had faced physical danger in the context of a presentation on Vietnam, Labor had its own and considerably more serious fright. In mid-1966, a disgruntled young man made an unsuccessful shotgun assassination attempt on Calwell's life, after the Labor leader had completed a powerful speech on Vietnam in Sydney. Labor could not restrain itself from reacting in a "people who live in glass houses should not cast stones" manner. When some ALP parliamentarians joined in a peace vigil outside Parliament House,

> several Government supporters stood on the parapet of the monument and continued to tell funny stories in very loud voices while the vigil for peace was going on. The culminating point came when a member of one of the Government parties seized the microphone and prayed for the success of the Government's actions in Vietnam. In other words, he prayed that people would be killed. This was an un-Christian attitude, an undemocratic attitude and a disgusting spectacle. I have not heard one Government supporter raise his voice in protest at this disgusting attitude of one of his colleagues.[7]

Expediency, Integrity, and the Party Dialogue

Vietnam and conscription have produced a basic confrontation of party positions. The personal style of Harold Holt helped to dramatize foreign policy, and especially the importance of Australia's "Asian exposure," at exactly the moment when Vietnam and conscription were most highly controversial. Vietnam and conscription have become widely debated topics in various political party settings. The controversy has converted political meetings and other encounters into exceptionally boisterous and emotional events. As the parties have clashed over Vietnam and conscription, they have hardly been content to limit themselves to sober, scholarly, undistracted presentations. The traditions of Australian political dialogue at large have run parallel to the colorful fencing match characteristics of political rallies, and foreign affairs have generally been more divisive than domestic issues, despite their traditional relegation to secondary electoral emphasis.

Vietnam and conscription have carried a very special potential for agitated party debate. The tone of the party dialogue on these issues has, of course, been influenced by other situational factors—the principal personalities involved on both sides, the forces operating within party decision-making structures, the facts of Labor's long-standing isolation from national office, and so on. These and other considerations have covered the debate over Vietnam and conscription with an especially heavy coat of personal, partisan, and insinuative language. There have been imputations of cheap and opportunistic politics, of deviousness and even of mendacity, leveled by the warring parties one against the other. Each side has claimed for itself the high ground of virtue and patriotism. The result, to many observers, has been highly unfortunate. Scare tactics and politics by innuendo not only conceal issues and thwart meaningful electoral choice but also inhibit the parties from adjusting with reasonable comfort to fresh circumstances. "The level of these [party] exchanges points up one of the ills in Australian politics today," commented the *Canberra Times* shortly after John Gorton assumed the prime ministership. "The war in Vietnam is too bloody, too destructive, too sickening for it to be tossed around in a game of political tennis. Both parties have taken up positions from which it is difficult to retire without loss of face."[8]

The very vigor of the party argument has nevertheless served to magnify the importance of Vietnam and conscription in Australian politics, even if it has smudged the issues and foreclosed certain policy options on both sides. If there is a single, outstanding partisan imputation which has repeatedly been laid during skirmishing over these related external affairs subjects, it is self-serving electioneering. The charge has generally emanated from Labor, if only because it has been the government, not the opposition, that has been able to time and to announce particular policy steps and House and Senate elections. In general, Labor has decided that government actions should be reacted to not only with substantive rebuttal, but with at least a touch of moral indignation added on. Thus, within a few weeks of taking office, Gorton and his government were being rebuked by Whitlam for viewing Vietnam "principally in terms of domestic politics"—Gorton was so callous that he was prepared to "let Vietnam be destroyed so long as the [L-CP] coalition may survive."[9]

A reading of ALP public pronouncements straight from the 1964

Senate election through the Senate election of 1967 indicates a profound suspicion in both Calwell and Whitlam that government judgments on Vietnam and conscription have represented an unconscionable substitution of electoral greed for national interest and parliamentary proprieties. When the government brought down legislation to authorize conscription for unrestricted service abroad, it did so less than a month before the scheduled Senate election. Labor castigated conscription as unnecessary as well as immoral. It impugned the forced service and possible slaughter of the flower of Australian manhood in unknown and perhaps ill-begotten conflicts. Why had the government sprung this surprise so close to an election? Labor's answer was that the callous politicians on the government benches were striving first to create an atmosphere of panic, and secondly to hide the shameful neglect to which the armed forces had for years been subjected. This was the L-CP's way, alleged Labor, to contest and very nearly steal elections, if needed at the expense of Australian lives and national interest; "the intention of the Government is not to win wars but to win elections. Its purpose is not to defend Australia but to defend its Parliamentary seats, and no more on any issue than on the issue of conscription."[10]

In 1966, once troops had been dispatched to Vietnam, Arthur Calwell insisted that the Holt government was deliberately shielding conscripts serving there from any serious combat exposure. The government was unprepared to pay the electoral price later in the year should an indignant public rebel against the waste of human life in that senseless, rotten, unwinnable war. After the election, Calwell predicted, it would be very different indeed. The government had refused to advise the Australian people as to what, if any, was the limit of its commitment. This "blank check" might well be filled in with huge numbers of young men; there was no point in trusting the government, since its intention seemed to imply placing Australia's manhood at the disposal of American policy-makers.[11]

In October 1967 the government authorized the addition of some 1,500 men to the Vietnam force. A Senate election was scheduled for late November. Whitlam, now ALP leader, alleged a history of government manipulation of foreign policy decisions to coincide with electoral campaigns. The government's latest step was part of a studied technique. "The Government believes that by appealing to people's patriotism and by making very proper tributes to the gallantry of Australian soldiers in Vietnam, it can obscure all other issues in the forthcoming Senate election. The Government is hoping to have a khaki election . . . ."[12]

Actually, Australia's Vietnamese buildup has come in steps which have fallen both before and after elections. But Labor has tried to have it both ways—to attribute electoral selfishness if troops are added before elections (alleged whipping up of patriotic fervor), and to attribute electoral cowardice if a fresh commitment is undertaken shortly after an election. In the latter situation, the government is charged with avoiding the unpopularity that is associated with casualty lists, while it lies in wait to increase the commitment in the political safety of a postelection period. But after President Johnson's 1968 announcement of an unconditional bombing reduction and call for talks, Labor felt that it had at last caught the government off its political balance. The old black magic of politically inspired timing where Vietnam and conscription were concerned was no more. Not only had the L-CP government been caught by surprise, but it had been caught moving in a different, more conservative direction than was now being followed by Washington. On returning home from an overseas visit, Labor's Deputy Senate Leader S. H. Cohen said that he had found it humiliating to be an Australian overseas—for an Australian government had committed itself to going all the way with LBJ without knowing the direction in which he would next move.[13]

The government parties have piously denied any improprieties, have spoken of the deep personal hurt which comes from being associated by Labor with such unworthy, calumnious behavior, and have turned the tables on the ALP. It has been Labor, not the L-CP, that should cover its head in shame. By appealing to mothers and the flower of Australian manhood, by invoking the twin specters of a "lottery of death" and of death in a Vietnamese charnel house, Labor has forsaken the most elementary standards of decency, playing to the gallery while off on electoral fishing expeditions. Calwell was "trying to win votes from people who otherwise would never have been attracted to vote for his policies on their merits."[14] This, of course, was contemptible for Labor to do; "To trifle with human lives and to trifle with the defence of this country is possibly the lowest act in politics."[15]

Any hint of a politically irregular motion by the government, and especially one which might earn the L-CP favorable publicity, has immediately caught Labor's attention. When Malcolm Fraser, the minister for the army, contributed a statement to the Australian army newspaper, refuting criticisms of the dispatch of conscripts to Vietnam, his action was seized upon as "an arrogant misuse of his position, a betrayal of his duty as a Minister in a Parliamentary Government and an attempt to establish a totalitarian climate in the army."[16] Labor has struck against certain official Australian publications which have presented the government's case in the most attractive light possible and which at least indirectly have discounted the principal anti-Vietnam and anticonscription criticisms. These booklets have been printed and circulated at public expense, and a number of them have been sent to prominent members of the community, including school headmasters, who have had the opportunity to request booklets in quantity for distribution to students. Labor has naturally cried "foul"; the government was using taxpayers' money to propagate untenable policies among impressionable schoolchildren, while the parliamentary opposition had no right to "equal time" for reply.[17]

Labor's temptation to expose the L-CP's proclivity for earning unfair political currency from Vietnam has not, however, been regarded in ALP quarters as something to undertake without some reflection, lest the backfire be worse than the benefits of the original assault, as was illustrated during Lyndon Johnson's visit to Australia in October of 1966, a month before the federal House election. The Holt government weighed the political effect the visit might have, and in balance it determined that the results would be productive. All the elements of a love feast between President and Prime Minister were present: similar national heritage, close bonds forged in the 1940s and continued by mutual involvement in Vietnam, an effusive Johnson and an equally effusive Holt. For Labor, it was damned if it did and damned if it didn't. If it complained too bitterly, it could be crucified for unfurling its anti-American colors at a time when America's foremost dignitary was honoring Australia with a visit. If Labor remained silent, it would allow the government to absorb the credit for a potentially spectacularly successful visit from its closest foreign friend and Vietnamese ally.

In the end, Labor turned in both directions at once. Senator J. B. Keefe, ALP federal president, issued a statement welcoming the President's visit. But he berated the government for allowing the visit to occur on the eve of an election, thus converting Johnson's presence into a "cheap political gimmick." He also urged Australians to apply all peaceful and constitutional means to demonstrate to the President Australia's opposition to the Vietnamese commitment.[18] For Dr. James F. Cairns, a prominent Labor parliamentarian, it was not only regrettable that Johnson had unwittingly been drawn into another country's partisan politics, but that any anti-Vietnamese demonstrations during the visit—demonstrations which he favored —would be twisted by the government to cast Labor in an unflattering light. Still, Cairns saw possible Labor advantage if Johnson were exposed to substantial Australian anti-Vietnamese manifestations, since such behavior could, *desirably*, further polarize public opinion on the great issues of the day.[19]

Most Laborites resented the timing of Johnson's visit, but were plainly afraid to make an issue of it, lest the party play into the government's hands. In the last analysis, the ALP federal parliamentary caucus endorsed the opportunity to greet the President and to explain Labor's thinking to him in person.[20] When Johnson came, there were anti-Vietnamese demonstrations from which Labor had difficulty in dissociating itself. Calwell and other members of an ALP delegation had a private conversation with the President. The discussants agreed not to issue a statement, but Johnson apparently had reemphasized the importance of the effort in Vietnam. In reply to journalists' questions on the effect of the Johnson visit on the forthcoming Australian election, Calwell blandly stated that there would be no effect, and he would be sorry if the visit should be regarded in that light. Thus, as John Bennetts of the Melbourne *Age* commented, the Laborites could wring little if any electoral mileage from the presidential visit. At best, "Their aim was, as far as possible, to sterilise it electorally." On the other hand, "The Johnson 'spectacular' is unlikely to damage the electoral prospects of the Government which stage-managed it."[21] It is impossible to establish the weight of the visit on the November election, at which Labor was severely mauled. But ALP resentment hung on. At the ALP federal conference in August 1967, Keefe's presidential address recalled sardonically the "disgusting spectacle" of a world leader being encouraged to come to Australia "to take part in a cheap and tawdry political campaign."[22]

In this climate of suspicion that the government has been enticed into exploiting the war for political advantage, it is natural that accusations of crude inconsistency, personal gain, and hypocrisy should have become fairly standard operating procedure. Labor has had a great many unkind things to say in this vein about the government's treatment of Vietnam and conscription. Much of this began in late 1964 with the introduction of the conscription legislation, which Labor found to be substantively wrong, an appalling admission of failure and duplicity respecting military preparedness, and at the same time an unsavory bid for electoral payoff. For years the government had been shouting "wolf" about international crises, for years it had been absorbing millions for defense, and only a few weeks prior to the decision to institute conscription it had been denying that conscription either was necessary or had been requested by the government's military advisors. Suddenly, everything changed, and without apparent rhyme or reason. Hence the ALP's insistence that the government was trifling with the people, with Australia's defense, with the very lives of young men, and Calwell swore that in the approaching 1964 Senate electoral campaign "my colleagues and I will go from city to city, from town to town, throughout the length and breadth of this continent, with one aim. We will expose the deceit and duplicity of this Government not only on defence but over the whole range of policy."[23]

As Australia assumed an increasing commitment in Vietnam, the ALP concluded that the L-CP government was intent on continuing its sleight-of-hand approach. Some of Labor's attack became personal and visceral, especially on Calwell's part. For instance, he insinuated that the government by and large invented Vietnam as a crisis to which Australia was being asked to respond with men and materials, since under ordinary circumstances most Australians treated the struggle there with almost complete unconcern, regarding Vietnam "as they regard Tibet."[24] Those in the government who advised the imperativeness of the Australian commitment were speaking from sheltered positions. They were "grizzly warmongers" who themselves would not need to risk their skins in combat.[25] Holt himself had "chickened out of the second world war and his three step-sons have chickened out of the Vietnam war. People who want to send others to war should be prepared to go themselves."[26] Increases in Australian troop strength in Vietnam seemed to be cynically ordered, according to the opposition; they were aimed at realizing such benefits as the placement of American orders for the manufacture of war materials in Australia.[27] Before the 1966 election, the ALP federal secretariat published a seventeen-page booklet entitled *Vietnam and Conscription.* The booklet's subtitle was "A Record of Deceit, Duplicity and Dishonesty," and inside was Labor's documented case against the government's alleged inconsistency and evasion on all major aspects of the Vietnam and conscription controversies.[28]

Partisan Politics and the Confluence of Issues: Chinese Trade and Vietnamese Policy

The most persistent jabbing at presumed government inconsistency and hypocrisy has dealt with Australia's commerce with China, and its elaboration here should usefully serve to spotlight the manner in which Vietnam has developed a capacity to merge with other features of public policy as the parties have fought to outscore and humiliate one another. The Chinese trade issue has been present for some years, but has acquired fresh pungency with the appearance of the Vietnamese war and Australia's contribution to it. It is also an issue in dispute on which Labor and the DLP have been able to achieve a rare, common foothold of agreement, though the agreement has come in terms of objections lodged against government policy, rather than on alternative solutions to prevailing policy.

Since the Communist seizure of power in China, Australia has never formally suspended trade with Peking. Trade during the Korean War was minimal but gradually picked up in the late fifties. The close of 1960 brought the first major wheat sale to China. Since then Australian exports to China have been considerable and represent an established part of Australia's overseas trade. In 1966–1967, Australian shipments to China were valued at $131 million (Australian), five times the value of goods imported from China in the same period.

The bulk of the Chinese trade has been in wheat, which the Chinese have purchased on credit and paid for with punctilious regularity. Wool and other primary goods and products have also been sold to China, as have some manufactured goods and processed and unprocessed metals. The government does not itself sell anything to China, but it does possess the legal power to bar whatever sales it might see fit. What the L-CP government has done is to maintain a "China differential," under which it applies a complex set of procedures which enable trade to continue, but with greater restriction on what can be construed as "strategic" than prevails among Western countries other than the United States, which imposes a total ban on commerce with Peking.

The ALP has always favored the expansion of commercial relations with China, and in fact in the late fifties frequently prodded the government to exert itself more energetically in this direction. Once serious trade with China had come about, however, the ALP reveled in exposing the government's hypocrisy in lapping up the foreign exchange which China paid and enjoying the disposal of embarrassing wheat surpluses at home, while identifying China as a major international threat and running a foreign policy designed to check the spread of Chinese influence. To correct this inconsistency, Labor called for a moderated foreign policy, not a cancellation of the Chinese trade. The DLP, agreeing with Labor that government policy on China was inconsistent and even hypocritical, recommended that the inconsistency be repaired from the other side— suspend the Chinese trade, but never slacken in pursuing a resolute foreign policy toward the Chinese menace.

The L-CP government has defended its ostensibly inconsistent position in several ways. Its plea that it cannot interfere in the trade sales as transacted by autonomous marketing boards or through private channels was and remains specious, but otherwise it has argued an entirely plausible case. The trade brings substantial income. It has never encountered Chinese defaults or political pressure. It is carried out in carefully screened goods and products, which have little if any strategic application. If Australia failed to sell to China, other countries would feel no compunction about doing so, and therefore a prohibition on the sale of Australian goods would leave China's interests unaffected. At all events, Australia has not been at war with China. In the long run, as a Western system and a close friend and ally of the United States, Australia might be rendering some small contribution toward alleviating China's sense of encirclement, thus pushing the door just a bit more open for some possible, future *rapprochement*.[29]

As long as the "Chinese menace" was a relatively remote consideration for Australia, the debate over Chinese trade seemed to lack real sting and conviction. But from 1965 onward, its focus became increasingly sharp. There is no evidence, direct or inferential, that Australia's continuing trade with China has impeded the prosecution of any aspect of the Vietnamese war, militarily, diplomatically, or otherwise. Nor have criticisms of the Chinese trade really refuted the government's own explanation of why the trade is valuable in its own right. But Labor and the DLP have, for their separate reasons, worked at invoking the "inconsistency" argument with renewed relish and pointedness. Labor has no direct chance of altering the L-CP's Vietnamese policy, but as an alternative government its interests are served by exposing the incumbent government before the voting public as less than fully sincere and committed to its own phrases about Vietnam's importance and the Chinese hand in manipulating the war there. In other words, it pays Labor to tarnish the government's credibility.

The DLP is not an alternative government. But it is unflagging in contending that a Labor government would be an unmitigated disaster for the country, particularly in foreign policy. Hence it wishes to strengthen the L-CP government's resolve in Vietnam, and to undermine Labor's appeal to the electorate. Contrary to the ALP, it insists on "consistency" so as to bring Chinese trade into line with foreign policy. By stressing the continuing danger from China and the stakes involved in Vietnam, it countervails the ALP's deemphasis on this danger and these stakes. It also has some hopes of altering government policy, if for no other reason than that the L-CP has committed itself so deeply on Vietnam that it would be easier for it to extricate itself from the Chinese trade than from fixed Vietnamese policies. This would obtain should the government find that the exercise of simultaneously juggling the balls of Chinese trade and anti-Chinese foreign policy was becoming too risky electorally, or was generating excessive tensions with the Liberal party's own right wing, or even conceivably was drawing the kinds of reprimands from America that have not to date materialized.

Since the ALP's purpose has been to hurt rather than, as with the DLP, to sustain the government, its attack on commerce with China has been especially biting. It was on Labor initiative that in August 1967 a special motion for adjournment was successfully raised in the Senate to consider the government's inconsistency over China, and it produced the single most detailed debate ever conducted in Parliament on the subject.[30]

The government defines China as Asia's preeminent source of discord, and in the final count a menace to Australia. It furthermore defines Vietnam as a classic example of the convergence of these factors. Trading with China is therefore tantamount to trading with the enemy; not a distant, potential enemy, but a clear-and-present-danger enemy. But when critics question the government's interpretation of the Chinese threat, or its insistence on the supreme importance of holding steady in Vietnam, they are scoffed at and treated as misguided or unpatriotic or both. Whitlam's taunt is worth quoting: The Prime Minister and his colleagues "condone a trade of hundreds of millions of dollars with a country which they stigmatise as the source of all subversion and aggression throughout our region, the indirect enemy in Vietnam. If there is a profit to be made, apparently there is no treason. When treason prospers, none dare call it treason."[31]

The Chinese trade becomes more ominous because, Labor has contended, the separation of strategic from nonstrategic items for authorized shipment to China breaks down in practice. While Australia does not sell guns and bullets to China, its wheat and its wool can be transshipped to Vietnam, North or South, to help feed and clothe those persons whom the government itself has identified as the enemy, and at whose hands Australian troops have been dying. Is it not by the government's own admission that China supplies moral, diplomatic, *and* material backing for the Viet Cong and the North Vietnamese? In this way, the government is portrayed not simply as inconsistent with its own principles. It is a knowing contributor to the military potential of the enemy and to the hardship and even personal danger of the men whom it has conscripted and compelled to wage the war. To make the irony complete, the government long argued the sanctimonious position that the bombing of the North, in the absence of positive signs that serious conversations could be undertaken, had to be continued. If it were suspended, more supplies would reach the enemy and Australian troops would face greater risks. Yet these supplies could very well have had an Australian origin, having been sold to China.

Equally reprehensible to its detractors is the apparent double standard which the government has encouraged respecting Chinese trade and Vietnam. The government cries out that Vietnam is critical to Australia's defense and implores the country's citizenry to make all needed sacrifices to uphold the cause—more taxes for defense, conscription, sacrifice of life on the battlefield. But when it addresses itself to trade, the accounting is done in dollars-and-cents terms, pure and simple. It seems perfectly fine for wheat growers or steel manufacturers to enrich themselves on Chinese gold while the community at large is implored to acquiesce in belt-tightening and casualties so that Chinese ambitions can be frustrated in Vietnamese jungles. "I wonder," asked the Labor senator who instigated the 1967 Senate debate, "how members of the Government Parties can sleep with their consciences when they know that these things are going on."[32]

The Politics of Loyalty: Aid to the NLF

Imputations of gross electoral deviousness, of toying with lives, of deceit and hypocrisy, and of political immorality have all become enmeshed in the party controversy concerning Vietnam and conscription. It is therefore not unnatural that the level of the debate has included charges that one side or the other is, in plain words, treasonable to Australian interests.

From the ALP have come accusations such as that the government is so obsessed with military solutions that it would be prepared to counsel the application of nuclear weapons in Vietnam, and would therefore contemplate with *sang-froid* the prospect of general nuclear war; so said Calwell.[33] From another Labor quarter came the insinuation that the American Central Intelligence Agency was probably subsidizing Labor's political opponents, in particular the DLP[34] (i.e., the charge being that one or more Australian parties were in the pay of a foreign power).

The DLP has not itself been short on such invective. The Labor party, its deputy leader alleged, has done its utmost to sabotage both the armed services' recruiting program, and to unsettle conscripts by spreading insidious propaganda about the wrongness of the Vietnamese war[35] (i.e., Labor has been subverting the Australian armed forces).

Nor has the government been negligent in exploiting opportunities to smear Labor with the tar-brush of disloyalty or something akin to it. According to Holt, "the external policies of the Labor Party are—to put it bluntly—suicidal"[36] (i.e., Labor was willing and/or trying to sell out the country). According to Minister for the Army Malcolm Fraser, a substantial swing from the government in the 1967 Senate election would be interpreted in Hanoi as a shift in Australia's attitude toward Vietnam, and Hanoi would also conclude that a similar wavering could occur in America[37] (i.e., to support Labor is to give aid and comfort to the enemy). Most succinctly of all, from Minister for Territories Charles Barnes came the assertion that, when a Laborite had advocated Australian withdrawal from Vietnam, "all I can say about his remarks is that if he is not for us, he is agin us, because he gave comfort to our enemies."[38]

The interplay of politics and patriotism in Australia was especially well illustrated when legislation was introduced in August 1967 to block the remission of Australian-controlled funds to the NLF and to North Vietnam. For the moment, our interest lies in noticing the party-political applications of this issue. While it has been an issue which has carried other important connotations, their treatment can best be deferred until the general themes of public protest activity and civil liberties are raised for analysis.

The notion of sending funds to the other side in the Vietnamese conflict was first broached in 1965, when the annual conference of the Australian Students' Labor Federation, a grouping of university-based "Labor Clubs," resolved in favor of sending medical assistance to the NLF. At its 1967 conference, the federation extended its intentions, placing itself on record as favoring the collection of moneys for "medical and other" aid for the NLF. Several university Labor Clubs as well as certain private individuals undertook the collection of funds, though it was at Monash University, in Victoria, that the collection of funds for purposes other than medical was most explicitly taken to heart.[39]

The impetus for governmental measures to prohibit such activity came from DLP Senator Francis McManus. He made it plain early in August 1967 that he found the practice of sending funds to an enemy which was responsible for killing Australians abhorrent and in direct contravention of Australia's national interest. Unless the government itself took appropriate steps to bar the transmission of money to the NLF and North Vietnam, he would move an urgency motion in the Senate, asking that those implicated be charged with treason.[40] The government did indeed take corrective steps. Legislation was enacted which imposed a maximum fine of two thousand dollars or two years in prison or both on those convicted of transmitting aid to the North Vietnamese government, the North Vietnamese Communist party, or the NLF. Those convicted of collecting or contributing money became subject to lesser penalties. The Australian Red Cross was exempted from these provisions and could transmit funds or goods to the International Red Cross. Direct transmission by the Red Cross of aid to the proscribed parties was, however, *de facto* invalidated by authority granted to the Reserve Bank of Australia to refuse to release funds overseas if it believed that the money was designed for remittance to these parties.

The debate in Parliament both before and after the introduction of what was denominated the Defense Forces Protection Bill constantly slid off the merits of such legislation and onto a jockeying for political advantage and insinuations of the worst order. It is likely that the government would have brought down legislation even if McManus had not threatened to create a *cause célèbre*. A Senate election was approaching, and there was every indication that Vietnam would again, as in 1966, dominate the campaign. Under Whitlam's direction Labor had just turned in a stunning federal by-election victory in the Victorian seat of Corio. It had also, however, just adjourned the Adelaide federal conference at which the party prescribed the rigid conditions under which an ALP government would be permitted to retain Australian forces in Vietnam. Consequently, this was an auspicious time for the government to begin the process of cutting Whitlam down to size, rubbing in the accusation that the new ALP policy on Vietnam was unalloyed humbug, and otherwise priming the L-CP for the forthcoming electoral battle. Then too, this was the time when both Labor and DLP outcries against the government's inconsistency over Chinese trade were at a peak. It therefore was good political sense to take some of the steam out of charges of inconsistency in trade by demonstrating consistency of Vietnam commitment and punishment for the rascals who were aiding the enemy in Vietnam.

In the House of Representatives on August 16, the same day that McManus in the Senate was bringing forward his special adjournment motion to discuss the need to curb funds for the NLF, Liberal Sir John Cramer asked the Prime Minister to make a statement on the subject. Judging by the nature of the question and of the reply, it was an arranged situation. Cramer did not simply ask if Holt was willing to offer a statement. He also asked, almost in the same breath, what measures could be taken against those responsible for the "traitorous" act of collecting money to aid Australia's enemies, whether the Labor Clubs were authorized bodies of the ALP, and whether Holt could explain the government's own attitude toward the Labor Clubs' fund collecting.

Holt was prepared with a lengthy reply. Yes, the fund collections constituted reprehensible behavior. No, he was "not able to say with any authority" what relationship the Labor Clubs bore to the

ALP. Yes, the government was planning prompt action to stop the collections. But the insinuation had been dropped; Labor and the Labor Clubs may have had some ties. Whitlam was quick to his feet. Quite correctly, he denied that the Labor Clubs were in any way related to the Labor party. In fact, only that afternoon, the ALP parliamentary executive had issued a statement on the subject. Hadn't the Prime Minister seen it? No, said Holt, he had not. But he was putting it to Whitlam that he did "not see all that much difference in principle between what these young students [in the Labor Clubs] are proposing to do and the terms that came out of the Adelaide conference in which the Leader of the Opposition joined in decisions to serve an ultimatum on the allies of Australia in Vietnam under threat of withdrawal of Australian troops if that ultimatum were not observed."[41]

And so the debate on the collection of funds progressed on the government side—Labor Clubs and Labor party, Labor party and humiliating, suicidal withdrawal from Vietnam—a neat package of innuendo about lack of patriotism and devotion to Australia's fighting men. This tactic was not well received around the country, even among those who favored legal sanctions against the collectors. Even B. A. Santamaria, a committed anti-Communist and one of the strongest spokesmen for the DLP cause, told his radio audience that the government "should stick to the issues and not try to make political capital out of the fruits of its own weakness."[42]

By and large, the government's attack threw the ALP onto the defensive. As a party, Labor supported and voted for the legislation, but without enthusiasm. It resented the insinuations made about its own concern for the safety of the country's forces engaged in Vietnam, and it accused the *government* of being the chief fund raiser: To realize cheap political marks, the government had inflated the issue of a few hundred students collecting money all out of proportion. It had created a crisis atmosphere which simply served to publicize and encourage what had been an insignificant group of misguided young persons. It could have quashed the flow of funds to the NLF by simple administrative expedients, not draconic legislation. Where possible, Labor went to the attack with the sharpest weapon then available to it, the Chinese trade. How cynical, how disgusting. The government allowed those whose goods were being sold to China—the presumed mastermind of the Vietnamese war—to line their pockets. But it had the temerity to launch a political extravaganza and to prosecute a handful of students who were contributing a few dollars to the NLF—mostly dollars not for killing, but for healing, since the bulk of the money was earmarked for medical supplies.[43]

Perhaps the most illuminating commentary on the party debate came from D. C. Hannaford, a South Australian senator who some months before had resigned from the Liberal party in disagreement over Vietnam, and was now sitting as an independent. He had no sympathy with those who collected funds for the NLF, but agreed with Labor that the government's bill had been unnecessary and politically inspired. While he in good conscience could not vote for the bill, he entirely appreciated why the ALP had to. It would have brought joy to the government had Labor decided to vote "no," for this would have been distorted as a denial of protection for the fighting men in Vietnam, to be "shouted from the housetops, on the hustings and everywhere else."[44]

Chapter 4. Vietnam and Conscription as Reflections of Labor's Internal Problems

The preceding analysis of the aid to the NLF debate supplies a convenient transition to one of the single most prominent aspects of the entire Australian party dialogue over Vietnam and conscription. The subject of the Labor party's own internal politics is a very large and evergreen theme within Australian political literature. Here only a truncated version of the many ramifications of ALP politics can be attempted, but it should disclose something of how and why Labor behaves as it does on the twin topics of Vietnam and conscription, both in the style and in the substance of its policy presentations. An appreciation of Labor's behavior can, in turn, elucidate how the conduct of the national political debate has come to be affected.

Criticisms of ALP Decision-Making Processes and Organization

It has long been the habit in Australian party politics for Labor's enemies to hit relentlessly at the manner and the men who decide party policy. According to Labor's detractors, the ALP is not to be trusted in office because it speaks with many and often conflicting voices. It cannot be trusted because the authoritative version of policy is not laid down either through rank and file party member participation, or by politicians, but rather by "faceless" and politically irresponsible men who control federal conferences or the federal executive, the latter being the interpreter of party policy between conferences. It cannot be trusted because those forces most prominently represented at conference or in the executive are manipulated by, obligated to, or otherwise influenced by trade union oligarchs who themselves are badly contaminated by extremist views.

Until the adoption of some minor organizational reforms in August 1967, the ALP's top decision-making body, the federal conference, was a tiny group of thirty-six persons, six from each state, and often bound to vote the instructions issued by the several state party organizations. Most of the delegates were not themselves political officeholders, and were selected in their respective states by means reflecting the trade union bias of the party generally and of the exceptional influence of key unions and their leaders in particular. The federal executive, composed of two delegates from each state until the 1967 reforms, spoke authoritatively for the party between conferences. While parliamentary tactics were the prerogative of the ALP parliamentary party and the parliamentary party enjoyed freedom of policy action on ground not covered by conference legislation and any executive emendations, all parliamentarians, including the leadership, were debarred from expressing attitudes which contravened conference or executive positions.

To the critics, no Labor government would therefore be its own master, and as a result would not govern on behalf of Australia's interests. Rather, it would be shackled to the directives insisted upon by "outside" radical forces.[1] While Calwell was ALP leader, the government parties and the DLP charged that he was the mouthpiece of the party machine. Once Whitlam had succeeded to the leadership, that charge was no longer particularly plausible, so the criticism was amended to read that no matter what Whitlam said about Vietnam, no matter how much he tried to squirm, to evade, to be all things to all men, to act the role of the "artful dodger," Labor policy remained organization policy, and organization policy was both wrong and the work of sinister elements.[2]

In the 1960s, ALP conference decisions were formulated amidst considerable controversy between the organization and the parliamentary party, or the parliamentary leadership, or both, on foreign as well as domestic policies. Vietnam and conscription helped considerably to accelerate intraparty efforts at achieving the connected objectives of instituting organizational and programmatic reforms. The protagonists of such objectives had various motives in mind, such as personal advancement, unhappiness with official positions which seemed irrelevant or impractical or simply ill-founded, and discomfort over what was construed to be unrepresentative and overrigid decision-making machinery. There were motives of electoral expediency, which seemed to teach that Labor was doomed to continue in opposition as long as its policies, fairly or not, could be assailed as bordering on national suicide, or its organizational framework, fairly or not, could be ridiculed as a case of radical power being wielded without the sobering tonic of political responsibility. Here was the setting for the clash of innovation and tradition, of personalism and collective judgment, and above all of expediency and principle.

Whitlam's Bid for the Leadership

The struggle for the ALP parliamentary leadership became central to any organizational or programmatic alterations, since the leading personalities had quite different perceptions of what, if anything, needed to be done. Following Labor's setback in the 1963 House election, Whitlam undertook what came to amount to a three-year campaign to differentiate himself from his chief, Calwell, and to install himself as leader. Twenty years Calwell's junior, and of a pragmatic persuasion, Whitlam did not conceal his view that Calwell's "image" was seriously wanting. Calwell's style was rough and unattractive. He was old fashioned. His policy commitments were not always the most defensible or electorally suitable. For a time, Whitlam's principal policy difference with Calwell and the party organization was over aid to parochial schools. By the second half of 1966, it had become Vietnam.

Whitlam's objections to Calwell's Vietnam-conscription approach were both substantive and stylistic. Calwell had never reconciled himself to forced service for any kind of overseas duty, and in 1942–1943 had actually opposed Labor Prime Minister Curtin's modest proposal to conscript for service within a narrowly drawn perimeter around Australia. When the Menzies government brought in its conscription bill in late 1964, a very deep-seated conviction in Calwell was offended. Once conscripts were assigned to Vietnam, Calwell's line became uncompromisingly hostile to government policy, and included the recall of all troops from Vietnam, with no apparent regard for the realities of the Vietnamese conflict, American reactions, or other unavoidable considerations. As 1966 progressed, Calwell became a constant name-caller and alarmist. The Prime Minister was personally accused of being "chicken" and a "warmonger." The government, in Calwell's mind, was conspiring with America in a manner that made pawns of Australian lives. Australian mothers would rebel against a government which sent their sons to die in a senseless war on behalf of a worthless South Vietnamese regime. Even Holt seemed pleased to have Calwell as an adversary, tearing

79

into him personally on the assumption that the Calwell image was a liability to the ALP.

Many months before the November 1966 election Calwell had promised he would vacate the leadership should Labor not be raised to office at the next election. Throughout most of 1966, therefore, Whitlam's job was no longer to force Calwell out, but to set the stage for a successful bid for the leadership once the election was over, and to create a climate in which necessary programmatic and organizational reforms could be undertaken under his own supervision. His first move was taken in August, upon his return from an inspection tour of Vietnam. He voiced reservations about the feasibility of separating conscripts from regular army men in Vietnam—party policy at that time being to ship the former home immediately but to delay the return of the latter. He also proposed a new ALP emphasis on civil aid to Vietnam, but it was so couched as to leave the impression that an armed presence would need to be maintained in the area if civil reconstruction were to make sense in the face of Viet Cong operations.[3] Later in the year he assumed a more elastic and open position than Calwell on negotiations with the United States to return regular Australian army personnel from Vietnam. Neither Whitlam proposal represented a radical departure from standing policy, but both were tuned to make Labor's promise about the troop commitment less dramatically certain, and more apt to prevent a rupture with the United States.

The parliamentary caucus rejected Whitlam's proposals, mainly, it would seem, because his basic intention was seen through, and loyalty to the incumbent leader and to official policy could not be cavalierly shrugged off. Shortly after the disastrous 1966 election, Whitlam's opponents in the party, including Calwell, maneuvered to embarrass Whitlam for having defied his leader and standing party policy on the troop withdrawal question. Their motive was not simply retribution, but an effort to allow the leadership to pass into the hands of a more doctrinally reliable and organizationally sensitive person, such as James Cairns.

Within the more doctrinally pure ALP circles it had long been understood that Whitlam, despite genuine disagreement with government rationales and policy, held no brief for a dogmatic position on Vietnam. Cairns himself had hit out against "saboteurs" such as Whitlam who would prevent the retention of an authentic, radical foreign policy alternative in Australian politics.[4] According to a publication reflecting the Labor left:

> The danger of a possible Whitlam leadership is that in the search for the "modern" smooth image, tailored to fit the editorial hectorings of the daily press and believed to be acceptable to the marginal voter, the little that is distinctly labour will be whittled away. It is doubtful, for instance, whether under Whitlam the ALP would withdraw troops from Vietnam. A tame-cat ALP that has traded its scant independence for the Treasury benches would forfeit claims to the traditional loyalty vote of the labour movement.[5]

The more hidebound elements in the party had, apparently, hoped to salvage something special from the anticipated electoral defeat in November. By their calculations, most Labor losses in the House would be in seats held by men leaning toward Whitlam. Therefore, defeat would be a blessing in disguise, for the chances of electing someone other than Whitlam to the leadership would be enhanced to the extent that the ALP parliamentary caucus would have lost some of its Whitlamites.[6]

One tack taken by Whitlam's opponents was to arraign him before the ALP federal executive on charges of having uttered a position on Vietnam which contradicted official policy. It is not entirely clear whether plans were to be made to expel Whitlam from the party or just to censure him and therefore weaken his bid for the leadership. Countermaneuvers by Whitlam's supporters, including warnings that a Whitlam expulsion would bring the breaking off of the entire New South Wales Labor party branch from the ALP federal party structure, managed to stave off a direct confrontation between Whitlam and the executive.[7] The episode is instructive, for it demonstrated the industry with which various party factions approached the leadership contest.

A second opportunity to embarrass Whitlam was quickly generated. Late in December 1966 it became known that Air Vice-Marshal Ky, then South Vietnam's premier, was to pay a call on Australia. Calwell's spontaneous reaction was to pour abuse on Ky and his government, for whom he had "nothing but contempt." Ky was a "miserable little butcher" and a "gangster Quisling," and his visit would shock every Australian except those "who condoned and tolerated murder, brutality and injustice."[8] While Calwell was undoubtedly sincere in expressing these sentiments, there was a possible political windfall to be earned as well. When Ky and his party arrived, there would need to be demonstrations. Calwell would march in peaceful protest. So would Cairns and F. D. Crean, both declared contenders in the impending ALP leadership contest. So should every other responsible Laborite who opposed the war and considered Ky to be a symbol of everything that was rotten in South Vietnam. Would Whitlam also march? "I hope all my colleagues will follow my lead," said Calwell. "Anyone who does not will incur the well-deserved wrath and contempt of all other members of the Labor Party."[9] In Vietnam during mid-1966 Ky had hosted Whitlam. Would Whitlam now attend any functions for Ky? Whitlam's response was silence and total noninvolvement. No marching, no attendance at receptions, no public statements. Discretion seemed in order on this delicate occasion.

When the parliamentary caucus, comprising all ALP House and Senate members, met in early February, the efforts to outmaneuver and weaken Whitlam proved futile. Whitlam had sufficiently prepared the ground for the showdown in caucus, and the party's losses at the November election hardly affected the outcome. Under an exhaustive ballot system, Whitlam won on the third round with thirty-nine votes, to fifteen for Cairns and fourteen for Crean.[10] Tasmanian Lance Barnard, also a moderate, was elected deputy leader in the House, defeating Cairns on the sixth count by the narrow margin of thirty-five to thirty-three.

Vietnam-Conscription and the Consolidation of Whitlam's Leadership

Whitlam's election was quickly followed by a number of further victories for the new leader within the parliamentary Labor party. Within three weeks of assuming the leadership, Whitlam floated a Vietnamese policy balloon. He said, in public, that he did not feel the time was opportune for Australian troops to be returned from Vietnam. Their return should be made contingent on a Vietnamese armistice or settlement—and the ALP's most immediate aim should be to press the government to search for a settlement.[11] There was some raising of eyebrows in the parliamentary caucus, but on a voice vote a resolution critical of Whitlam was overwhelmingly defeated.

Many of Whitlam's critics were obviously unwilling to start a wrangle with a leader who had barely unpacked his bags.[12]

Whitlam wasted little time in exploiting the "era of good will" to the fullest measure. He assigned himself primary parliamentary spokesmanship for foreign affairs, and gave Barnard responsibility for defense. When caucus balloted for ALP parliamentary committee membership, moderates received heavy representation on the External Affairs and Defense Committee. It was Whitlam's wish to abandon the Evatt-Calwell line of refusing ALP participation on the Joint Parliamentary Committee on Foreign Affairs. The government made a few concessions in the management of committee affairs, and Whitlam was able to persuade caucus to waive other conditions which had previously held the party back from consenting to participate. Left-wingers in caucus boycotted nominations for the eight committee positions to which Labor was entitled, with the result that all Laborites elected by caucus were Whitlam supporters.[13]

But in the months following his assumption of the leadership Whitlam's successes were by no means entirely limited to the arena of the parliamentary Labor party. What Whitlam also needed to assert his command over the party was both stature and concrete successes where, in politics, success matters a great deal—on the hustings. June and July of 1967 provided some pleasant rewards along these lines. In June, while in the United States, Whitlam met with some of the most influential figures in the country, including Senators Mike Mansfield, William Fulbright, and Robert Kennedy, Assistant Secretary of State William Bundy, Ambassador Averell Harriman and, last but not least, President Lyndon Johnson. Labor had been excoriated by the government parties and the DLP for an allegedly lunatic Vietnamese policy. Now Whitlam was consorting with the crème de la crème of the nation his party was accused of wishing to betray. To be sure, Whitlam did not emulate Holt's exuberant "all the way with L.B.J.," and instead sidestepped public questions by declaring himself unwilling to become involved in political controversy outside his own country. Not only did he commit no errors, but he scored handsomely when the President described him as the "young and brilliant leader of the Australian Labor Party."[14]

In July came the federal by-election in the Victorian seat of Corio. It had previously been easily held by a Liberal, who in November 1966 had taken some 43.6 per cent of the popular vote to Labor's 37.7 per cent. When the Corio by-election tally was in, Labor had captured the seat. It was the first Victorian seat taken by Labor from the government in fifteen years. The swing to Labor was a phenomenal 11 per cent plus. There were many reasons for the reversal of party fortunes. For instance, the previous sitting member had been especially popular, while the new Liberal aspirant was an unknown. Labor's candidate was both known and popular. Labor stressed domestic, not external issues, while the government was far more concerned with foreign policy. This was Whitlam's chosen emphasis. He campaigned in Corio on a virtually nonstop basis, projecting himself, his candidate, and the positive qualities of the ALP to the fullest degree possible. Even Holt had to admit that Whitlam's presence had been decisive, though he would not have admitted to the judgment that "it was proved once and for all that with a superb vote-getter in Mr. Whitlam and the confidence of the people that he is out to reshape his party, anything is possible electorally."[15]

Whitlam was indeed arming himself for an effort to reconstitute the ALP's decision-making structures and to induce changes in standing policy. But the period between his election as leader in February and the convening of the ALP conference in Adelaide in August was not for him a series of unalloyed triumphs, free of rancor and full of opportunity to do exactly what he wished. Very early in his tenure as leader, the party was backed into two separate Vietnam-related controversies during which Whitlam pretty much allowed nature to take its course, rather than staging a conspicuous and personal intervention.

The first affair concerned the manning of the Australian National Line ships *Boonaroo* and *Jeparit*, scheduled to carry munitions and other stores to Australian forces in Vietnam. The Seamen's Union declared that its members were prohibited from manning these ships, since what was entailed was the supply of instruments of war for an unjustified, despicable conflict. The Seamen's Union, however, was in a very special and isolated position on this score. It was a union which included heavy Communist influence in its leadership. An informal poll taken among *Jeparit* seamen indicated that they were willing to sail. The Australian Council of Trade Unions (ACTU) and various individual unions denounced the ban and urged that the ships be allowed to proceed as planned. Ultimately, the ships did sail, but the *Boonaroo* was taken over by a Royal Australian Navy crew, and the *Jeparit* by a mixed RAN and merchant marine crew.

The ship episode was not strictly an ALP problem, but a union problem. However, for some time Labor had been professing the view that, while it wished to return Australian servicemen from Vietnam, it would do nothing to interfere with their safety or efficiency while they were still in the combat zone. The Seamen's Union position was *de facto* designed to deny Australian troops necessary materiel. Also Labor's special organizational ties to the union movement, and especially to the ACTU, suggested that an opinion from the party might very well be in order. However, Whitlam confined himself to a brief, unrehearsed, parliamentary interjection. He reaffirmed the established Calwell view that his party did not believe in interfering with the troops in the field. When the government finally decided to staff the ships with RAN crews, he conceded that he wanted the Seamen's Union to cooperate in manning the vessels.[16]

The second incident on which the ALP Leader maintained a conspicuous silence concerned the party's connections with the Association for International Cooperation and Disarmament (AICD). The AICD had, by early 1967, become one of the foremost Australian organizations for directing anti-Vietnam and anticonscription operations. It contained members virtually from across the political spectrum, including Laborites, Liberals, and Communists. In late March, the state executive of the New South Wales ALP branch decided to proscribe the AICD (N.S.W.). ALP members in New South Wales would need to resign from the AICD and work for peace through other channels. The AICD had not confined itself to its stated objectives, it included Communists and Liberals on its directorate, and it otherwise was harming Labor's electoral image, especially on Vietnam and conscription.[17] But before the ban could go into effect, a special meeting of the ALP federal executive was convened. There, by a ten-to-two vote, the New South Wales executive's action was rescinded, nominally on grounds that a 1963 federal conference decision had awarded state party branches the right to draw the presence of improper peace groups to the federal executive's attention, but the federal executive held the final authority to judge their legitimacy.[18] Whitlam was present at the executive meetings as a nonvoting observer. During the controversy he failed to make any public comment, even though his own state of New South Wales and its own "moderate," Communist-dissociated position on Vietnam was involved.

Whitlam's reticence to become embroiled in the ship ban and AICD cases would, on balance, appear to reflect something other than indifference or pusillanimity. In neither dispute was it likely that his intervention could have made any difference in the outcome. If anything, his interference, even in the *Boonaroo-Jeparit* argument, could have caused otherwise avoidable ripples of resentment in party circles at a time when Whitlam was eager to round up as much support from all quarters as he possibly could for his party reshaping projects. For instance, the Victorian secretary of the Seamen's Union, B. Nolan, held a seat on the ALP Victorian state executive; so did Calwell and Cairns, both of whom had opposed Whitlam's accession to the party leadership. A Whitlam attack on the Seamen's Union would have been an attack on Nolan, and therefore could have embarrassed and upset Nolan's influential colleagues on the Victorian executive. Regarding AICD, it appears that this was no ordinary moderate-extremist confrontation at various levels of the party hierarchy. The New South Wales executive's decision surprised and irritated many ALP figures in the state, including ranking party members who were in AICD and were not necessarily foreign policy dogmatists or willing collaborators with Communists. All states save New South Wales voted together in the federal executive, and among those supporting the majority was Whitlam's own parliamentary lieutenant, Lance Barnard. There were some real reservations held even among moderate federal executive members both as to the substantive and the procedural appropriateness of the New South Wales move.

The two cases are instructive not so much because they reveal any real inconsistency in Whitlam, but rather his determination not to become bogged down in marginal disputes whose course he could hardly hope to channel. His objectives were to assemble maximum good will in the party and to conserve his political ammunition for basic showdowns—to effect organizational and programmatic renovation in the party. As a shrewd tactician, Whitlam appreciated the dictum that one does not fight in all places on all occasions and with all commitment of available resources.

The 1967 Adelaide Conference: Organizational Alterations

Whitlam did not need to wait long before some skirmishing on these fundamentals opened up. When upon assuming the leadership Whitlam spoke in revisionist language about Vietnam, he escaped any serious challenge. In May, Whitlam dispatched Barnard to Vietnam for a firsthand assessment, and this time it did not pass unchallenged.

Barnard reported that while the ALP's foreign and defense policies were well conceived, they had been "overtaken by the march of history in South-East Asia." While he disagreed with the dispatch of Australian conscript troops to Vietnam and urged a halt in the bombing of the North, he was persuaded that this was a major war, not simply a guerrilla operation, and that North Vietnam had launched a sizable invasion of the South.[19] Critical reaction was swift. Most prominently it issued from F. E. Chamberlain, the Western Australian party secretary, a member of the ALP federal executive, an inordinately powerful figure in the ALP generally, and a dedicated exponent of hard-line leftism. In a circular addressed to party branches and unions throughout the country, Chamberlain defended established party policy on Vietnam and asked for its preservation. He rebuked Barnard for having breached party thinking, and for having reached his judgments on the basis of what amounted to "cocktail party evidence." He also complained that Barnard's remarks could undesirably influence party decision-makers who were about to meet in state and federal conferences.[20]

The Chamberlain memorandum elicited from Whitlam a lengthy and pointed reply. He was about to undertake a systematic selling campaign in the party for structural and programmatic reforms, and was now firing his first major shot. Whitlam accused Chamberlain of really attacking him, Whitlam, via the criticism of Barnard. In March Chamberlain had denounced Whitlam's advocacy of refurbishing the party's organizational base. Now he was advising Whitlam on Vietnam, since Barnard had been sent to Vietnam as Whitlam's personal envoy. Whitlam pounced on Chamberlain's assertion that Barnard's views might affect party conferees, state or federal. It was precisely his point, Whitlam claimed, that ALP decisions should be taken out of the hands of bureaucrats and invested in the rank and file. What was required was fewer "autocratic and idiosyncratic" machine people such as Chamberlain and more representative party decision-making. On questions of substance, Chamberlain was protracting, not shortening, the Vietnamese conflict, since his tenets were dogmatic and impractical. "The defence and diplomatic shortcomings of the Holt Government sent Australian conscripts to Vietnam. The rancorous ramblings of men like Mr. Chamberlain have kept them there."[21]

In a sense, Chamberlain had stumbled into a Whitlam trap. He had provided a convenient catapult for Whitlam's party reform campaign. He had offered Whitlam opportunity to denounce party oligarchs, and therefore to press the case for widening the ALP's decision-making process. He had taken an uncompromising stand on Vietnam, offering Whitlam the chance to paint the party dogmatists in the color of reactionaries rather than progressives. Whitlam made his argument with Chamberlain into a personal issue, both to discredit Chamberlain, and to enhance his own prestige in the weeks ahead. It was a prestige which he had sedulously cultivated for months, and had been unwilling to dissipate in peripheral scuffles such as the ship-manning ban and AICD.

During July and August Whitlam exerted himself to bring about his desired party structural and policy alterations at the forthcoming Adelaide conference. Appropriate structural change would, in its own right, facilitate both short- and long-range policy shifts, something that was critically needed in Labor's foreign policy. Also, it would relieve Labor of the extremely poor public image which had been cast and so strenuously exploited by opposing parties. Improved policy and improved image meant improved electoral power. Eventually, electoral power would bring national office, and with it the actual ability to institute changes in Australian public policy, as for instance regarding Vietnam.

Whitlam was especially attracted to an outline of structural reforms submitted some time before by the ALP's federal secretary, Cyril S. Wyndham. It was a plan whose essence was a greatly expanded conference, composed of delegates directly chosen from the various federal House electorates and from labor unions. Such a scheme would endow the party with a more broadly representative decision-making organ, render cliques at conference much less likely, and would stimulate rank and file party involvement. Whitlam's prime object was to convince the delegates to the Adelaide conference to endorse the appointment of a special commission to give detailed study to the Wyndham plan. In the interim, he was interested in gaining acceptance of a limited expansion of conference and the executive, particularly to include on them state and federal ALP parliamentary leaders.[22]

Whitlam understood that all his hopes would come to grief unless a majority of the existing thirty-six-person conference stood with him, which implied persuading the state party organizations to commit their delegates behind him. Fighting—and winning—the Corio by-election was helpful, for it was a sign that Whitlam was an asset, and a man whose views and methods had to be taken seriously. But Whitlam knew that he had to convince the party elites that it was in their own interest to accede to reforms whose effect would be to dilute their present weight in conference and therefore in the party.

Most ALP state branches were conducting their own conferences, and Whitlam used the opportunity to speak to them as plainly as possible, arguing time and again that politics without power equals impotence, the continuation of L-CP rule, and disastrous Vietnamese and other policies.[23] New South Wales and Tasmania had for some time been known to stand behind Whitlam's reform project. Victoria was unqualifiedly opposed. South Australia leaned against Whitlam. Western Australia and Queensland were uncertain quantities. The state conference in Perth, repudiating Chamberlain, the Western Australian secretary, swung into place, and Whitlam was also hopeful of tying down some Queensland delegates.

It was before the Victorian conference that he was most outspoken, lashing the Victorians for their unmodern, unrealistic, ostrich-like behavior on both organizational and policy questions. He had known for months that Victoria would never support him. It was in Victoria more than in any other state that any semblance of party vitality and democracy had disappeared. It was the Victorian party that in 1966, nearly on the eve of a federal election, had subjected an incumbent ALP federal member, Sam Benson, to public denunciation. It eventually was instrumental in his expulsion from the party for his moderate views on Vietnam and conscription, and for his membership in the Defend Australia Committee, a nonpartisan organization which favored a strong Australian foreign policy.[24] It was the Victorian executive that contained some of the strongest voices raised on behalf of condemning Whitlam after the 1966 election. It was the Victorian executive that applauded the public demonstrations against the Ky visit, and which tried to trap Whitlam into an embarrassing predicament.

Whitlam's purpose in going to Victoria and hitting out with all he had was to dissociate himself completely and publicly from the Victorian party. Some of this was for internal party consumption, but it was also arranged to allow Whitlam to operate in total disregard of the state organization during the forthcoming Corio campaign, at which he neither asked for nor expected any favors from the Victorian party. The smashing ALP victory in Corio was partially made possible because this dissociation had been achieved. With Corio won, Whitlam felt more confident than ever that wavering state organizations and delegates would close ranks behind him in Adelaide.[25]

But at Adelaide Whitlam had to settle for half a loaf. Despite furious eleventh-hour negotiations, he could count only on New South Wales, Tasmania, and Western Australia—exactly half of the conference delegates, and therefore no majority. A compromise was effected. Whitlam lost his plan for a thorough review of the Wyndham proposals, but gained an enlargement of the federal conference and executive. Leaders and deputy leaders from the House and Senate and a delegate from the Northern Territory were added to both bodies. The conference was further augmented by the six state parliamentary leaders. Tradition, a reluctance to break the strength of entrenched interests, fears of widespread programmatic changes, plus a resentment of the driving, *allegro vivace*, one-man band performance Whitlam had so long been staging brought him less than total success.

Tremendous energy, successful electoral performance, cogent argument, and the injection of a fresh, exciting breeze of optimism had, however, brought for Whitlam the most important party organizational reconstruction since 1915, and it was a reconstruction agreed to unanimously; even the Victorians rode along, despite their lack of enthusiasm. Conference and the executive would henceforth be larger and contain built-in representation from among ranking and visible Labor politicians. Quite possibly, the reconstructed executive might itself order the very type of broad Wyndham-plan examination on which conference had demurred. Whitlam proved himself to be less than a master tactician, but hardly a slouch; "by cooly performing the art of the possible, Mr. Whitlam saw that the conference was not ready to go so far so soon and, by a neatly-timed face-saving operation for the party, if not for himself, Mr. Whitlam was able to convert what could have been a nasty public setback into a display of solidarity. 'It is the opinion of the whole conference and it is my opinion, too,' he was able to say of the new set-up."[26]

The 1967 Adelaide Conference: Programmatic Alterations

Party reorganization was complementary to the drive to alter Labor's Vietnamese and conscription policies. Particularly after becoming leader, Whitlam was especially well placed to give it focus and direction, but his thinking was shared by an increasing number of people in the party generally, and he was as much a catalyst as an innovator.

During 1966 a number of Labor parliamentarians visited Vietnam, and concluded that this was no black-white situation which could be resolved by dramatic yet simpleminded solutions such as an abrupt withdrawal of Australian forces. Similarly, there was something of a shock treatment effect when Prime Minister Lee Kuan-yew of Singapore, a socialist and nationalist of unimpeachable credentials, told delegations of visiting ALP parliamentarians and officials that the protection of Vietnam from Communist absorption was in the interest of Southeast Asian countries. Then there was the Benson affair, which dramatized the determination of one Labor man to stand and speak out on behalf of an outlook quite differently premised than was the official party line.[27] Barnard's 1967 Vietnamese impressions were therefore additive to an ongoing reconsideration of party policy.

The impetus to alter the party's foreign policy stemmed from feelings that established policy was inherently impractical if not counterproductive to Australian interests, and that the policy was electorally damaging to the party—a sentiment openly voiced by certain ALP parliamentarians defeated in the 1966 election, and in moderate union circles.[28] Whitlam put the two factors together during his appeals to the party in mid-1967, reasoning that while Labor retained a dismally doctrinaire foreign policy it could not expect election to national office, and therefore could not expect to modify the incumbent government's tragically mistaken Vietnamese policy. His ideal was to achieve flexibility on Vietnam, which meant that the party had to forego categorical and/or highly detailed, binding pronouncements on the subject.

Those reluctant to allow serious revision of Vietnamese and conscription policy represented a somewhat more complex set of motivations. Conscription, especially for overseas service, had always been an exceptionally delicate issue for Australian Labor. An early 1957 survey of a sample of ALP elites in Queensland disclosed that anticonscription sentiment was very strongly lodged among *all* ideological groups in the survey population, were they right, left, or in between.[29] Australia's position on Vietnam became a point of principled outlook in some sectors of the party because of the many special, even moral, doubts that it raised. When conscripted Australian troops were assigned to fight there, there was an understandable hardening of attitude.

For some in the ALP, holding fast to a righteous albeit electorally questionable position on Vietnam was therefore the result of a principle and a very particular, historically conditioned content. For Calwell, for instance, when the electorate rebuffed Labor in 1966, it was displaying its cowardice and selfishness[30]—and for the party to emulate these traits would have constituted a perversion of the ALP's role as a movement of beliefs and a genuine alternative to status quo policies. One variation on this theme was that if Labor adopted an essentially bipartisan approach on Vietnam, the government would then become even more supportive of American policy, since it could not offer the excuse that the official opposition, representing 40 per cent of the electorate, imposed certain restraints on an "all the way" approach. Once committed to material support of the allied effort in Vietnam, a subsequent Labor government would find that, just as in America, investments for desirable domestic programs would have to be written off.[31]

Opposition to a swing in policy inevitably became personalized. Whitlam and others felt that standing policy had been made even more untenable by Calwell's viscerally evangelical presentation of it. As Whitlam began to separate himself from this policy and laid plans for its interment, there were some who rallied to the support of a policy which, by its specificity, would deny Whitlam freedom in interpretation. Throughout various ideological persuasions in the party there had long been a widespread sense of genuine devotion to and solidarity with the party, and therefore a reluctance to dispute openly and/or casually abandon what had been decided by prescribed means. The corollary of this syndrome has been that no man is greater than or above the party, particularly in a way that would entitle him to be the tail that wagged the party dog.

As of the Adelaide conference, therefore, there were conflicting party moods as to how far if at all the ALP should move toward overhauling its Vietnam and conscription policies, and especially granting Whitlam considerable room for maneuver. The federal party's Foreign and Defense Committee, despite containing a majority identified as "leftist" and hostile to basic change, brought before conference a recommendation which, while condemning the Vietnamese war and calling for all military efforts there to halt, failed to demand the withdrawal of or prescribe terms for the retention of Australian troops in Vietnam. Also, it recommended that in times of emergency conscription be permitted, and that service for the armed forces could be extended to areas necessary for Australia's defense.[32]

But the conference would not accept such highly elastic and permissive policy. Very exact conditions were spelled out under which Labor could countenance the retention of Australian forces in Vietnam. Conscription was allowed, but only in the event of a threatened attack on Australia or its overseas territories. Conscription for service in Vietnam or anywhere outside Australian territory was prohibited except in time of *declared* war. These modifications of the Foreign and Defense Committee's recommendations, while favored by the "immoderate" forces in conference, did not necessarily reflect a straight "left wing" against "right wing" confrontation. The motion to require that certain very precise conditions obtain before Labor could retain the Australian contingent in Vietnam was moved by a moderate Tasmanian delegate, and had been approved by most of his delegation before they came to Adelaide.[33] The clause forbidding conscription for Vietnam or anywhere else outside Australia except in time of declared war, while seconded by Chamberlain, was moved by a moderate member of the Western Australian delegation, who spoke for his motion in temperate language.[34]

The end result was, as with Whitlam's party reform proposals, some dilution of established practice and policy, but less than Whitlam had sought. Labor was henceforth not committed to an almost automatic return of troops from Vietnam, but could retain them only under carefully prescribed circumstances. Conscription was not per se outlawed, but could be instituted only if voluntary recruiting failed and an attack on Australia or its territories were threatened. Conscription for overseas service was accepted—even in Vietnam— but only in time of declared war.

Beyond the Adelaide Conference

With the close of the Adelaide conference, Labor had new policies on Vietnam and conscription. The question now arose how the party, and especially Whitlam, would present it. On August 2 the sitting Labor member for the Queensland seat of Capricornia died, meaning that a by-election was very shortly to be fought. More importantly, it was widely understood that a Senate election would soon be called—which it was, for late November. Whatever else he did, Whitlam therefore needed to plot a strategy which would enable the ALP to maximize electoral benefits because, or despite of, the new conference rulings.

His first step was to assert his own authority, without which he could not develop a rational electoral strategy. When after the conference various Labor personalities offered public interpretations of the Adelaide decisions, he came to the ALP caucus, reminded his colleagues that he was their leader and official spokesman on foreign policy, and stated that he would not wish to be embarrassed by hearing conflicting viewpoints ventilated for critics to exploit.[35]

If he could clear the path to becoming Labor's authoritative voice on foreign policy, what then? His strategy was twofold: First, take Vietnam off the centerstage and into the wings of public discussion; second, when Vietnam arose, use it to expose the government's deficiencies, rather than creating forums for arguing what Labor wished to do, except to unveil the more constructive and popular features of the officially prescribed policy. He wanted to de-escalate the Vietnamese debate, to keep the government on the defensive, and to accentuate the positive whenever possible, starkly unlike Arthur Calwell's approach of one year earlier.

In Capricornia, Whitlam campaigned vigorously. He emphasized central Queensland state development, accused the government of neglect in this area, and deflected attacks on ALP Vietnamese policy at every turn. Labor retained Capricornia with an increased majority, though it fought against heavier opposition candidate odds than in the 1966 general election.[36] In October, Whitlam deliberately avoided an opportunity to debate (and therefore oppose) in Parliament the government's announcement of the assignment of an additional fifteen hundred men to Vietnam. During the following month's Senate campaign, his stress was on the government's credibility and performance in the handling of delicate key issues. One of these was the ostensible government reluctance to encourage the participation of the NLF in Vietnamese negotiations—something that the United States had announced in the United Nations that it would be prepared to accept. This Whitlam gambit was designed to make Labor appear more consistent with American policy on Vietnam than government policy was. It also dovetailed with a Labor emphasis on those *selected* aspects of the Adelaide program which were pleasantly wholesome and generally noncontroversial—such as commitment to the United States alliance and the desire to bring the war to a speedy and honorable conclusion. When Holt and other government spokesmen tried to pin Whitlam down on whether the Adelaide platform in fact meant that Labor would withdraw the troops unless America met the stipulated, near-to-impossible conditions, Whitlam darted out. He turned the dialogue back onto the L-CP and in effect claimed that the government, being politically responsible, stood in the dock. Being the opposition, Labor did not care to wind itself up in discussing hypothetical situations.

A prominent ALP newspaper advertisement published on the eve of the Senate election read like a model of American comradeship and punctiliously responsible foreign policy. Labor regards the ANZUS alliance as essential. It was Labor that in both world wars mobilized the nation and its resources to achieve ultimate victory. Labor supported the deployment of Australian troops as part of the United Nations effort in Korea. Labor will defend Australian territory to the limit of the nation's ability. Labor never has and never will let Australian fighting men down. Labor urges an end to the bombing of North Vietnam, and encourages an atmosphere in which meaningful discussion for a settlement could occur. Not one word on conditions governing the troop commitment, or on conscription for this kind of service or another.[37] When the tally was in, Labor had some 5 per cent more votes than it earned exactly one year earlier when Arthur Calwell directed a blistering, no-holds-barred campaign over Vietnam and conscription. While Whitlam had not overtly contradicted the Adelaide program during the Senate campaign, he generally ignored it, except to stress some of its more palatable sections out of the context in which they had been written.

But Harold Holt was drowned in December, and the Liberals selected John Gorton to lead them. Gorton resigned from the Senate to contest Holt's now vacant Victorian seat of Higgins. Hence there was another by-election to be fought, but against a new man with slightly different perspectives on Vietnam. There was little preaching from Gorton about unconditional support for America, and a promise that for the visible future the Australian military commitment in Vietnam would not be raised. Higgins was an ironclad Liberal seat, and Gorton was easily elected. The Whitlam line was not much different from what it had been in November. To wit: If Gorton felt no new troops could be dispatched, if Australia was going to be a loyal though not necessarily uncritical ally, the next and logical step for the government was to urge that attrition against the North be halted and negotiations opened. Again, Whitlam refused to be baited into an across the board defense of the Adelaide decisions.[38]

Gradually, however, Whitlam began to address himself to the stubborn problem of what was to be done with the "unmentionable" features of the Adelaide program. Before the Tasmanian state ALP conference in February, he remarked that "we ought to have learned that it is unfruitful to dot every *i* and cross every *t* in advance. No conference can write a policy speech on foreign affairs or any other matter. We don't try to write a policy speech on the social services two years ahead."[39] Ten days later, in a television interview, Whitlam asserted that in 1966 both Holt and Calwell had "debauched" the political debate by their stridency. He said that if an American administration failed to acquiesce in the stated Labor conditions for de-escalating the Vietnamese conflict, an ALP government would have to *consider* withdrawing Australian troops. But unlike Calwell, he did not start with the proposition that Australia should disengage: "I would withdraw Australia's troops if I believed that America was taking no notice of us at all. But I believe America is taking notice of Australia. Australia has more influence on America than any other allies." The problem, according to Whitlam, was that Holt had not seized this opportunity, nor was Gorton seizing it.[40]

Whitlam's increased willingness to disfigure and even openly challenge established party policy was probably activated by wishes to maintain the momentum of his own prestige, to deny his party critics an opportunity to preempt or dominate an intramural debate over "inappropriate" interpretations of Vietnam policy, and to plan for officially sanctioned reconstitution of both party policy and party organization.

For some months after the Adelaide conference, the more militant sectors of the party tended not to interfere with Whitlam's exposition of Vietnam and conscription, perhaps to avoid the kinds of personal and wound-opening barbs that could have cost the party at the polls.[41] Whitlam did lead the party to commendable electoral performances, but he did so by pressing what to some minds was a heretical version of policy. A vigorous and popular leader became the symbol of party and electoral success, but success apparently scored by the expounding of an unprepossessing version of policy. If Whitlam was left unreprimanded too long, he and the policy emphases he cultivated could become the *de facto* and inextricably joined image of the ALP. This would be wrong because an individual had robbed the party of its authoritatively *collective* role in formulating policy, and because an unprincipled and mistaken foreign policy was being peddled.

Arthur Calwell was among the first to speak up, averring that a conspiracy, so far unchallenged, had been concocted in the press and elsewhere to stampede the ALP into altering its Vietnamese policy. He was eager to bring Labor to office, but the drift toward bipartisanship which he perceived was reprehensible, and he would apply whatever influence he held to check the spreading corrosion of the Adelaide guidelines. If the choice were between further defeat at the polls and the preservation of a principled Labor policy, he would choose the latter.[42] Calwell did not take lightly Whitlam's attribution to him of "debauchery" in the 1966 electoral campaign. His position had been both right in substance and sustained by responsible party organs, hence he categorically denied any and all imputations of irregular, "debauched" behavior. If irregular behavior was present, it lay elsewhere. In April 1968, Calwell filed before the federal executive charges of disloyalty and unworthy conduct against Whitlam.[43] Charge and countercharge between Whitlam and Calwell over the handling of Vietnam and conscription contributed to probably the most severe party crisis since the great split of 1954–1955.

Since the Adelaide conference, the Victorian branch of the ALP had been relatively circumspect in addressing itself to foreign policy questions generally and to Whitlam's revisionism in particular, except for a move in October 1967. It invited Prince Sihanouk of Cambodia to send a personal representative to an anti-Vietnam protest rally scheduled to be held in Melbourne the following month, and it advised all ALP groups in the state to support and assist the rally in full measure.[44] Eventually, the Victorians became increasingly impatient with what the parliamentary leadership was doing. In February, the Victorian executive issued a special statement underscoring the dangers of pursuing any course on Vietnam other than the one already ingrained in formal party policy.[45] In March, Whitlam announced that he would appear before the Victorian executive to charge the state party's secretary, W. H. Hartley, with a breach of faith. Hartley, Whitlam explained, had verbally agreed to refrain from any comment on federal affairs during the preceding month's Higgins by-election, but instead had published material on Labor's Vietnam policy.[46] Actually, this alleged Victorian trespass on Whitlam's self-invested prerogative to delineate party foreign policy was only part of a larger problem. The Victorians' foreign policy attitudes were for Whitlam symptomatic of the organizationally decrepit, ideologically hidebound and electorally self-defeating party conditions in the state, and he was determined to challenge the Victorians without further delay.

But two could and did play this game. In March, Whitlam made his promised appearance before the Victorian executive, presenting his own indictment of party malpractices and programmatic intrusions. In April, with the Calwell-Whitlam rhubarb at flash point, the Victorian executive, on which Calwell held a seat, announced that it would request a meeting of the federal executive to consider Whitlam's criticisms of Victorian party conditions—i.e., to force a showdown with the federal leader. The federal executive which convened later in the month now included the ALP federal parliamentary leaders and deputy leaders from the House and Senate. But the alignment of forces was still hostile to Whitlam. The leader and deputy leader in the Senate, both of them now *ex officio* executive members, stood against Whitlam, and Deputy Senate Leader Sam Cohen was also a member of the Victorian executive. Calwell's grievance against Whitlam was not specifically acted upon, though the executive implicitly sustained Calwell by repeating a considerably earlier decision in which it had congratulated him for his conduct of the 1966 campaign. By a series of maneuvers and resolutions, the executive refused to sanction an immediate investigation of the party situation in Victoria, and instead raised a host of criticisms against Whitlam himself.[47]

Whitlam thereupon resigned as parliamentary leader and announced his intention to seek re-election by the parliamentary caucus; he required a reconfirmation of his acceptability as leader, and of his desire to renovate the party organization.[48] His announced opponent was James Cairns, Whitlam's strongest competitor for the leadership somewhat more than a year earlier. Cairns's explanation for challenging Whitlam was that Whitlam had succeeded only in dividing the party further by his refusal to accept majority decisions when they went against him. Whitlam had tried to subordinate the party to himself; his behavior had raised the question, "Whose Party is this—ours or his?" According to Cairns, such haughtiness would not help to lift Labor into power, but would only excite such internal disorder as to push it further into the political wilderness—hence, he turned around Whitlam's proposition that the party had to be fundamentally remodeled in order to gain power. He also mentioned that, with new foreign policy currents blowing in Washington, it was his position (i.e., along the lines of the Adelaide declaration), not Whitlam's tightrope walking efforts, that were about to be vindicated.[49]

Cairns's stand on Vietnam had been well established for some time, and plainly re-emphasized just before the leadership contest developed. In March, he insisted that Australia should withdraw unconditionally from Vietnam, a position hardly in line with Whitlam's countless embellishments.[50] In early April, following Johnson's announcement, he said that he would resign from the ALP if the party came to office after the next House election and continued any policy of limited intervention instead of withdrawing from Vietnam.[51]

When on April 30 the ALP parliamentary caucus met to fill the leadership vacancy, Whitlam was re-elected by thirty-eight to thirty-two. He had won, but the vote was close. In caucus at large, Whitlam's moderate view undoubtedly commanded considerably more support than the thirty-eight to thirty-two vote distribution might have suggested. But caucus members voted as they did for various reasons. Foreign policy preference was one impulse. Another impulse was a calculation over whether Whitlam or Cairns could patch the party's internal discord well and long enough to bring the prospect of election to federal office closer, and on this count, *faute de mieux*, it may have been a standoff. Some parliamentarians could not help but be concerned about the reaction of their respective state parties, and therefore about their own prospects for renomination and re-election, if one man or the other won the leadership race.

Finally, regardless of his electoral skills, telegenic qualities, aura of "modernity" and the rest, Whitlam was resented by some moderates as well as by leftists. In a very short time, he had moved incredibly fast on a whole range of fronts to stamp the party in his own image, wheeling and dealing, upbraiding Calwell, the Victorians, and others frontally whenever it suited his purpose, and even after being counseled by his friends and admirers to apply restraint. As one observer wrote before the taking of the caucus ballot,

Normally the party would tell Mr. Whitlam to go to hell. Certainly it would do so if it was any person but Mr. Whitlam who was doing the asking. Indeed, it still might. A majority of his colleagues don't like what he is doing—to be more correct, they don't like the way he is doing it. They see his actions as arrogant misuse of the authority of a Federal leader. He has outraged and shocked all but the totally committed. The rationalisation that the end justifies the means sits uneasily with Caucus members.[52]

The intraparty feud of April 1968 settled very little. Whitlam's Vietnamese position seemed to enjoy majority endorsement among his parliamentary colleagues, but his methods, both in redefining official party policy and in punching at those whom he identified as impediments to formal programmatic revision, to organizational vitality, and eventually to electoral success, had brought their share of resentment. When the balloting in caucus was over, the Victorian executive resumed where it had left off. It reaffirmed its standard Vietnamese position, reprimanded Whitlam for his interference in state party affairs, and authorized its leaders to tour Australia to mobilize forces against Whitlam's avowed intention of imposing reforms on the Victorian party through some form of federal party intervention.[53]

Foreign policy differences within the party may not have been the sole or even overriding stimulus for the party infighting and the collection of pools of bad blood. Foreign differences were probably overshadowed by the quest for political power by various individuals and echelons within the ALP. But the contribution of Vietnam to the party dispute, like its impact on party life for several years preceding, was evident. More pronouncedly than any other issue, Vietnam divided exponents of principle and of what in shorthand can be termed pragmatism. Vietnam conspicuously actuated Whitlam to seek organizational reforms, so that the party would evolve more "realistic" and electorally beneficial policies, and therefore it was Vietnam that evoked a reaction against Whitlam's efforts. Despite the translation of leadership from Calwell to Whitlam, the Adelaide modifications in program and conference and executive membership, and an at least temporary reversal of electoral fortunes, Australian Labor continued to be bedeviled by endemic internal controversy—an endless, open-ended debate over external policy, crystallized and magnified by the overreaching issue of Vietnam.

Labor's style of sorting out its own policies and presentation of Vietnam-conscription has contributed directly to the style of the national debate on this subject, and has made that debate more conspicuous, colorful, and intense.

Chapter 5. Organized Public Protest Activity: General Characteristics

In Australia, as in a number of other nations, Vietnam as an issue in controversy quickly spilled over from the arena of organized politics into the arena of public expression. The present chapter will attempt to characterize the anti-Vietnam and anticonscription movement as a whole, while the succeeding chapters will deal with particular groups and categories of protesters. Altogether, the aim will be to provide the basis for some judgments of general political bearing. For instance, have Vietnam and conscription so excited the Australian public's imagination as to have evolved a large-scale involvement in organized protest groups? What meaning, if any, can be drawn from an assessment of the kinds of people, or categories of people, who seem to have become vociferous and active in this cause? Is there reason to believe that the protest movement has affected the general level of public awareness on these subjects, or the tone of the controversy generally? Have the outspoken dissenters produced any change of mind among the voting public, or within the political parties?

The Australian Experience with Public Protest Activity

In the Australian context, historical precedent indicates that, while public protest or revisionist movements concerned with external problems have appeared, they have been infrequent, severely limited in membership, ephemeral, relatively placid, or some combination thereof. This is hardly surprising either for Australia or for comparable political systems, given the broadly consensualized nature of the society and the absence of widespread interest in external affairs, though something of the peculiarly Australian experience in this area requires mention.

The most acerbic public protests in Australian experience relating to external matters came during the conscription controversy in the First World War. At the beginning of the war, small established radical or pacifist groups expressed their predictable criticism, but against a war which commanded considerable popular support throughout the country. However, as conscription for overseas service intruded into the public debate, other groups, of much larger following, entered into the field—mostly to combat Hughes's conscription plans, but also to raise increased doubts about the wisdom of unflinching backing for the war in its own right. The trade union movement's presence was strongly felt, and the closing years of the war were marked by conspicuous work stoppages designed to intimidate the proconscriptionist forces.

In the late 1930s Japan's belligerency against China drew considerable popular resentment in Australia. This was at a time when a non-Labor government was pretty well confining itself to moral reproval of Japan, despite undertaking a rearmament program. There was some generalized organized protest, including efforts to boycott Japanese goods, but the most tangible expression took the form of refusals by Australian waterside workers to load war materials on ships bound for Japan. A decade later, the waterside workers were again in the forefront of protest action when they declined to load or service Dutch ships during Indonesia's efforts to gain independence from the Netherlands. This time, Labor was in office, and its sympathies were with the Indonesian cause.

Under L-CP governments since late 1949, and until Vietnam conscription appeared, organized protest on foreign issues was noticeable but in no way striking. The trade unions, the churches (especially Methodist), and the Returned Servicemen's League (later Returned Services League) issued occasional pronouncements on foreign and defense subjects. The League was especially vocal in pleading its case for a strong defense establishment and a firm anti-Communist posture. Some union officials and churchmen associated themselves with sporadic causes such as opposition to South African apartheid or to nuclear testing in the Pacific, or with broader "peace" and disarmament movements, but there was little sense of broad and sustained public involvement. Even such a specific subject group as the Australia-China Society, which aimed to spread information about mainland China, to encourage the movement of people and trade between the two countries, and to effect a relaxation of official Australian diplomatic policy toward Peking, lacked the zest and spirit of urgency that could have labeled it as a genuinely activist "protest" organization. It did enroll several hundred people in several states and from various callings and political backgrounds, but it remained a special interest group whose cause failed to exercise the great majority of the public.

The Australian peace movement requires special attention. Its base was the Australian Peace Council, organized in Melbourne in 1949. It was formed with Communist inspiration but with "progressive" non-Communist elements included. Peace councils were formed throughout the several Australian states. Peace congresses were staged intermittently in the fifties, again with mixed Communist and non-Communist endorsement and participation, with a variety of subject-matter interests and invariably with a known, Communist-favorable outcome in the adopted resolutions. In 1958 the prevailing approach was modified so as to reduce the visibility of Communist influence, and to broaden public acceptance of the movement and its purposes. It was on this basis that the Australia–New Zealand Peace Congress was staged in Melbourne in 1959, and the Australian Congress for International Cooperation and Disarmament in Sydney in October of 1964, just as Vietnam was surfacing as a public issue.

Some prominent people from the ALP, from the unions, from among church bodies, and from science and education were attracted to these congresses, supporting such positions as advocacy of a nuclear-free zone in the Southern Hemisphere, opposition to the installation of the American naval signal station in Western Australia, and condemnation of apartheid. The ANZ Congress sponsored a massive, country-wide "peace petition" movement in 1962, and on occasion was instrumental in organizing marches. But the 1959 and 1964 conclaves remained closely tied to the old Peace Council establishment. The discussions and resolutions at the congresses were invariably steered toward positions congenial to the sponsors. Even among a number of genuine progressives, there was considerable disquiet that the congresses had been stage-managed, or basically Communist-manipulated, or unrealistic in their policy formulations.[1]

Therefore, when the Vietnam and conscription issues developed, there was no particular Australian tradition of widespread public involvement in durable, directly appealing causes, free of the taint of Communist manipulation, or of the inordinate conspicuousness of some one activist element such as the waterside workers. There had been an instance of considerable public dissent, but that had been half a century earlier. It was an issue that was unmistakenly and even intimately felt by nearly all Australians, an issue relating to war—an Australian, not just someone else's fought war—and relating to the constraints under which men were to be sent to fight, and if need be, to die.

Here the parallelism between the conscription argument in the First World War and the argument over Vietnam and conscription fifty years later takes form. In both cases, organized politics were in a heatedly divided state. In both cases, and unlike during the war against Japan, there was spoken doubt about the very premises dictating an enthusiastic Australian commitment of men and resources against "the enemy." The "Great War" was greater than the Vietnamese war, but Vietnam assumed the potential to spiral into a conflict whose consequences for Australia could be more far-reaching, and destructive, than anything the Kaiser could have arranged. In the First World War, Australia enjoyed freedom of choice as to how to recruit its troops and how many of them, and which ones, to dispatch overseas, the same as in the Vietnamese war. But half a century ago Australia lacked international sovereignty and the capacity for an independent foreign policy. These it now possesses, and therefore arguments over whether it should or should not follow a particular Vietnamese policy are not academic or otherwise beside the point. The fact that they *do* lie within the ambit of meaningful public discussion serves to sharpen the already aggravated, historically conditioned differences over conscription for overseas service. It is in this light that the character and course of contemporary Australian protest activity need to be appraised.

Programmatic Emphases

The present chapter is concerned with a characterization of the contemporary protest movement at large, and especially with the characteristics of the inclusive-membership groups which compose it. The question arises as to what, exactly, such protest groups have been objecting to or espousing—in other words, their programmatic emphasis. In the widest sense, their aim has been a more peaceful world, especially in the Asian-Pacific environment, and including advocacy of more reliance on an accommodative Australian foreign policy. In context, this means the search for a more accommodating policy in Vietnam, or an elimination or transformation of the conscription system, or both. Some of the groups began with and never really departed from an undifferentiated opposition to Australia's Vietnamese policy and the introduction of conscription for overseas service, and the subsequent dispatch of conscripts to Vietnam. Still others drew the distinction, stressing either Vietnamese policy or conscription. But the distinction proved to be a very fine one, particularly for groups whose original rationale may have been opposition to conscription for overseas duty. Such, for instance, was the case with Save Our Sons (SOS), a woman's organization, Youth Campaign Against Conscription (YCAC), and the Draft Resistance Movement, groups composed mainly of young people.

Steps leading to the founding of SOS, for example, reach back to late 1964, when the Menzies government introduced its conscription legislation, but before there was any Australian combat commitment in Vietnam or, for that matter, before Vietnam as such had become an exceptionally contentious issue. The SOS's statement of aims remains quite simple—membership is open to those who oppose conscription into the armed services for duty in overseas war, on humanitarian, religious, or pacifist grounds. The group will strive to amend or repeal the existing National Service Act.[2] But SOS has almost of necessity argued and publicized its case in the Vietnamese frame of reference. Vietnam has been described not as a war for freedom, but as a blundering and wasteful conflict, sapping efforts at mobilizing peace generally and forcing Australian conscript troops into a deadly and pointless encounter. As an SOS leaflet asks rhetorically, "Which is the Greater Crime—Burning Draft Cards . . . Or Burning Children?" Technically, of course, there is a distinction to be made. Australia could have followed a hard-line policy on Vietnam while stopping short of conscripting for service there or elsewhere. Or, it could have assumed a tame Vietnamese policy while conscripting for future, unspecified overseas service. But policies on Vietnam and conscription did in real life merge and come to complement one another, and the Australian protest groups have probably been more successful at attracting members and propagating their cause because their presentation has *de facto* been composite, not based on hairline distinctions.

While most contemporary Australian protest groups view their concern as a composite of Vietnam and conscription, they have differences in program, and even wider differences in tactics and approach. Consider the Association for International Cooperation and Disarmament (AICD) in New South Wales which, as the preface to its own constitution admits, "has been established to continue and extend the work initiated by the Australian Congress for International Cooperation and Disarmament, held in Sydney, October 1964."[3] Its Vietnamese program has been quite close to Hanoi's own long-standing terms for entering substantive negotiations. AICD has urged the Australian government to withdraw its troops from the area, to demand an immediate cessation of American bombing in both the North and the South and a termination of "all other offensive military operations," to call for the removal of all foreign troops and military bases from Vietnam, and to insist on equal status for the National Liberation Front in any settlement discussions.[4] In practice, the AICD has seldom made public appeals which have encapsulated all of these demands, and was criticized by some members of associated protest groups for concentrating on the cessation of bombing in the North and the arrangement of a cease-fire.[5] It will be recalled, however, that it was the AICD that in early 1967 had difficulties with the New South Wales branch of the Labor party, which ordered its members to disaffiliate from the AICD.

The Vietnam Action Campaign, which works in close liaison with the AICD, has made fewer concessions to moderation. Its organ, *Vietnam Action*, speaks in very strident language, including praise for the movement to collect funds for the NLF, and it has consistently been uncharitable toward any dilution of Labor's own Vietnamese policy, especially its application by Whitlam.[6] After President Johnson's dramatic announcement of an unconditional bombing halt over much of the North early in 1968, the Vietnam Action Campaign responded by calling for massive demonstrations against Secretary Rusk, who was about to pay a call in Australia. The Johnson gesture was reviled as an act of duplicity. The bombing halt was not being comprehensively applied to North Vietnam. "Because Johnson is losing his war against the Vietnamese people he calls for 'peace.' But he still increases the U.S. troop commitment. And he puts pressure on America's 'allies' for greater commitment. Dean Rusk arrives in Sydney Friday night to put pressure on Gorton for more Australian troops. GO HOME, RUSK! . . . U.S. GET OUT OF VIETNAM NOW!"[7]

A rather different tack has been followed by other groups within the protest movement, among them the Campaign for Peace in Vietnam, which was organized in South Australia in mid-1967, considerably later than most anti-Vietnam groups now operating in the country. Its literature and advertisements make it quite plain that its sponsors, while advocating de-escalation and negotiations with the NLF, are tortured by doubts about how to arrange an outcome to the conflict that will not result in capitulation and an outright Communist takeover. Because it has not felt confident that any particular set of programmatic specific could be set down in advance, because it has wished to embrace opponents of the war who might among themselves adhere to quite different solutions, it has deliberately limited its objectives to working toward an end to the Australian military commitment in Vietnam and toward a closing down of hostilities. "Given agreement on these basic issues, any other differences of opinion about the war are at present negligible. For this reason, too—because we need one large organization—THE SOLE CONDITION FOR MEMBERSHIP OF THE CAMPAIGN IS WILLINGNESS TO JOIN."[8]

Method and Strategy in the Protest Movement

The Australian protest movement has not been a tightly knit, closely coordinated phenomenon. A number of the groups have branches in most and even all states, while others are considerably less developed. Some groups had at least a measure of inspiration for their appearance from a wider parent organization. For instance, SOS, YCAC, and Vietnam Action Campaign were encouraged by the AICD. The Campaign for Peace in Vietnam, on its part, had an independent origin. Some organizations, such as the Vietnam Coordinating Committee (formerly Vietnam Day Committee) and the Project Vietnam Committees have assumed special responsibility for providing a measure of coordination for various protest groups and their members in such areas as the staging of demonstrations, the transmission of propaganda through the news media, and the collection of funds. There is, however, a fair amount of membership overlap among the constituent parts of the protest movement.

Because the member parts of the protest movement have not been single-minded either in programmatic emphasis or in organizational character, the tasks and methods they have set for themselves, while generally complementary, have themselves hardly been identical. On the conscription side, both pacifist and nonpacifist groups have strived to acquaint draft-eligible men of their rights to conscientious objection under prevailing law. The SOS, whose quarrel with conscription for overseas service rests much more on political than on pure pacifist grounds, has acted in a more generalized protest capacity, though it has retained such special interests as legal aid to objectors. More recently, the Draft Resistance Movement has stepped in with the avowed purpose of *destroying* rather than simply opposing conscription: "We are opposed to the war in Vietnam and we intend to resist conscription of Australian youth by all available means"—which entails resort to passive resistance, rowdiness at political meetings, encouragement to flaunt the law on National Service registration and call-up, advice on how to perform draft-dodging maneuvers such as deliberately failing medical examinations, and so on.[9]

Within the protest movement generally there has been considerable diversity of approach and method, often dictated by the size, resources, radicalism, or special interests of the groups concerned. Some of this diversity has been intentional, so that the impact of the expressed dissent would be felt as widely and as prominently as possible.

Some of the activity has been given a highly reasoned, even scholarly tone. The AICD in Sydney maintains a research library of Australian and foreign materials for the use of both formal protest group members and other interested parties. Books and pamphlets on Vietnam are given wide publicity, and their sale is facilitated for potential buyers. Some of these publications are Australian in origin, and represent some of the better collections of public and private statements and anti-Vietnamese essays to be found anywhere.[10] It should be noticed that the protest groups have frequently alluded to the supportive remarks of highly respected critics of the war, ranging from Pope Paul to Charles de Gaulle to U Thant to William Fulbright.

Other material has been designed more to dramatize than to inform. An AICD pamphlet entitled *We Cannot Support a War Against Children!* was stocked with ultrarealistic photographs of maimed and burned Vietnamese children. The message: "There are certain issues beyond political considerations. The killing of children is one of them." In late 1967, the Vietnam Information Centre in Melbourne issued an anti-Vietnam foldout in the form of a Christmas card. On the front was a caricature of Lyndon Johnson, dressed in a Santa Claus costume. His Christmas sack contained bombs rather than presents of peace, and he was yodeling, "HO HO HO HO HO HO CHI MINH." The leaders of SOS have moved farther than most in the composition and circulation of poems, personal testaments, and the like. While Arthur Calwell in 1966 tried to persuade mothers that their sons were about to be cut down in a senseless Vietnamese war, SOS has worked to link Australian sons with the image of sons of troubled mothers everywhere. Wrote an Australian mother of five sons:

I think of the mothers of Vietnam, of the suffering and anguish, the tortures and destruction that have been their portion for so many years. . . . Society at the moment is raging against the hoodlum, while at the same time our country is engaged in a war which is the ultimate vandalism, destroying man, woman and child, body and soul, and the good earth as well . . . . We in the Save Our Sons Movement know we cannot save our sons from the common fate of death. But we will fight against them being forced to commit evil because they have no choice.[11]

For the loyal followers, as well as for others who might wish to learn, many of the protest groups have published newsletters. More elaborate magazine publications such as AICD's *Pacific* and the Vietnam Action Campaign's *Vietnam Action* have provided readers with editorials, original and borrowed articles, news of past and forthcoming protest events, reports of protest activity overseas, announcements of books, book reviews, and so on.

Members of protest organizations have constantly been enjoined to talk to neighbors, write letters to newspaper editors, place Vietnam-conscription topics on church, social, fraternal, and other meeting agenda, sign and circulate petitions, and to form deputations and approach parliamentarians and other public figures. They have been encouraged to display car stickers bearing such legends as "Escalate Opposition to the War in Vietnam," and to carry placards at rallies with eye-catching slogans such as "Stick to Killing Fish, Harold," an allusion to the late Prime Minister's proclivity for fishing.

The staging of massed public displays of protest has become one of the more pronounced features of the Australian protest movement. A number of the more militant dissent group members have been among those who provided the pyrotechnics at Liberal party election meetings in 1966 and 1967. The new Draft Resistance Movement became the first protest organization publicly and unabashedly to announce as policy its intention to disrupt meetings of unwelcome public figures. John Gorton was given a taste of these tactics within a few weeks of being inaugurated as prime minister. Disturbances at an electoral meeting he was addressing brought some seventy police and a number of Commonwealth security men to the scene and resulted in a number of scuffles and in sixteen arrests.[12]

Violence as part of the contemporary Australian protest movement has, however, been the exception. When it has flared up, it almost invariably has not been instigated by the sponsors of protest events, nor condoned by them after the fact. Marches and rallies have been held throughout various Australian cities from 1965 onward. Sometimes there has been no occasion for such displays, save the determination to designate a particular day as a target for mobilizing protest. Sometimes demonstrations have been planned around an event, such as the visits of Ky and Johnson, the American Fourth of July independence holiday, or the celebration of the Moomba Festival in Melbourne, where thousands of onlookers would be witness to expressions of anti-Vietnam dissent manifestations. Outdoor meetings and parades have varied in turnout from hundreds to thousands, with the Sydney October Mobilization Rally in 1967 attracting possibly up to ten thousand persons.

Such demonstrations have often begun on notes of solemnity, or profundity, or fraternal casualness, or some combination thereof. Prayers for peace and good will among men have frequently introduced a rally, program, or vigil. Distinguished Australian and foreign political, academic, and other celebrities have come to speak. Participants have been invited to bring bag lunches. Folk songs have been sung. Vendors have strolled about selling ice cream and soft drinks. But when marches have gotten under way, or celebrities who were the objects of criticism were subjected to placard-bearing, chanting demonstrators, the mood has sometimes become angry. The rehearsed or spontaneous sit-ins at public or congested locations, the inevitable traffic jams, the arguments between demonstrators and other-minded spectators, the concern of police for the safety of persons and property have sometimes precipitated violent confrontations and arrests.[13]

In the last analysis, what has the protest movement wished to accomplish? Certain objectives, such as counseling young men about conscientious objection opportunities, or supplying money for the legal defense of those who are arraigned for violations of the National Service Act, can be accomplished apart from public policy reorientation. But to answer that the protest movement has aimed to reorient Australian foreign and defense policy is rather to beg the question, since such change is possible only if politically responsible persons are prompted to do so. The protest movement feels this is a feasible though admittedly difficult objective. It finds the need to create and maintain a momentum of active protest, even if only a small portion of the national population is intimately involved. Ideally, this core of activists should be composed of as many prominent figures as possible, and reflect membership across the spectrum of the churches, trade unions, professions, university communities, and so on. Having enrolled respectable people from a cross-section of backgrounds, the movement has planned to apply its tactics of publicity, persuasion, and overt demonstrations so as to jog the general public into an appreciation of how manifestly important the issues of Vietnam and conscription are, and to move to the next step of dramatizing the validity of the movement's own position on these issues. As a complement to working on public opinion, it has wished that its presence and fervor would be taken to heart by the political parties. As a capstone to the above steps, the protesters have hoped to bring on their ultimate aim—namely, policy change. If an incumbent L-CP government cannot find its way to reversing its settled thinking on these issues, either because it cannot be persuaded of the merits of a contrary policy or because it does not fear electoral retaliation for pursuing settled policies, then it must be removed. In practice, this means replacing it with the ALP, which in turn requires that Labor itself must not compromise its foreign and defense policies, and the electorate must be induced to support it.

It is in this context that efforts have been made within a number of protest group circles to undertake petitioning and demonstrating before politicians, and even more substantially to behave as a pressure movement to realize the election of sympathetic candidates for parliamentary office. Hence, before the 1966 election, the AICD worked in marginal constituencies to elect declared antiwar candidates, and distributed 150,000 copies of a pamphlet designed to acquaint the public with the inhumanity of the Vietnamese conflict, while in Victoria the Vietnam Day Committee made special efforts to purchase television and radio time and newspaper space. Labor's dramatic setback in the 1966 House election was disheartening, but some comfort could be taken from the fact that official ALP policy on Vietnam and conscription had provided the electorate with a crisp, undebased alternative to the government's own allegedly calamitously mistaken approach. Comfort could also be gained from the appearance and surprising popularity of Liberal Reform (later Australian Reform Movement), and from the fact that the membership base of the protest movement was, if anything, widening, particularly as progressive Catholics, business people, academics, and ex-servicemen enriched its ranks.[14]

Still, it was widely felt that by clever repetition of scare phrases and imputations of disloyalty toward Labor, by tricks and media manipulation, the government parties had struck at the public's weak spot. "Perhaps it was the case, then, that the 'Australian voter' simply responded to the repeating pattern like the Pavlov dog, an additional jerk being added to the reflex action by the question of Vietnam."[15] As the AICD confessed, "Seemingly, no matter how much we petition, march or demonstrate our protests make little impact upon our Governments and the war proceeds to escalate regardless."[16]

While it was understandable that the movement suffered some loss of morale, there was another, potentially ominous consequence of Labor's electoral failure, which by implication had been a failure for the protest movement as well. With the ostensible failure of prevailing positions and measures, tendencies arose within the movement on behalf of heightening militancy in future operations. The New South Wales AICD's secretary's report to the general meeting, filed in June 1967, addressed itself to this situation. It cautioned against allowing such pressures to impose themselves upon the movement as a whole, since

> such a development could lead to a process of polarisation and serious barriers to the movement's widening composition and mass development. It must be said, however, that equal care needs to be taken to ensure that under the guise of adhering to the principle of non-domination there is no violation of the principle of non-exclusion by pressures to exclude or discriminate against radical minority groupings.

Concluding his assessment of the problem, the secretary wrote that

> an essential prerequisite . . . [for adding converts to the movement's cause] will be a capacity to accommodate a diversity of approaches, emphases and methods of participation. Diversity needs to be seen as an essential characteristic of the movement. Without prejudice to the diverse views of individual participants, A.I.C.D. regards the purpose of the movement as being not to change the social system but to safeguard world peace.[17]

Hence the protest movement faced a set of dilemmas about what to do and how to do it. The alteration of established, official policy seemed to require a change of government, which only the ALP could provide. But an ALP committed to a drastic change in policy had just been badly defeated, in part because its policies were interpreted by the protest movement itself as unpopular with the electorate, thereby entrenching the government and its settled policies more firmly than ever. Established protest group approaches seemingly had failed to achieve their principal purpose. One option was to intensify and radicalize protest activity, but this would drive out the very people whose presence was regarded as necessary for the movement's credibility and influence. Another option was to avoid radicalization and perhaps even to scale down the intensity of protest, but this tack would undermine the movement's *raison d'être* and perhaps contribute to Labor's own dilution of policy. Diluted policies might help Labor to achieve office, but unless the party was willing to institute drastic changes in foreign policy, its election to office would lose its relevance.

Composition and Membership

In asking who belongs to and who controls the protest movement, at least among those portions of it which are inclusive in membership, it is proper to begin by inquiring into the Communist presence. Organized Communism in Australia actually has two parts. There is the parent Communist party of Australia (CPA), with a membership of not much over four thousand, and an offshoot CPA (Marxist-Leninist), which is "Chinese" oriented, with under a thousand members. It is primarily the former group which concerns us here, not simply because it is by far the more numerous, but because its professed approach to relations with non-Communists has direct bearing on the functioning of the protest movement.

The CPA has for some time espoused a "popular front" approach to politics, meaning participation in reform and protest causes to which the left sector of the ALP, the trade unions, intellectuals, certain progressive churchmen, and others would be attracted. Such cooperative action, in which Communists would be present and influential but not numerically dominant or even particularly visible, would relieve the party of isolation and therefore of impotence at relatively minor cost.[18] This "accommodationist" view of conducting radical causes has persuaded the CPA that even a Vietnam-conscription policy such as was officially expounded by Calwell on the behalf of the ALP in 1966 was acceptable, and so long as a Whitlam-type of revisionism could be staved off. But the support of a clearly alternative, radical foreign policy was by itself insufficient. Vietnam and conscription were also publicly emotional issues, generating related problems such as civil liberties observance and the allocation of national resources—the "butter *versus* guns" issue. On Vietnam and conscription, therefore, wrote its president, "The Communist Party believes that unity in action of people and organisations, irrespective of their political or religious views, is the most effective form of struggle and would do most to consolidate the opposition to the Government."[19]

Even before Vietnam arose, there was considerable Communist encouragement and sponsorship in the peace movement, but with Communists generally in the background. AICD's appearance after the October 1964 congress was carried forth with considerable Communist initiative, while supportive groups such as SOS and YCAC, which arose almost simultaneously, were given Communist encouragement. The Australian protest movement has by now proliferated considerably, and includes numerous old, new, and refurbished organizations, some very tiny, others relatively large—such as the AICD in New South Wales, which carries a formal membership of some one thousand. Since the protest groups at large are outwardly nonpartisan and open to persons of any leaning or affiliation, Communists are sprinkled about in most of them. In no known instance, however, do they control the leadership levels or represent anything approaching a majority of the rank and file membership. The New South Wales AICD, for example, includes two or three Communists among its officers and committee, a body totaling twenty-five persons.

Nor does that CPA compensate for its lack of numbers in protest organizations by serving as a generous financial contributor. Virtually all of the clerical, organizational, and materials distribution work in the protest groups is performed by unpaid volunteers. In order to attract and retain a maximum of paying members, membership dues are kept low. Expenses incurred in connection with stationery, printing, postage, the hiring of halls, purchase of television and radio time and newspaper space, occasional fees for visiting speakers, and so on, constantly impose financial burdens on the groups, and elicit appeals for special contributions, however small. A typical appeal will read: "The necessary finances for the ever-increasing momentum of the Campaign can only be raised at the cost of individual *sacrifice*—no one can ever 'spare' money. You are asked to consider carefully just how much the cessation of the war means to you, to Australia and to the world. And having decided, CONTRIBUTE!"[20] Most contributions arrive in small amounts, and not from wealthy donors. To supplement out-of-pocket donations, nearly all the protest groups have resorted to special fund raising devices, such as white elephant sales, raffles, and cake-bake sales. Whether by design or necessity, therefore, the Communists are not the financial backbone of the protest movement, though it can plausibly be argued that the movement's penurious condition and interminable appeals for money suit their overriding purpose. They endow the movement with pride of independence and a sense of members' self-sacrifice that generate spirit and momentum, and excuse the Communists from charges of dominating the movement through control of the purse.

Communist attendance at protest rallies and marches would seem to be another story. A random sample survey of persons involved in the October 1967 march in Sydney provides considerable suggestive data about the composition of such mass protest group efforts. Among those surveyed, 18.3 per cent were found to hold formal Communist membership, in the ratio of about three "regular" CPA members to every one "Chinese" party Communist.[21] This of course is a figure enormously higher than the proportion of Communists to the Australian population at large or in New South Wales itself, where there are some 1,900 CPA members in a population of over 4,300,000. Although the aggregate Australian and New South Wales data respecting Communist membership in the protest groups are very imprecise, the figure of 18.3 per cent from the sample tested (n = 109), if at all representative, would appear to be rather higher— perhaps by 50 per cent—than the Communist membership in the protest group organizations. The inference to be drawn is that Communists are more dedicated, more apt to take the trouble to sacrifice time and energy for their cause, than others are, and that in degree they serve as an important energizing nucleus for protest demonstrations.

In its earliest stages, the organized Vietnam-conscription opposition was considerably stimulated by the CPA and individual Communists, both in terms of retooling established groups and founding fresh ones. After that, and partly by the Communists' own choosing, non-Communist membership widened, direct Communist influence decreased, a number of organizations appeared with little if any Communist inspiration, and the movement developed a style in keeping with its heterogeneous character. In one commentator's words, written as early as April 1966, "A hunt for Communists in the peace movement now is too late. In a way it both over-estimates and under-estimates the party's role; over-estimates it because they are no longer the leading or even significant moving force; under-estimates the party's influence because it ignores the patient groundwork of moulding opinion when the peace movement was still confined to the political fringe."[22]

If the Communists do not in fact run or heavily populate the various protest organizations, then who does? In terms of the membership's political party voting preference, it is the ALP that dominates. Nearly all the ranking secretaries of the more conspicuous groups are electorally Labor, and by far the most prominently represented party-associated element on protest group executive committees is Labor-preferring as well. There is, however, a vast gulf between the rank and file electoral supporters of the Labor party and the ALP-voting protest movement members or participants, which the telescoping of various survey data vividly illustrates. While Ky's visit to Australia was overwhelmingly opposed by the protest groups, and many of their members joined Calwell and others in staging demonstrations when Ky arrived, only 33.8 per cent of ALP voters around the country opposed the visit; 52 per cent favored it, and 11.7 per cent were undecided.[23] A July 1967 survey indicated that most ALP supporters felt it had been wrong to dispatch conscript troops to Vietnam—25 per cent endorsed the decision, 67 per cent opposed it, and 8 per cent were undecided.[24] The preceding May, however, ALP followers were distributed as follows on the question of whether Australian troops, now that they were there, *should continue* to fight in Vietnam, or be returned home: 45.7 per cent for continuing, 38.1 per cent for pulling out, and 16.2 per cent undecided.[25] In November of 1967 a Gallup survey asked whether any countries posed a threat to Australia's security, and if so, which ones. Among ALP respondents, 42.5 per cent felt that some country posed a threat, 39.5 per cent believed there was no threat from any quarter, and 17.9 per cent could not say. Of the total ALP group surveyed, 7.4 per cent included North Vietnam, 10.8 per cent included the Soviet Union, 22 per cent included China, and only 3.1 per cent selected the United States as constituting such a threat.[26] A September 1967 survey revealed that only 12.3 per cent of Labor voters believed that collections of funds for distribution to the Viet Cong, except under the sponsorship of the Red Cross, should be allowed. Among ALP supporters, 81.6 per cent were opposed and 6.1 per cent undecided.[27]

In the October Mobilization survey, it was learned that among those interviewed who had voted in the 1966 election, three-quarters had cast their ballots for a Labor candidate. The sampled population at large was asked to name the country most responsible for world tension. Among ninety-nine respondents, ninety-three named the United States, three named Australia, three chose China, and one selected the Soviet Union. Only 5.5 per cent said they objected to any kind of Australian aid being rendered to North Vietnam, and only 6.4 per cent disapproved of assistance to the NLF. Of those favoring some type of assistance (medical, economic, military), only 8.2 per cent indicated they would not personally contribute toward this end. The vast majority expressed a preference for a political outcome of one united Vietnam. Of this group, 88.9 per cent opted for a solution according to the Vietnamese' own choosing, 10.1 per cent leaned toward a neutralist system, and only 1 per cent (one respondent) preferred a pro-Western government in a unified Vietnam.[28]

While the all-Australian Gallup polls and the October Mobilization survey questions were not identical, it is quite apparent that those who attended the protest rally, the bulk of whom held formal protest group membership or had associated themselves with previous marches and rallies, and the overwhelming majority of them Labor voters, were totally untypical in their attitudes compared to Labor voters generally. They were far more radical, and more categorical in their opinions.

Activists are more committed to their cause than mere followers, but it is noteworthy that the presence of a very numerous ALP-voting component in the protest movement does not confer upon the movement the sort of mildness of outlook which is associated with ALP supporters collectively. The untypicality of the ALP-voting persons in the movement shows up in still another way, namely, in the meagerness of *formal* ALP membership found among the October

Mobilization survey group. The largest element by far in that survey population belonged to no political party. Among those who did have formal party membership, there were more Communists than ALP members, the latter representing only 10.1 per cent of the sample.[29] One inference is that non-Communist voting members of the protest movement are not in practice activists in party politics. Another inference is that a number of protest group members vote ALP less out of any real attachment to the party and its programs than out of a feeling that Labor offers the least distasteful voting option. On foreign policy, at least, they stand not at the center but at the left fringe of the ALP.

No wonder that the presence of ALP people in the protest organizations has created occasional headaches for the ALP and political opportunities for other parties. We are reminded that the ALP's New South Wales branch attempted to disallow membership in the AICD, partially to spare the party political embarrassment. Likewise, to embarrass Labor, the L-CP and the DLP have enlivened the debate over Vietnam and conscription by pointing to the association of some Labor figures with protest-group-sponsored demonstrations. Some of Labor's leaders were said to be "inciting impressionable young Australians to irregularities and near-treason. They are giving positive support to the youth of this country blindly following Communist agitators . . . . Is anyone . . . naive enough to believe that the demonstrations which we see breaking out in all parts of the country are spontaneous expressions of the normal Australian outlook?"[30]

While the more militant sector of Labor represents the most prominent ingredient among protest group members and demonstrators, there are others besides Communists who are involved. There are a very few Liberal supporters who formally belong to the protest groups and who join in rallies. But it is the Australian Reform Movement (ARM) that stands out. It is a party which endorses much of the work of the protest groups and emulates a number of their tactics; however, it can hardly be characterized as a collection of unreconstructed leftists, pie-in-sky idealists, and sons of soil and factory who rebel against having their sons disposed of as cannon fodder in capitalist wars.

Australian Reform has published open letters in newspapers, circulated handbills and more elaborate literature in opposition to the war, encouraged its supporters and listeners to join in both silent and not so silent demonstrations, and has enrolled some of its people within the ranks of protest organizations. It does not propagate what some would describe as an "appeasing" or "neutralist" doctrine, though some of its detractors have identified it as "neoisolationist." What separates the ARM from the more stereotypically antiwar activists is its composition and target of electoral appeal. Its founders, operatives, candidates, and financial backers do more than wear a white rather than a blue collar—they wear silk ties as well. Its candidates for office bristle with professional status and academic degrees. Its party branches, originally limited to New South Wales and Victoria and extended late in 1967 into Queensland, have reflected this middle-class and academic image. As of the close of 1967, most of the New South Wales branches were in Sydney's fashionable North Shore area, and its first two Queensland branches were established at the University of Queensland and on the Queensland Gold Coast.[31] Money has been no problem. Business patrons have not been lacking. The recommended individual "tithe" from interested persons for the 1967 Senate election was ten dollars—a considerable request by Australian standards. For the 1966 House and 1967 Senate elections, available campaign funds compared favorably with Liberal and ALP resources. Prior to the 1966 House election, interviewed ARM-intending voters were found by a Gallup survey to be more than twice as heavily represented among the "upper" classes as in the "artisan" and "lower" classes combined.[32] Only business leaders were invited to a sumptuous luncheon staged by the ARM to launch its Senate campaign in New South Wales. Gordon Barton, the moving force behind the ARM, averred that he was a businessman and had never felt ashamed of that fact. Businessmen were needed in the country's politics. They were practical men with a stake in Australia's future; "I myself have got beyond the stage of wondering where my next meal is coming from"—on which theme a newspaper observer was to write that "the chortles that followed that remark reminded us that we were indeed among the affluent radicals."[33]

The appearance of the non-cross-sectional ARM on a prominently anti-Vietnam platform is a helpful introduction to the socioeconomic composition of protest group members generally. The testimony of some leading figures in the protest movement and impressionistic observation suggest that these activists are atypical of the population at large, and are borne out by the Sydney Mobilization Rally survey findings. The population of the Sydney survey was found to be inordinately well educated, concentrated among skilled, white-collar, and professional occupations, resident in middle-class suburbs, and young. By the test of religious affiliation, it was inordinately independent-minded. While only about 3 per cent of the general population could be classified as lacking a religion or being hostile to organized religion, the interviewed Sydney group was found to be composed of 28.4 per cent who were members or adherents of church bodies (including Quaker and Humanist), and of 71.6 per cent who identified themselves as without a religion, or as agnostics or atheists.[34]

Those Australians who have involved themselves in protest movements and expressions are predominantly neither old-line and committed Communists or Labor party radicals, nor persons with histories of political involvement generally. The Sydney survey's finding that the vast majority who participated in the rally had no formal party connections pointed this up. The protest movement has attracted concerned individuals who, for reasons of conscience or their own pragmatic assessment of the dangers of the Vietnamese war, have now become politicized. The more cosmopolitan, broadening tendencies which have affected Australia in recent years have been a predisposing influence in this direction, helping to account for the middle-class, educated, and young-in-age qualities of the protesters. People of this type may or may not care that there is a Communist or radical Labor presence in the movement. What appears to matter most is a wish to manifest opposition to the war and to its foreseen consequences. The salience assigned by them to Vietnam and to conscription for overseas service, which *de facto* means service in Vietnam, has made the commitment to protest activity worthwhile. Just as the Communist and radical ALP components of the protest movement feel that the movement should not overradicalize itself for fear of alienating these middle-class, party-politically unattached persons, so these persons are willing to cooperate with the older brand of peace seekers on the basis of high common cause.

It is tempting to scoff at these "new radicals" as a mélange of bored housewives, maladjusted youths, frustrated intellectuals, hyperidealistic religionists, and the like. Here it is adequate to write that, whatever its temperamental propensities, the bulk of the new radical, protesting population is not concerned with martyrdom and is impressively sincere in outlook. To quote from a letter written to the author by a prominent "new radical" spokesman for one of the protest organizations, "Not one of our members will be proud to call ourself an Australian until we as a nation have repaid for our wrongs in Vietnam. We don't know what to do to impress [this] on our largely apathetic people, full of sun and sport, overfed, well paid, selfish yet fearful; the latter conditions played up to by a Government which realises the value of playing on peoples basic fears and instincts."

Chapter 6. The Churches, Veterans, and Vietnam-Conscription

With the general characteristics of the Australian protest movement in mind, we can proceed to a more specific treatment of particular categories of protesters. In the present chapter, two important types of voluntary associations and their followers, the churches and veterans organizations, are selected for special attention.

Dissent Among Protestant Churches and Protestants

Applying indices of religious belief and church membership to gauge sentiment on Vietnam and conscription, it is plain that, relative to their numbers, those without religious attachments represent a much more "oppositionist" body of opinion than do Protestants or Roman Catholics. The October 1967 Sydney survey revealed that well over half of the questioned rally population was not committed to any body of formal religious beliefs. Gallup surveys have consistently noted that, compared to the general population, nonreligious respondents have held much less enthusiasm for prosecuting the Vietnamese war vigorously, for maintaining Australian forces there, and for the principle of conscription for overseas service as such.

There has also been strong anti-Vietnam anticonscriptionist sentiment among certain small-membership, traditionally "progressive" Christian groups. Australian Quakers, who number about fifteen hundred, subscribed to the 1966 American Friends Service Committee report "Peace in Vietnam," which called for ending the bombing, other forms of de-escalation, discussions with various interested parties including the NLF, eventual political self-determination, and an internationally guaranteed status of neutrality for the entirety of Vietnam. Australian Friends and others were urged to write to the prime minister, asking him to give the American report earnest consideration.[1] The Fellowship of Reconciliation, an international Christian pacifist organization with an Australian membership of four hundred, encouraged all Australians to "rebuke the government over its policies on Vietnam and conscription. Such chastening will make it a better political party"—and it suggested that electoral support be thrown behind candidates who would work toward ending the war and withdrawing conscription legislation.[2]

But it is the remainder of the Australian Christian Protestant churches, which embrace some 65 per cent of the total national population, that requires special attention. External affairs had not been entirely neglected in the fifties and sixties by Protestant, and especially nonconformist, churches. There had been expressions of church body and individual clergy opinion on such topics as South African apartheid, the Hungarian Revolution, and nuclear testing. The organized post-World War II peace movement in Australia had consistently included some prominent clergymen, both as spokesmen for causes being served and as members of peace group governing bodies.

Since the arrival of Vietnam and conscription, Protestant involvement in foreign policy has grown both in depth and in breadth. One index has been the clear, sometimes ardent spokesmanship of ranking Protestant clergymen. The number of prominent clergymen who have publicly advertised their support *for* the government's established position on Vietnam has been slight. Most of those who have chosen to speak out have taken a moderate or an oppositionist view of one inflection or another. Among the oppositionists have been men traditionally associated with political activism, but they have been joined by men who seldom if ever recorded themselves on foreign policy questions. They have included men of real standing in their respective churches, and who have been generously represented not only in the nonconformist churches but in the more staid Anglican Church as well—for instance, the former bishop of Tasmania,[3] the bishop of Canberra and Goulburn,[4] the archbishop of Perth,[5] and the archbishop of Brisbane,[6] who is also the Anglican primate of Australia. Among those who in June 1967 issued a public statement which advocated a far more accommodative government posture were the president-general of the Methodist Conference on Australasia, the moderator-general of the Presbyterian Church of Australia, the president of the Federal Conference of the Churches of Christ, and the Anglican primate of Australia.[7] One of the first notable public confrontations between Vietnamese critics and the government occurred when, in March and April of 1965, letters were exchanged between a group of New South Wales Protestant clergymen and Prime Minister Menzies.[8]

123

Protestant church state conferences, assemblies, and synods have not assumed any single position on Vietnam, but a few illustrations should provide some appreciation of the spirit which has pervaded the Protestant churches. Consider the results of a spate of church conferences conducted in October 1967. The General Assembly of the Victorian Presbyterian Church called upon the Australian government to commit itself to negotiations with all parties involved in the Vietnamese conflict.[9] The Methodist conferences in Victoria[10] and New South Wales[11] condemned the war effort in Vietnam, requested a halt to the bombing of North Vietnam, and called for immediate negotiations. The New South Wales Anglican synod took a fairly conservative stand, arguing that allied forces should hold in Vietnam until a negotiated settlement could be achieved,[12] but its Victorian counterpart, though not explicitly condemning Australia's Vietnamese participation, urged an end to all foreign intervention in the country.[13]

The Australian Council of Churches, representing eleven Anglican, nonconformist, and Orthodox churches, wrote to Holt in April 1966 that it had reservations about conscription for service in Vietnam, reminded the Prime Minister that there was strong feeling in the national community that Australian participation in the war might not be justified, and endorsed all possible initiatives for a settlement.[14] In another letter addressed to Holt, this time in October 1967, the council urged a cessation of bombing in the North, participation of the NLF in speedily arranged negotiations, and the eventual withdrawal of American and other allied forces from the area.[15] Early in 1968, the council petitioned the government to undertake a drastic overhaul of the National Service Act, and in particular recommended the liberalization of the treatment of conscientious objectors and alternative options to military service of which objectors might avail themselves.[16]

Individual clergymen and church bodies have done more than simply comment on what they have regarded as imperfections in government policy, or to suggest counterproposals for Vietnam. Many have formed strong opinions on the need for expanded official civil aid to Vietnam and have made substantial efforts toward arranging privately contributed assistance to Vietnam. Clergymen have joined non-church-affiliated protest groups, and some have found their way to executive positions in them. Others have walked in demonstrations and have participated in peace vigils, while still others have stood on street corners distributing some of the most flamboyant literature found anywhere in the files of the protest organizations.

It has been difficult for the government and its political allies to attach a Communist or fellow-traveling label to these churchmen as a group, or otherwise to impugn the sincerity of men and organizations who have invoked the names of God and Christ to wage their campaigns against what they have defined as misguided, if not immoral, policy. Because of the relative insulation of the churches from such politically originated denigration, the question arises whether the public positions of these clerics and church bodies have had an influence upon parishioners, i.e., the Protestant public at large.

In a sense, the question is impossible to answer, since people form opinions based on a host of influences. Then, too, many Protestant Christians in Australia, as elsewhere, are more nominal than practicing, and therefore would not be likely to place any special weight on the foreign and defense policy positions and behavior of their clergy, or of ranking laymen who attend and pass resolutions at conferences. Nevertheless, it is difficult to avoid the hypothesis that the vigorous and relatively widespread activity on Vietnam has in some measure helped to socialize the Protestant public in the issues under debate, serving as still another channel of exposure. The presence of clergymen in protest groups and at rallies has on balance endowed the organized anti-Vietnam campaign in Australia with greater respectability—and therefore a capacity for progressively enlarging its ranks—than if the Protestant churches and their leaders had remained silent, or as a group had assumed an identifiably conservative posture.

Also, it is tempting to speculate that the attitudes, and possibly the voting behavior, of some sectors of the public have been influenced by the attitudes of the churches, though Gallup attitudinal data reveal only very tenuous clues. Of the major Protestant denominations in Australia, the Methodist Church has probably been the most vociferous in its opposition to established government policy on Vietnam. The September 1966 poll which inquired whether the United States ought to begin to withdraw its troops, carry on at present level of fighting, or increase the strength of its attacks against North Vietnam, revealed that Methodists, though only by a slight margin, were the *least* disposed to encourage escalation. The other tested and reported Christian categories in the poll were Roman Catholics, Anglicans, Presbyterians, Baptists, and "other Christians."

Among these categories Catholics favored escalation most—27.4 per cent of them. Next were Anglicans—24.1 per cent. Lowest were Methodists—19.8 per cent.[17] Four months later, in February 1967, another survey seemed to substantiate the presence of relatively accommodationist thinking among Methodists. The question was whether the allies in Vietnam should press for a complete victory or a compromise peace. Among the several religious groups just listed, Methodists evinced the lowest incidence of support for a complete victory (23.6 per cent), and the highest incidence of favor for a compromise solution (66.7 per cent). Baptists were the strongest for complete victory (37.1 per cent), while "other Christians" were weakest for a compromise (54.9 per cent).[18] In November 1967, the proportion of Methodists regarding North Vietnam as a threat to Australia was only about half as great as the figures for other Protestants or for Christians generally, and Methodists ranked lower than any other category of Christians in their evaluation of China as a security threat to Australia.[19]

While there seems to be a slight positive correlation between the strongest Protestant clerical and church-body sentiment opposing established Vietnamese policy, and that denomination of Protestants least hawkish in its views on Vietnam and associated subjects, the hypothesis that leaders and church bodies have contributed to tempered views among the Methodist public must be a guarded one. In a number of instances, the survey data have shown no *marked* difference between Methodists and other Christian denominations, or no difference at all. Also, it is fair surmise that those who become Methodists may very well already carry characteristics which predispose them toward accommodationist outlooks in foreign policy.

The Catholic Response

For a considerable period after Vietnam and conscription had become controversial public issues, organized and hierarchical Roman Catholic opinion in Australia seemed either becalmed or, where it was forcefully presented, to be decidedly supportive of official policy. Identifiably critical Catholic opinion was centered on a group of progressive Catholics who adhered to the position of the *Catholic Worker*, a Melbourne-based lay Catholic journal with a national circulation of some five thousand or was scattered about the ALP itself. Within the ALP, of course, there are prominent figures who may be

Catholic (as Calwell), Protestant, Jewish, freethinking, or otherwise, though the party has over the years included many more Catholics in its parliamentary and organizational echelons than has the L-CP.

The other, conservative, side of the Vietnam question was for long far better represented among Catholic leaders and groups. There was the DLP, disproportionately Catholic both in leadership and popular following, with its steadfast ideas on Communism, China, Vietnam, and related topics. Considerable publicity for a pro-DLP line has long been supplied by the National Civic Council, an all-Catholic offshoot of the movement which in the late forties and early fifties worked to purge Communists from trade unions, and whose influence became a precipitant factor in the 1954–1955 ALP split. Through its organ, News Weekly, and other publications, and the voluminous writings, public appearances, and television broadcasts of its president, B. A. Santamaria, the National Civic Council has provided a consistent, fiercely anti-Communist, pro-Vietnamese commitment exposition.

The Catholic hierarchy in Australia has in past not been bashful about dipping into politics. Archbishop Mannix and other Catholic churchmen were among the controversialists during the World War I conscription battles. More recently the church has taken a special interest in such intimately Catholic-related issues as governmental assistance to parochial schools, and of course has opposed Communist influences at home and abroad. The Labor split in turn split the hierarchy. Traditionally, the church had been close to the ALP, for reasons which included the party's own heavy Catholic composition and progressive social ideas which served lower-income Catholics well. But the Labor split carried many moderate and right-wing Catholics out of the party. The surviving ALP swung to the left, while the new DLP, most prominently in its attitudes on domestic and foreign Communist influence and on foreign policy, veered to the right. Some Catholic dignitaries kept their own counsel. Still others quietly stood by the ALP, at least in those states where the ALP managed to settle into a moderate posture. Such, for instance, became the relationship between the archbishop of Sydney, Norman Cardinal Gilroy, and the New South Wales branch of the ALP. Elsewhere, and especially in Victoria, where the postsplit ALP became vigorously leftist and the DLP was especially prominent, ranking church officials assumed unconcealed hostility toward Labor and supported the DLP. The principal exponent of this position until his death late in 1963 was Archbishop Daniel Mannix of First World War notoriety. Two days before the 1958 federal election, Mannix praised the DLP's stand against Communism, warned that "every Communist and every Communist sympathizer wants a victory for the Evatt party,"[20] and went on to abuse Labor in every imaginable way, including condemning the ALP's advocacy of the recognition of mainland China as "morally reprehensible and politically mistaken."[21] Mannix gave aid and comfort to the DLP and the National Civic Council in various ways. The *News Weekly* was sold in many Victorian churches on Sundays, and Santamaria delivered a regular television broadcast under the Victorian hierarchy's sponsorship until Mannix's death.

Mannix's successor in the Melbourne archdiocese, Archbishop Justin Simonds, followed a generally neutral position in partisan politics. But his auxiliary bishop, Arthur Fox, stepped into the limelight just prior to the 1966 election by announcing that the peace and security of Australia were the "supreme and paramount" considerations in the election, that there was immense danger in compromising with Communist aggression, and that Pope Paul's recent call for peace in Vietnam had been distorted all out of proportion by those seeking political gain.[22] Generally, the hierarchy's voice had lapsed into almost total silence on Vietnam, punctuated only by occasional expressions of implicit support for allied policy. It was a condition that was to prevail for several months beyond Fox's intervention on the eve of the November 1966 election.[23]

This combination of quiescence and occasional blessings for status quo policy in Vietnam was perhaps to be expected. The Australian hierarchy had, as a group, been over the years far better recognized for pastoral than for intellectual or broadly ranging public consciousness contributions to national life. It had tended to be cautious and conservative, rather than innovative, and earned a reputation for close alignment with Irish and Spanish delegates at the Vatican Council. But the Vietnamese war, and Australia's involvement in it, were eventually to prove a considerable tonic, not only for bishops and archbishops, but for ordinary clerics and the lay people as well. As of 1967–1968, the hierarchy had, collectively, expressed itself in constructively peace-seeking terms over Vietnam. A reconciliation between the church and the ALP, tenuous even after Mannix's death, seemed to have been effected. Prominent Catholic newspapers became skeptical of government policy on Vietnam. Articulate laymen organized to question the war, and even priests became involved in protest activities and in the public defense of conscientious objectors who refused to serve because of reservations about Vietnam. At least among a sector of Catholic opinion, a very different climate became evident.

The best place at which to begin the account is to start with the chronologically earliest efforts to express views which, save for the people associated with the *Catholic Worker*, challenged the stereotypic Catholic position of timidity among bishops and exalted anticommunism in the DLP and the National Civic Council. Early in 1966, a handful of Catholic women, impressed by the humane, conciliatory, peace-seeking gestures of John XXIII and Paul VI, collected and mailed such papal writings to priests, teaching brothers, and nuns in New South Wales, and to all Australian bishops. A second round of mailings was conducted, this time to newspapers. Because of interested response among lay persons and some priests, permanent organizations were established in New South Wales, in Queensland, and in Canberra under the title "Catholics for Peace," and in Victoria under the name "Pax," with expectation of extending the movement throughout the country.

This Catholic peace movement was not organized as an explicitly anti-Vietnamese or anticonscription drive, nor is it by design or membership pacifist as such. However, the overwhelming majority who enrolled have been severely critical of official Vietnamese policies, and many if not most have stood out against conscription for overseas service. Vietnam and conscription therefore provided exceptional incentive for the formation and subsequent development of the Catholic peace movement. Guided by progressive Catholic writings, by the increased emphasis placed by popes upon social responsibility in such encyclical letters as John's *Pacem In Terris* and Paul's *Christi Matri Rosarii*, depressed by what they have regarded as the sprint of events toward confrontations in international affairs, the Catholic peace movement people have dedicated themselves to reflective study and public action. The New South Wales group defines itself as "a group of Catholics pledged to the search for peace, justice, and freedom throughout the world,"[24] while the Victorians speak of themselves as "an association of Catholics pledged to quest through prayer, study and action, for peace with justice for the whole human family."[25]

While the Catholic peace movement's activities include seminar discussions and other self-improvement measures, the stress from the outset has been on action. Some of it has been of a fairly predictable sort—distribution of literature to lay and church people, staging of public debates on Vietnam and Christian responsibility, appearance before Catholic women's groups and Catholic school gatherings. But some of it has been quite unconventional. The Catholic peace movement has assumed the initiative for launching and popularizing Catholic-Marxist dialogues on philosophical and sociopolitical questions—the first time such enterprise has had any momentum in Australia.[26] Catholic peace movement members have assisted conscientious objectors and have exerted themselves to demonstrate that conscientious objection in the context of Vietnam is perfectly defensible by Catholic standards. They would agree with the *Catholic Worker* that "we must deplore the fact that some Catholic priests are still telling young Catholic men, who wish to object to involvement in Vietnam, that it is their 'duty to fight Communism.' We advise anyone who is told this to consult a better informed priest at once."[27] They have, furthermore, joined other, nondenominational Vietnam and conscription protest groups, and have participated in marches and other forms of public demonstrations, actuated by their substantive beliefs and their commitment to the ecumenical spirit.

Who are the Catholic militants? By far the greatest number are lay persons of both sexes. Most have exhibited little if any previous political activism. Most are of the educated middle class, and in fact relatively conservative on economic questions, a "bourgeois" quality that is confirmed by the location of the Catholic study groups—the better suburbs and the universities.[28] These are among the very same group characteristics found in so many of Australia's "new radicals" who have organized to protest against the Vietnamese conflict.[29]

What is particularly striking is the presence of ordained Catholic priests in the movement, some of whom have been there since its inception. As of the latter part of 1967, the Sydney group of 120 contained 6 priests, and the Melbourne group 8 out of 150—priests representing a new, rebellious element among the clergy who "see themselves as the conscience of the Church and the State. They are social hot-Gospellers who demand the freedom to act and speak as their consciences dictate," absorbed in the excitement of church renewal and ecumenism.[30] It is these Young Turk priests, literally young and usually with advanced educations, who for the first time have inserted themselves among Protestant clergymen and lay people of various faiths to collaborate in public protest parades and vigils, who have often sparked the Christian-Marxist dialogues, and who have written and spoken critically and at length, fusing moral, pragmatic, and academic arguments, about Vietnam and conscription.[31] It is from among them that the Reverend John Burnheim, Ph.D., rector of St. John's College at the University of Sydney and a prominent Catholic philosopher, has emerged to present himself at court hearings to explain and defend the consistency of young Catholic men to plead conscientious objection, be it for service in Vietnam or generally.[32]

While the Australian hierarchy has not even approached the pitch of militancy found in the Catholic peace movement, it was probably given a shove to the left by the movement, and has contributed to the continuing progress of the movement and of Catholic reflection on the war generally. When in 1966 the Catholic peace movement was first taking shape, the reactions of contacted bishops, the author understands, were usually carefully diplomatic, but when the group decided to arrange a series of university-based lunchtime forums, "extreme displeasure" was manifested from the "highest official quarters." But when the activists wrote to Cardinal Gilroy of their intentions to create a permanent organization and requested his blessing, he complied. The Catholic militants therefore proceeded to organize and to publicize, and especially to publicize the relevance of Pope Paul's message in which he cried out "in God's name . . . stop"; a settlement in Vietnam must be scrupulously pursued by all parties, "even at the expense of some inconvenience or loss, for it may have to be made later in train of bitter slaughter and involve great loss."

By early 1967, therefore, while the war in Vietnam was rapidly escalating, the Pope had publicly declared himself on behalf of a reasoned settlement, and lay protest activity in Australia was well under way, having been granted the cardinal's approval. When the Catholic bishops of Australia assembled in April 1967 for their annual conference, these considerations were in mind. The apostolic delegate to Australia, a strong advocate of the Pope's position on Vietnam, was in attendance, but the initiative for a progressive declaration on Vietnam came from Gilroy himself, a man who in past had leaned toward the official, status quo Australian approach. After considerable debate and committee work, the Pope's statement was endorsed by a resounding majority, and it was an endorsement without reservations.[33]

The impact of the bishops' resolution cannot be construed as having dissolved all previous conservative sentiments among members of the hierarchy. Some bishops, such as Fox, continued to express their felt conservatism which, at least in spirit, departed from the Sydney declaration.[34] The South Vietnamese ambassador to Australia complained to the hierarchy about the presentation of anti-Vietnam papers at a June 1967 forum at the University of Sydney. At least some of the priests who have participated in the more pronounced protest activities are known to have been subjected to pressures and reprimands from their superiors. It is also known that in the second half of 1967 two priests were dissuaded from presenting controversial papers before Pax sessions because of the opposition of the new archbishop of Melbourne, James Knox.[35]

It was the very same Archbishop Knox, however, who received Gough Whitlam on a "courtesy call" in October 1967. Whitlam did not request, expect, or receive promises of active assistance for the ALP. But personalities and conditions had changed during the previous few years. Knox was no Mannix, and Whitlam was neither an Evatt nor a Calwell. To be sure, Calwell was a devout Catholic and Whitlam was a Protestant. But while Calwell as leader had fought tenaciously on behalf of unceremonious withdrawal from Vietnam, Whitlam was playing very moderate variations on Labor's new Adelaide program. Furthermore, as the DLP was at that time showing some signs of electoral decline, Labor under Whitlam was apparently advancing, and no longer was there the aid to church schools controversy, which for several years had exacerbated church-ALP relations. Neutrality, or perhaps quiet sympathy toward Labor by the chief church dignitary in Victoria, was at least partially a recognition that Labor's Vietnam policy, despite differing from the government's, was acceptable.[36]

The church in Australia has traveled a considerable distance since the days of quarrel with the ALP. Despite reservations of various kinds among members of the hierarchy, the church in April 1967 formally committed itself to an accommodationist approach to Vietnam. Lay persons and clergymen alike have, sometimes in the face of public abuse or of hierarchical criticism, organized themselves not only for study, but for action. The principal Catholic metropolitan newspapers in Australia, the *Catholic Weekly* in Sydney and the *Advocate* in Melbourne, have been according considerable space to news of ecumenical and church renewal developments the world over, as well as to reports of Catholic protests over Vietnam in America and elsewhere. Their own editiorial policies became opposed to escalation in Vietnam, and in favor of fresh initiatives toward a settlement.[37]

These tendencies in the Catholic community, as is true of protest expressions among Protestants, have variegated and rendered more respectable the Australian anti-Vietnam and anticonscription movements at large. Because of the historically more disinterested or rigid positions of organized Catholics and ecclesiastical authorities than has been true in some Protestant quarters, the change is all the more profound. The change probably contributed to making the Whitlam-version ALP and its Vietnamese policies more palatable to the Catholic electorate, which in recent years has been deserting the ALP for either the DLP or the Liberals. Since DLP foreign policy is the most intransigently conservative of the three parties, it is not likely that many DLP followers to whom foreign policy was salient would vote Labor simply because Labor has become more malleable on Vietnam and conscription, or because there were signs of lay, clerical, and hierarchical Catholic uneasiness over a hard-line government policy.

But the ALP's recovery of recent losses to the Liberals, or otherwise the picking up of swinging or new voters, is more imaginable. The Australian Catholic electorate at large hardly deviates from overall national opinion on Vietnam and related issues. In February 1967, on the question whether the United States and its allies should press for a complete victory or a compromise, the all-Australian and Catholic response figures were, respectively, 26.5 per cent and 27.6 per cent for complete victory and 62.0 per cent and 60.6 per cent for a compromise.[38] In May 1967, on the question whether Australia should retain its forces in Vietnam or withdraw them, the figures for the two groups were 62.2 per cent and 59.9 per cent for retention, and 23.5 per cent and 24.8 per cent for return, respectively.[39] In November 1967, Catholic opinion on whether China represented a threat to Australian security was nearly identical to national opinion—32.7 per cent and 30.8 per cent, respectively.[40] In June 1968, following the unconditional partial bombing halt of North Vietnam, Catholic and general population responses to options of full bombing resumption, status quo, or the elimination of all interdiction against the North were virtually identical. Indeed, as compared to Anglicans, Presbyterians, Methodists, and Baptists, Catholics were *least* disposed to resume full bombing, and *most* disposed toward a total suspension of bombing.[41]

A survey carried out in the Isaacs (Victoria) electorate during the 1966 election indicated two interesting, interrelated phenomena. By far the largest concentration of replies that the vote was being affected by Vietnam and conscription came from persons who were swing, genuinely independent, or new voters. Additionally, it was learned that while solid Liberals were nearly unanimous in endorsing the "Australian involvement in Vietnam and the use of our troops there," among swing Liberals the distribution was quite close—56 per cent in favor and 44 per cent opposed.[42] All-Australian Gallup surveys found that Catholic and general population appraisals of the personally held importance of Vietnam and conscription as issues influential in determining one's vote in the 1966 House[43] and 1967 Senate[44] elections were nearly identical. Here is at least one clue that an ALP Vietnam policy critical of the official position yet free of doctrinairism of the 1966 Calwell variety, combined with gathering Catholic spokesmanship on behalf of accommodation, could be a factor in winning over Catholics who might be politically uncertain, recently defected to the Liberals, or just coming of voting age.

Vietnam-Conscription and Interfaith Cooperation

It is also profitable to comment on a factor which, while only incidentally related to *anti*-Vietnam protest, has resulted in Vietnam serving a special, Australian ecumenical cause. Christian ecumenism in Australia has of recent taken impressive forward strides. Many reasons can be offered, including the gradual socioeconomic homogenization of Protestant and Catholics, the virtual elimination of the divisive aid to parochial schools issue of the early and mid-sixties, and of course the conciliatory Vatican gestures of recent years. The proportion of either Protestants or Catholics prominently engrossed in the Vietnamese protest movement has been small. Still, the very fact of collaboration in a cause of this magnitude, transcending religious affiliations, has supplied a new interdenominational home to a particular portion of the population, and perhaps has impressed a sector of the nonmilitant public generally. It is also instructive that on January 1, 1968, in Perth's Roman Catholic St. Mary's Cathedral, for the first time in Australia, leaders of all Christian churches joined at a Catholic church in common prayer for peace.[45] The trigger had been the Pope's personal appeal for common Christian endeavor on behalf of peace, and the most preoccupying issue of peace and war, for the Pope and others, was the conflict in Vietnam.

This celebration of Christian solidarity, however impressive, was after all symbolic, but through the medium of nonofficial civil assistance for Vietnam, the conflict there has provided a concrete boost for the objective of Christian cooperation in Australia: "Australian opinion remains deeply divided on many aspects of the Vietnam war, but there is no mistaking the swelling support for efforts to relieve civilian suffering. It has gained strength from being largely non-ideological and non-political—the simple concern of individuals for their fellows overtaken by the savagery of war and lacking the means to help themselves."[46] Voluntary Australian assistance for the relief of hunger, physical displacement, underdevelopment, and other symptoms of a troubled world existed long before Vietnam became the scene of massive dislocation. Also, much of the effort of both denominational and nondenominational agencies operating on a permanent basis has been funneled to Asia, either directly or through coordinating international agencies. In recent years, however, the principal developments in the field of voluntary overseas assistance have reflected increases in amount and variety of aid provided, a diversion of considerable aid resources to Vietnam, and cooperative action among various types of aid-granting agencies and interested individuals, Protestant and Catholic alike.

Because of the growth of Australian overseas donations, the number of organizations involved, and the obvious need to effect reasonably close liaison with Australian federal and state governments and the United Nations and its specialized agencies, an Australian Council for Overseas Aid (ACFOA) was formed early in 1965. The impulse for the new coordinating body was general rather than Vietnamese. The same could be said for the Overseas Service Bureau, designed as a central reference pool for Australians interested in employment in developing states, and as the manager of the Australian Volunteers Abroad, a group of volunteers who donate their services abroad for minimal compensation. The federal government has provided funds for administrative upkeep of ACFOA and for the shipment of certain privately collected goods to developing countries. The principal burden of financing the aid program, however, remains private, and more especially falls on ACFOA member groups, since ACFOA is not a fund-raising agency. A special campaign launched by the Melbourne *Age* to collect funds for Vietnamese relief, for instance, designated ACFOA and its member bodies as recipients.

Since Vietnam became an area of acute dislocation and civilian hardship, voluntary overseas aid has been increasingly directed there. In 1966, ACFOA agreed to a request from the Department of External Affairs to coordinate private assistance activities in Vietnam. Following a visit to Vietnam by an ACFOA team, a Vietnam Aid Committee was formed, and projects have been assembled for presentation to member agencies and the public for support.[47] The member groups include both church- and non-church-related organizations. Among the most prominent church bodies are the Australian Council of Churches and Australian Catholic Relief. Between them, these two groups in 1967 provided almost half of the voluntary Australian assistance of more than $200,000 (Australian) contributed to South Vietnamese relief. They and other bodies have worked together in ACFOA, and have profited from the coordinative and project-recommending activities of ACFOA. They have also lent keen support to common, Vietnam-oriented voluntary aid programs such as "Project Concern," which has sent medical personnel to Vietnam and has supported a hospital, and they have joined in endorsing other cross-denominational efforts such as the Australian Committee of Responsibility for Children of Vietnam.

As various groups with interests beyond Vietnam have begun to devote more energy and money to Vietnamese relief, Catholics, Protestants, Jews and others, comprising virtually the entire Australian political spectrum, have cooperated smoothly and freely. At the turn of 1967–1968, several member groups of ACFOA constituted themselves into Australian Care for Refugees, or AUSTCARE, with the intention of launching a nationwide appeal for refugee relief, Vietnam included. Here was an initiative involving Protestants, Catholics, and other groups to coordinate Australian refugee assistance in Vietnam and elsewhere and which, for the first time, entailed an inter-organizational fund appeal.

The vast majority of Australian voluntary aid to Vietnam has, understandably, been directed to *South* Vietnam. Some of the aid distributed in South Vietnam has, however, benefited persons who may be NLF members or followers, since the assistance generally has not involved the asking of questions of needy civilians about their political allegiances. Also, some of the Australian aid organizations —including the Australian Council of Churches' division of Inter-Church Aid, and Australian Catholic Relief—contribute to their parent international bodies which, in turn, have diverted some assistance to churches and needy persons in the North. It is rather significant that when in 1967 the government was introducing legislation to bar aid to the NLF or Hanoi save through International Red Cross channels, much of the initiative for requesting a wider aid allowance emanated from Australian church quarters. The Quakers complained, and so did the Inter-Church Aid group. The representations from Inter-Church Aid spoke directly for Protestant-derived assistance, but implicitly on behalf of others as well. A telegram to Holt from a representative of Inter-Church Aid specified that "I speak only for Inter-Church Aid, but I am concerned also for Catholic relief services with whom we share projects in (South) Vietnam, and for whom we also recruit Australian workers."[48] In February of 1968 the Australian Council of Churches announced in the plainest language that it was sending eighteen thousand dollars to the World Council of Churches for distribution on behalf of Vietnamese relief, with no limitation being placed on its use in either part of the country.[49] The following month, AUSTCARE, composed of a dozen member groups—secular, Protestant and Catholic—explained that its forthcoming campaign would collect money for refugee relief in various parts of the world. Vietnam was scheduled to be allotted a sizable share, and no distinction was planned between North and South Vietnamese distribution.[50]

Voluntary Australian assistance for civilian purposes in Vietnam has therefore given testimony of the impact of the conflict upon the community at large. It has also opened fresh avenues of cooperation between members and organizations of various faiths, regarding relief activity as a human, rather than as a political, pro- or anti-Saigon regime, South or North Vietnamese problem. Vietnam as a healing rather than a war-making concern has therefore in its way contributed toward the progress of interdenominational harmony in Australia.

Veterans and Their Organizations

Ex-servicemen's organizations offer another instance of how the Vietnamese war and conscription for overseas duty have affected associational groups in Australia. By far the largest and most influential veterans' group in the country, founded in 1916, is the Returned Services League of Australia (RSL), formerly known as the Returned Sailors', Soldiers' and Airmen's Imperial League of Australia. While it limits membership to those who served in officially designated theaters of war rather than enrolling ex-servicemen at large, the league contains a quarter of a million members, with some two thousand branches in every Australian state and territory.

Many of the RSL's activities have focused on the social and economic advancement of returned servicemen. In fact, the RSL has for many years had excellent access to the federal government in what are referred to as matters of "repatriation" of veterans, and has frequently succeeded in having its politics implemented. The league has also declared itself on subjects of broader national policy, and has carried such representations to the government. Communists are barred from RSL membership, but otherwise its rank and file political composition is believed to reflect the distribution of party preferences found throughout the community generally. It has studiously avoided alignment with any particular political party, preferring to maximize its influence as a pressure group opposite whichever party might be governing at any given time.[51]

Despite this devotion to partisan nonalignment, the league's formulations on foreign and defense policy have been decidedly hard-line. It has been a consistent advocate of a powerful military establishment, of conscription, and in 1962 endorsed a nuclear capability for Australia. It has been profoundly disturbed over international (and domestic) Communism, and has applauded Australia's efforts at blocking the advance of Communism through diplomatic and military measures alike. On Vietnam, the RSL early condemned the unrest in the South and unmasked it as a manifestation of Communist aggression, no different in objective than had been instigated in Korea in 1950. The RSL argued that "it is worthy of note that Communists, both at home and abroad, are campaigning for an allied withdrawal from South Vietnam. This fact alone indicates the need for questioning the wisdom of such a move. It would be a rare event indeed if the best course of action from our point of view was the one advocated by our enemies."[52] Ranking RSL figures have expressed frequent and barbed criticism of Vietnam protesters and their tactics.[53] The league has become associated with the Australian Friends of Vietnam, a procommitment group to which the Vietnamese conflict gave rise, and one of whose central committee members is RSL National President Sir Arthur Lee.

However, the costly and seemingly stalemated nature of the Vietnamese conflict created some countertendencies among Australian former servicemen. The RSL itself, while continuing to interpret the war as dangerously Communist-inspired, finally progressed to a more balanced appraisal and set of recommendations. It expressed the need for a heavy civil aid commitment in Vietnam, imploring the government to "substantially increase its contribution to the general programme designed to combat social and economic backwardness."[54] It also took the task of civil aid to Vietnam to personal heart, joining in a 1966 national campaign on behalf of "Operation 'New Life' Vietnam" to collect clothing, tools, and utensils for use by the Australian army in its own civic action work in Vietnam. Later, as part of a general Southeast Asia aid project, the RSL created a special fund to help finance welfare grants and technical experts, and to provide aid for persons entering Australia for study purposes.

More dramatic has been the RSL's redirection of thinking about the resolution of the war. At the October 1967 National Congress, the president's report stipulated that Vietnam was as much a political as a military operation, the "unfortunate political implications of the bombing [of the North] cannot be ignored," and the government should constantly be searching for a "satisfactory alternative" to the bombing.[55] In February 1968 the league's national executive made a formal submission to the government to this very effect, making it the major item in a two-hour discussion held with the minister for defense.[56] The RSL did not urge the immediate and unconditional end of bombing in the North. But its public position reflected unease about untempered military measures in the conflict, a departure from its characteristic firmness on questions involving confrontations with Communism in Asia.

In 1966, however, the RSL's militancy on Vietnam proved too much for some Australian veterans. In October of that year, while attending an anti-Vietnam-war, Methodist-sponsored rally, a World War II combat veteran met a Catholic woman who was a moving force in the New South Wales Catholic peace movement. After some discussion, it was agreed that there were a number of veterans who shared powerful anti-Vietnam convictions, and that they might be amenable to organizing themselves.

From this the Ex-Services Human Rights Association of Australia was born. Its platform is broadly defined in terms of seeking peaceful solutions to international conflict, rather than aiming exactly at Vietnam. But Vietnam inspired the formation of the group, and has been its dominant concern. As with most Australian protest groups, the Human Rights Association people are basically political amateurs, groping their way to give maximum publicity to their cause at large and to the fact that ex-servicemen are not necessarily reflexive militarists. They meet, they talk and study, they publish a newsletter, and occasionally take on a major program, such as a rally in Sydney Town Hall in March 1968 with Arthur Calwell as featured speaker. As of the beginning of 1968, the organization had about three hundred members in New South Wales, two hundred in Victoria, and one hundred in Queensland. As in most protest organizations, there are Catholics, Protestants, humanists of assorted kinds and outright atheists, most members vote Labor, and there are some Australian Reform Movement people and a handful of Communists.

Most of the organization's members do not belong to the RSL, but some do, and here lies an interesting tale. In the first half of 1967, very shortly after the association had been founded, a considerable flap arose in the New South Wales branch of the RSL. Les Waddington and Ashley Pascoe, two of the more vocal association members and both RSL members in good standing, were subjected to an investigation by the RSL branch in New South Wales. Their outspoken views on Vietnam, aspects of conscription, and other related topics were found to be subversive to RSL policy and incompatible with continued RSL membership. Waddington was expelled from the RSL and Pascoe was suspended for five years. These events in New South Wales immediately precipitated a nationwide furor within the RSL organization and among its members. Hundreds of RSL members, not themselves involved in the new, anti-Vietnam Human Rights Association, resigned from the RSL. Protests were received from ranking Labor parliamentarians, themselves RSL members. The Victorian branch of the RSL pointedly announced that it would undertake no action against any of its own members who took exception to official RSL policy on Vietnam and conscription.[57]

The RSL's national executive refrained from formal intervention in the case, but it did underline the right of all members to dissent from official league policy. The New South Wales branch, taking into account this judgment as well as the heated protests which had been generated across the country, finally rescinded Waddington's and Pascoe's punishments, though it announced that its decision was based on legal grounds—the RSL barred membership to Communists, but permitted membership in other organizations and the freedom to challenge standing RSL policies.[58] It was reassuring, as one editorial suggested, "that an organisation with the great political and social influence of the RSL is, like any other, subject to the rule of law, and that diverse opinions will not be stifled. This in turn must help prevent a hardening of the League's arteries"[59]—which could also be said of the RSL's gradual modification of its own position on the appropriate manner to handle the Vietnamese war.

Within the churches and among ex-servicemen, therefore, Vietnam-conscription have made a considerable impact. These public policy questions have provided an induction into political sensitivity/action for persons previously uninvolved. These issues have induced noticeable change in mood among groups such as the Roman Catholic hierarchy and the RSL. While prompting the formation of such offshoot groups as the Pax movement and the Human Rights Association, they have also fostered the harmonization of important voluntary associations, most notably in the area of interfaith cooperation. Lastly, the demeanor of these groups and their elites has supplied yet another stimulant for interesting and possibly affecting the attitudes and politically relevant behavior of the mass public.

Chapter 7. Vietnamese Protest among Academics, Artists, and University Students

It has already been suggested that the Australian protest movement absorbed a disproportionately high number of educated and professional people. It is therefore appropriate to emphasize the role that has been played in the Vietnam-conscription controversy by certain key sectors of the Australian intelligentsia—academic persons, members of the artistic community, and by university students.

The Changing Milieu of Australian Academics

It is probably fair to suggest that Australian academics as a group have not enjoyed a tradition of confident, imaginative, political involvement, and at least some of the determinants of this condition should be cited.

The very small university enrollments before the Second World War meant very small faculties, and therefore an unduly low academic population opposite the general population. Even by 1964, when university enrollment had reached seventy-five thousand, there were only about five thousand staff people of all grades throughout the country. Traditionally and to a degree in the present, the university emphasis in Australia has been on vocational training, meaning that the climate in universities was not overly conducive to encouraging freewheeling, socially questioning faculty enterprise. The Australian academic community also suffered from a mixture of professional isolation, inbreeding, and institutional rigidities which detracted from widespread and vigorously expressed sociopolitical activism. Professional associations were slow to form. The majority of academics was found at the two oldest and largest universities, Sydney and Melbourne, while the faculty at other universities, being at small institutions and far removed from one another, suffered from an isolation which carried both professional and personal consequences. The Meccas of higher education were for very long Oxford and Cambridge, since graduate (and especially doctoral) education at home was essentially a development of the 1950s. Departmental organization in Australia was far more British than American oriented, with a single professor per department whose authority was far greater than *primus inter pares.* A tradition of commitment to consistent, original research and distingiushed scholarly publication was missing. It was not helped by the condition that achieving a professorship by working one's way up through the ranks was extremely rare, while denial of "tenure" in the American sense for reason of defective or inadequate scholarship once an appointment was received was nearly unheard of. These considerations depressed the flowering of a vigorous intellectual atmosphere which could have carried over into articulation of and noticeable involvement in social and political controversy.

There were other reasons as well, some of the academics' own making, and some not. Australian society itself, with its severely egalitarian bent and suspicion of elites and establishments of whatever sort, was not the perfect milieu in which academics could develop self-pride and confidence. The quest for professional overextension and excellence was not among Australia's highest-regarded virtues. Academics themselves were not valued as people of exceptional professional standing. This generated a syndrome of conventionality in behavior and routine of job execution which carried "nine-to-five" working hour connotations among academics. The Australian academic was inclined to typify rather than diverge from the practical, bourgeois orientation of his nonacademic middle-class compatriots. When he felt he had something special to contribute, "Australian conditions sharpen[ed] the inevitable conflict . . . . His isolation in an unsympathetic society-at-large has its reflection in a certain inner loneliness [though one should probably not call it isolation] in the very community which might have been expected to sustain him. That is the cause of his recessiveness, of his absence from public affairs, of his recurrent self-doubt."[1]

The sense of "loneliness" was for some time aggravated by the academic's impression that he has lacked appropriate forums through which to contribute to an invigoration of public policy. While most nonscientific academics have been temperamentally or ideologically closer to the ALP than to the other parties, they have found the ALP inhospitable. They have been inclined to "distrust the Liberal Party, hate the Democratic Labor Party and despair of the Labor Party; usually they would feel detached from party politics; they detest anti-semitism but often are suspicious of all Catholics; they fear McCarthyism."[2] Their aversion to Labor has been based on their own perception of the party's trade union influenced, cliché-dominated, organizationally stultified character, and on the party's ill-concealed disdain for intellectualism. The result has not only been a withdrawal from active party-political involvement for academics; "This lack of communication with an influential Left intelligentsia is a tragedy for the ALP," it has been suggested, "as it has deprived it of the thinkers and theorists (such as Tawney, Beveridge, the Webbs, Titmus) who have, in Britain, provided many of the party's radical policies and initiatives."[3]

Australian academics, and especially social scientists, have also felt a denial of access to nonparty outlets. There is no long habit of co-opting academic experts into government positions or for important consultative roles. Excessive secretiveness relating both to documentary material and to the willingness of public servants to talk with relative candor to researchers, while a somewhat exaggerated complaint among academics, has not been entirely unfounded. Additionally, Australian academics for some time felt discriminated against in the lack of regular opportunities for dissemination of their opinions through news media—media which they lamented for their alleged undersophistication, pliant conventionality, and overcommercialism.

Conditions in Australia and within academia have, however, undergone a fair amount of transformation within a short period of time. Universities have grown in number, in size, and in the variety of their offerings, including new emphasis on the social sciences. Potential academics now look to Australian universities, to America, and to British red brick institutions for their advanced training, as well as to Oxbridge—thus stimulating far more professional and even personal cosmopolitanism among Australian university faculties than in the past. Demand has developed for more academics with better, more specialized and refined training, departmental organization has begun to evince increasing openness, and incentive for professional productivity has climbed. New journals of opinion have sprung up, both commercial and public radio and television have increasingly drawn on academics to explain events or offer positions, the press has moved toward a wider and more depth-oriented political coverage and has welcomed academic contributions, and government has begun to grant improved recognition to academic advice. The very nature of Australian society has been in process of reorientation, given its exposure to a heterogeneous migrant population and to intensified contacts with Asia and Asians—and with the parallel raising of perceptions and tastes through swings in pretertiary education and the content of media presentations. It has, in sum, become a more congenial and receptive climate for academics in which to work and self-confidently express themselves.[4]

Academics and Vietnam-Conscription

The emergence of Vietnam and conscription for overseas duty as controversies has encouraged more academic involvement in public affairs and has invested the controversies themselves with more weight and sharpness because academics have been willing to step in and be counted. Some of this academic activity has been nearly or entirely nonpartisan, but nonetheless noticeable. For example, the World University Service, an international voluntary organization of students and faculty, has operated at Australian universities, and in 1967 had a target of nine thousand dollars for assistance to South Vietnamese students and universities.[5] In 1967, twenty-nine staff members at the Australian National University, representing a wide range of views on Australia's commitment in Vietnam, organized a "University Vietnam Civil Relief Appeal," whose object was relief and rehabilitation on behalf of South Vietnamese civilian war victims.[6]

A number of interested academics have publicly taken sides on Vietnam-conscription, and within this group by far the most have been critical of established government policy. Here the prevailing biases of social scientists and humanists have been able to crystallize around issues of pre-emptive national importance, providing opportunity to activate such underlying academic predispositions as close bonds with emerging Asia, less reflexive reaction toward Communism, less sycophancy toward the United States, and a sense of idealism respecting accommodation among peoples and nations.

One favorite Vietnamese forum for academics became the teach-ins, which proliferated among universities across the country. Their importance lay not simply in the fact that academics were participating in open and vigorous presentation of a salient public question. More importantly, the teach-ins were among the first major stages on which spirited, contentious discussion of Vietnam occurred in Australia, a stage which pulled the Vietnamese debate away from the sometimes stilted quality common to partisan parliamentary debate or the generally unchallenged expressions found in the press. Ministers of government, prominent opposition spokesmen, journalists, and others joined academics for give-and-take exchanges, and in so doing contributed materially to interesting and informing the public at large.

Academics have also been active in various aspects of the organized protest movement. They have been prominent at rallies and demonstrations, both as ordinary participants and as featured speakers. They have contributed to the membership of protest groups, and the lists of founding or executive committee persons in such groups is usually prominently sprinkled with academics, many without reputations as professional cause-chasers or even as political activists generally.

Academics have been among the professions most heavily represented in signed letters, petitions, and advertisements entered in newspapers and periodicals. The signatories to such manifestoes have understandably been drawn mostly from among the social sciences and the humanities, but not entirely so. The most graphic illustration of anti-Vietnamese sentiment among other academic and academically related people appeared in a statement entered in the November 1967 issue of the *Australian Journal of Science*. This statement called upon the United States and Australia to heed U Thant's call for a cessation of bombing in the North, the scaling down of all military activities by all parties within South Vietnam, and the expression of willingness to negotiate with all belligerents. The statement was subscribed to by 677 Australian scientists, many of them, including 61 professors—a considerable figure for that rank—members of university faculties. The two organizers were a physiologist and a histologist-embryologist at the University of Sydney. Included was a group of scientists employed by the government's own Commonwealth Scientific, Industrial, and Research Organization (CSIRO), and a member of the CSIRO executive.[7] About a year earlier, in a full-page anti-Vietnam newspaper declaration dominated by Victorian academic and professional signatories, a third of the listed Melbourne and Monash University academics were found to be in the physical and biological sciences, and in medicine.[8]

Two faculty surveys are available to the author—one comprehensive (ten universities) and the other confined to the University of Tasmania. Their results are complementary, but both, and especially the first, require very qualified treatment.

The first survey, conducted in 1966 at all major universities save Western Australia, put certain questions about Vietnam to all faculty people of all grades from lecturer upward. It revealed that of those responding 54 per cent opposed the Vietnam war, 30 per cent supported it, and 16 per cent declined to state their position or gave only comments. A clear majority against the war was found at all universities polled. Biological-social scientists and humanists were most strongly opposed—64 per cent and 61 per cent, respectively—though more opposition than support for Vietnam was found among all academic categories. Various other questions revealed comparably serious reservations about the tenets governing the government's Vietnam policies.[9]

While this survey should not be discounted out of hand, it suffered from two powerful flaws. First, only 36 per cent of those approached replied at all. Therefore, the above findings were based on barely a third of the eligible respondents. Second, the statements to which faculty persons were being asked to react were couched in stark and loaded terms. It is fair to assume that this feature of the survey kept responses very low, and also screened out a large number of persons who were not adamant opponents of, and perhaps were supporters of, government policy.

The other university faculty Vietnam-conscription survey known to the author was conducted in 1967 by students of the Tasmania University Union. The survey needs to be treated with caution in several respects. The total group contacted was small. Only sixty persons, representing about 50 per cent of those who were sent questionnaires and who were able to reply, in fact did so. The organizers of the survey themselves surmised that the majority of those abstaining was most likely "to be the conservative established element who in general are not kindly disposed to student enterprises of this kind. On the other hand, those who answered are more likely to be the younger liberal generation." While the survey was interdisciplinary, it might also be true that persons in the scientific fields, ordinarily more conservative than those in the social sciences and the humanities, were disproportionately represented among the abstainers. Those who did respond, however, were overwhelmingly opposed to official premises and policies governing Vietnam and conscription. The Australian commitment in Vietnam was opposed in the ratio of more than four to one, the system of dispatching conscripts to Vietnam in a ratio of five to one, and nearly half favored the sending of nonmilitary aid to the National Liberation Front by Australian students. Interestingly, both the L-CP government *and* the ALP—the latter by a five to one margin—were felt to have inadequately stated their reasons for their respective positions on the Australian involvement in the conflict.[10]

The Artistic Community

Australian performing and creative artists were also stimulated to undertake protest activity by the war in Vietnam. Like the academics, they have signed letters and published petitions, sometimes as a discrete group and at other times in conjunction with politicians, trade union officials, clergymen, and others. They have participated in demonstrations, and have offered to supply politically slanted presentations at such events in the form of songs, dances, and poetry readings. For the 1967 October Mobilization activities in Sydney, even the convenors of the event seemed pleasantly surprised by the number and caliber of artists who volunteered to lend their services —people not normally associated either with political action or with radical causes in particular.[11] One of the more celebrated individual protest steps was taken by Glennis Tomasetti, a folk singer, who attempted to withhold that share of her income tax payment which was earmarked for federal defense spending.[12]

Publicity (and income) for the protest movement has also come from more systematically organized artistic activities. There was *On Stage—Vietnam*, a theatrical production which played to capacity audiences in major cities. Incorporating skits, song and dance routines, and other vehicles, its aim was to portray the inhumanity of the Vietnamese war and the wrongness of conscription, and to satirize important American and Australian personalities.[13] Later came *Childermas*, a play commissioned by the Australian Committee of Responsibility for Children of Vietnam. Although its theme was basically antiwar rather than anti-Vietnam, it nonetheless was a part of the theater's role in deprecating the Vietnamese conflict.[14]

Another significant artistic protest effort was a touring "Artists on War" exhibition, organized with the cooperation of the Contemporary Art Society of Victoria. Executed in various media, it contained pieces bearing such titles as "Requiem for the Dead by Napalm," "Death in the Jungle," "Confrontation," "Children Finished Screaming," and "Do You Realise a Truce Could Escalate Into All Out Peace?"[15] One reviewer felt that the display was "so well intentioned and so awful that it needs careful handling. . . . Bad paintings don't

become good paintings simply because they carry the right sentiment."[16]

Good or bad, however, the art exhibition was symptomatic of a
mood which had increasingly spread across the Australian intellectual community. It did not represent willful service to Communists
who were endeavoring to broaden and make more respectable the
base of anti-Vietnamese and conscription protest. It was not a pre-
meditated effort to mobilize support for the Labor party politically,
especially since conventional party politics were of small concern to
many of those included in the protest manifestations. It was not, at
least among those who spoke, wrote, marched, sang, painted, or
otherwise visibly protested, anywhere close to a majority of those
who in the country could be labeled members of the academic, intellectual, or artistic communities. But it did demonstrate the power
of an emotional, overriding issue, to pull many people out of apathy
and noninvolvement, to raise for common effort intellectuals and
trade unionists, pacifists and ex-servicemen, churchmen and atheists,
party activists and political amateurs, and to dramatize the issue before politicians and public alike.

The Range of University Student Protest Involvement

Vietnam and conscription have left their marks not only on the
staffs, but on the student components of Australian university communities, whose protest expressions have spanned an extremely wide
gamut.

University of Western Australia students burned crosses and fes-
tooned the war memorial with toilet seats. The University of Adelaide
United Nations Students' Association arranged a Vietnam War
Crimes Tribunal. Students in Canberra publicly burned an Australian
flag—and, far more charmingly, supplied well-endowed coeds in
"Make Love Not War" sweatshirts for demonstrations against the
Johnson visit to the capital city in 1966. A student crowd mercilessly
jeered and paper-dart bombarded Holt during a formal invitational
lecture he was delivering at the University of Melbourne in mid-1967.
A month later, when Holt arrived for a lecture at Monash University,
his entry was greeted by hisses and catcalls. An inscribed copy of
the *Thoughts of Mao Tse-Tung* was thrust into the Prime Minister's
hand. He began his address by remarking, "I entered this place and
was handed a copy of the thoughts of Mao Tse-Tung. I am asking you

here to listen a while to the thoughts of Harold Edward Holt." That saved the day, and the audience accorded him an uninterrupted hearing.[17]

It was at Monash, and at the University of Melbourne and at the ANU, that the aid to the NLF movement was strongest. Monash witnessed some of the sharpest Australian teach-in activity. A group of Monash students in 1968 initiated a series of Saturday morning public discussions on the Vietnamese conflict in Melbourne's city square.[18] It was the Monash Students' Representative Council that collected one thousand dollars from within Monash, Melbourne, and the Royal Melbourne Institute of Technology to send a Monash graduate student on a personal observation tour of South Vietnam so that he could report back to a prearranged Monash teach-in.[19] Students from Victorian universities were instrumental in the founding of the Draft Resistance Movement, the group which was committed to "wrecking" (and not simply "opposing") conscription, and which elicited such tactics as a "chain-in" at a military reception center.

At the University of New South Wales, and then at the University of Sydney, impetus was given by students and some cooperating faculty to the organization of groups such as the Vietnam Objectors Group, whose purpose was to assist those young men seeking National Service exemption on the specific grounds of objection to the Vietnamese War. A reliable informant has suggested that perhaps 80 per cent of those who have claimed exemption on nonpacifist, and more especially anti-Vietnam grounds, or who have simply refused to register, have been university students. The Vietnam Objectors Group in New South Wales and its offspring elsewhere have emphasized the preparation of men for facing court hearings when Vietnam objection was involved—an opposition which long lacked legal success, but which eventually managed to yield some results.[20]

At New South Wales universities and at the University of Queensland the Students for a Democratic Society (Society for Democratic Action at Queensland) became most firmly entrenched, spreading later to Victoria. Disenchanted both with the sociopolitical assumptions of conventional politics and with traditional radical solutions, the SDS has encouraged the avoidance of National Service registration, expressed hostility toward involvement in Vietnam, continued collection of funds for the NLF and—a fresh twist—early in 1968 announced a campaign to collect funds for the construction of a high school in Hanoi to replace one destroyed by American bombing raids.[21]

A number of university Students' Representative Councils and student newspapers have gone on record opposing Australian participation in the Vietnamese conflict, and the National Union of Australian University Students (NUAUS), which formally represents the hundred thousand university students in the country, has long shared this view. In October 1966 NUAUS organized "protest day" activities in most Australian capitals, urging opposition to the deployment of conscripts in Vietnam.[22] By February 1968, NUAUS had adopted resolutions which branded the war "unjust" and a danger to world peace; it deplored the presence of Australian troops in Vietnam and urged their withdrawal.[23]

Early in 1968, the Australian Student Christian Movement passed several motions condemning Australia's part in the Vietnamese war and the National Service Act. It called upon all Christian bodies, students, and university staff to "participate in any action seen as useful, and purposeful towards bringing about an end to the Vietnam war."[24]

The most reverberative student behavior concerned the collection of funds for civil aid to the NLF and to North Vietnam. Literally tens of thousands of dollars for such assistance were collected from nonstudent sources in the second half of 1967, largely through the instigation of an adult, one Francis James, a prominent Anglican layman.[25] Still, it was the student actions that leapfrogged the controversy into the political arena and brought passage of the Defense Forces Protection Act—despite a hurriedly adopted student Labor Club qualification that "unspecified" assistance was more than medical but excluded military aid.[26] After the enactment of the legislation, student organizers of the aid project continued their work, seeking to circumvent the law by transmitting funds through indirect foreign channels. To close such loopholes, the authorities were impelled to issue more restrictive regulations.[27]

Through their ingenuity in finding channels for such funds, the student activists became unwitting contributors to an international incident between Australia and a foreign power. The first act in the episode occurred when a delegation from the Monash Labor Club's committee for Aid to NLF paid a visit to the Cambodian ambassador in Canberra. The students did not ask that the Embassy or the Cambodian government serve as a conduit for the transmission of NLF-

intended funds, though they did inquire whether Cambodia supported their aid project, and whether they could mail money to the
NLF representatives in the Cambodian capital of Phnom Penh. The
Cambodian ambassador provided a diplomatically proper reply. Because Cambodia was unwilling to interfere in Australia's internal
affairs, and because of Cambodia's wish to preserve strict neutrality,
no support could be given to the students, though the students could,
without Cambodian reproval, mail their funds in care of the NLF
representatives in Phnom Penh.[28]

But members of the University of Melbourne Labor Club had written personally to Cambodia's Prince Sihanouk, requesting contact
with the NLF and enclosing a check as a token contribution to the
Front. The letter specified that any reply from the Cambodian Chief
of State would be treated confidentially. Sihanouk replied, expressing
"keen sympathy" for the students' efforts and providing them with
an address in Cambodia where the NLF could be reached. But the
correspondence leaked out in early September and became public
information.[29]

Hasluck regarded the Prince's action as indiscreet, and expressed
his "disappointment" to the Cambodian ambassador that, while the
aid to the NLF issue was running strong in Australian politics, a
foreign government should have interposed itself in this manner.[30]
Cambodia already had its differences with Australia, since the latter
had agreed only to "respect" rather than "recognize" Cambodia's
ambiguous and diplomatically sensitive borders with its neighbors.
It is difficult to weigh the relative importance of Cambodia's pique
over the border issue and its NLF aid differences with Australia. Still,
almost immediately after Hasluck had rebuked Cambodia for interfering in Australia's domestic politics, the Cambodian ambassador
was called home and the Embassy in Canberra was evacuated except
for a single officer. For several months Austral-Cambodian relations
remained cool, and not until February 1968, when Australia reversed
itself on the border issue, did Cambodia express interest in restoring
normal relations.[31]

Student Activists: Their Strength and Character

Australian student protest has been dramatic, has aroused considerable interest, and has impacted itself upon domestic politics and
even upon Australia's foreign policy. Nonetheless, *activist* behavior
has been confined to a very small minority of Australian university

student bodies. On the basis of a 1961 study undertaken at the University of New England, in New South Wales, researchers concluded that perhaps 1 per cent of the second and third year students were members of any political clubs.[32] More recently, based on investigations carried out in 1966, one writer concluded that an upper-level estimate would find 2.5 per cent of Australian university students enrolled in political clubs. "On any reckoning the activist core is small. Total nominal membership in the political clubs in a good year is very unlikely to exceed 350 in the big universities; the clubs are actually run by a few handfuls or less; and those who flutter in awe or anticipation around the edges of the organisations amount only to further handfuls."[33] A 1967 survey of University of Sydney students disclosed that 4 per cent were active in political clubs—as against 21 per cent membership in cultural societies, 21 per cent in academic societies, and 28 per cent in sports clubs.[34] Among the political clubs which enroll some of this small band of activists are organizations not of the "left" in overall persuasion or actively anti-Vietnam or anti-conscription more particularly—for instance, Liberal and DLP clubs.

Further confirmation of this trend may be found in a selected breakdown of groups which have worked to upset the government's foreign policy. At the beginning of 1968 the SDS groups, then present at six or seven universities, contained a membership of about 350, of whom perhaps 40, according to one of the group's spokesmen, were genuinely "activist."[35] At the ANU, with a student body of about 2,700, there was a publicized difference of opinion as to whether those who had voted to aid the NLF had numbered 50 or only 14.[36] At the peak of the NLF aid controversy, the Monash University Labor Club contained about 250 members, from among a student population of 7,500. As was explained in Parliament,

> There are 7,500 students at Monash but the proportion involved in controversial issues of this kind is very small indeed. Only thirty-odd students in the Labor Club voted to raise funds for the NLF. . . . Only three were prepared to defy the Vice-Chancellor's ban by collecting for this fund on the campus. Only seven students and one girl who worked in the bookshop have been prepared to contravene the Defence Forces Protection Act.[37]

One Monash student underscored the heterogeneity of the Labor Club at his university in explaining that "it is a rather loose coalition including Maoists as well as more frequent Whitlamites, and—I suspect—some whose dispositions would make them Australian equivalents of the British Conservatives Bow Group."[38]

Where Students' Representative Councils at various universities have assumed militantly anti-Vietnam postures, or even in the instance of the position endorsed by NUAUS, such decisions have been adopted by very small numbers of students, themselves activists, and by no means necessarily reflective of student body opinion. At the ANU, a struggle developed in mid-1967 over whether the local SRC should make political comment on behalf of the student body. The debate was precipitated by a strongly worded anti-Vietnam resolution sent by NUAUS to the ANU for ratification. The issue seemed to actuate considerable interest at the ANU, and was accorded banner publicity by NUAUS. Forces favoring a nonpolitical role for the ANU SRC, except where student opinion had been explicitly ascertained, won out. Those ANU students who attended a general meeting on the subject and were recorded as voting divided 218–127.[39] In other words, interest as evidenced by attendance was not substantial, and the 127 who voted against, of whom most could be suspected to have been activists and supportive of the NUAUS resolution on Vietnam, were a meager number compared to the total student population.

What kind of people are the student militants? The previously mentioned 1966 study entailed in-depth interviews with sixty-eight University of Melbourne students who joined formal party clubs in that year—two ALP clubs, a Liberal Club, and a DLP Club. It was a group representing about 65–70 per cent of the year's new members in those clubs. A very large proportion—over 80 per cent—were enrolled in law, arts, or commerce faculties, rather than in science or engineering faculties. As a group, the surveyed students did not have an inordinately high level of political affect, i.e., involvement in politics, or of political knowledge. Most joined not for reason of burning cause, but for personal or social reasons. Despite these considerations and differences connoted in the students' selection of ALP, Liberal, or DLP affiliation, a pattern emerged. "The joiners are generally hard on Australian politicians, sometimes hard on Australia, mostly hard on America, but soft on social and political reform: they seize on odd issues—education, hanging, independence in foreign policy—but rarely have an eye for the system as a whole, and rarely invest the views they do have with the bitter affect which is reserved for America or, in some cases, Australia."[40] Among the ALP club respondents, there was considerable restiveness about the party itself, and about the difficulty in deciding whether the ALP was in fact deserving of their electoral support.

In other words, a visible trait among the political club members was considerable cynicism about standard party politics and politicians. This expressed itself particularly on the "left," or ALP, end of the three-party club array, and from where potential protest focused on Vietnam and conscription would be most apt to derive. Despite lacking any exceptionally strong political affect or knowledge, the survey group tended to be outwardly disenchanted with the United States and with what that nation represented, a reaction found among nearly half of the Liberal and DLP respondents, and more pronouncedly among ALP club members. This represented a potential for turning against the Australian commitment in Vietnam, which officially was being justified so very heavily on grounds of protecting the American alliance.

These propensities of skepticism about conventional politics and dislike for America have been accentuated among persons, such as Labor Club and SDS members, who are considerably more militant than the members of the orthodox political party clubs, and who harbor an uncommon distaste for the Vietnamese conflict and Australia's involvement in it. Judging by their actions and their pronouncements, the militants have carried party politics cynicism to considerable lengths, thinking that the "great issues" are issues of conscience and humanity, not conflicts between states and governments. They deplore what they interpret to be the clichés of office-seeking politicians, the clichés of professional, old-line radicals, such as might be found in the Communist party, and the relative apathy of the general public. Even the Vietnamese protest movement, many of these student militants believe, eventually declined into routinized exhortations and gestures.

The Monash Labor Club promoters of aid to the NLF wrote that Labor's "heavy defeat in November [1966] and the subsequent election of Mr. Whitlam to leadership of the A.L.P served to demoralise opponents of the war. We felt that it was vitally important to re-raise the whole issue of our involvement in Vietnam and to raise it in a completely new context."[41] According to the ANU Labor Club, enough has been had both of the "bibles on the left"—be they from Marx or Mao; enough has been had of the ALP's "deception, opportunism, and the trivialisation of public affairs"; indeed, "the public no longer believe anything that Holt, Whitlam, or any other bureaucrats tell them. They sense only the opportunism of the rulers, and the drive towards world war."[42] For Sydney SDS chairman C. H. Jones:

> We became completely disenchanted with the right wing of the Labor Party—completely frustrated—and sick and tired of being involved in united front organisations with the communists. We want to evolve as a radical alternative to both the Labor Party and the Communist Party, we regard ourselves now as the conscience of the peace movement—fighting the nine-to-five big-business attitude within it. . . . In America, the students always *react* to the Government, but we're getting out and attacking. The Government will react to us.[43]

Hence the emphasis on "Don't Register for Conscription" and "Help Hanoi Program"—undisguised, personally self-sacrificing entreaties on behalf of startling, even illegal measures.

In April 1968, the Queensland SDA newsletter—rather aptly entitled *Student Guerrilla*—prominently flashed the caption "YESTERDAY KING, TODAY DUTSCHKE, TOMORROW US!" It read, in part, that "the attempted assassination of student leader 'Red' Rudi Dutschke was more than an example of what can happen to anyone who confronts the state and who finds that social justice and truth are in conflict with the values of the establishment. It is a warning that the established system will not willingly give way to the forces of social change."[44]

Australia's radical student groups, despite differences in outlook throughout the various states and universities, have begun to demonstrate increasing common effort. At a radical student conference held in Brisbane early in 1968, a measure of division of labor was agreed upon. Full-scale attacks were to be launched against the National Service Act by the Monash Labor Club, the Queensland SDA, and the Sydney SDS. The Sydney SDS was encouraged to promote its "Help Hanoi" scheme, while the Monash Labor Club was to launch a fresh campaign to collect medical funds for the NLF, in open and deliberate defiance of the Defense Forces Protection Act. Radical student organizations generally were to pool their energies for an April "National Liberation Week," during which intensive anti-Vietnam campaigning was to be undertaken on various university campuses.[45] By mid-1968, plans were set afoot to establish a broader, coordinated radical student organization throughout Australia, drawing primarily on SDS–SDA–Labor Club membership.[46]

To the Australian student militants, action on behalf of conscience is both a duty and a political elixir. To their critics, they are simply advertising their weakness of "isolation and subsequent alienation."[47] While striking out at the irrelevance and impotence of available political alternatives, they are missing the entire point of what meaningful political action is all about—their problem "is to translate political idealism into political possibility, and this can only be done in co-operation with those who have at their disposal political power."[48]

General University Student Opinion on Vietnam and Conscription

Australian university students who participate in political organizations are a distinct minority. Those who join the standard party clubs are skeptical about much of the conventional wisdom surrounding politics and, literally, of neatly packaged images of Australia and America. The radical-activist students project this skepticism and rejection of stereotypes much farther, and lace it with a certain stubborn idealism, which helped to spark far-out positions and tactics on Vietnam and conscription.

What of the general university student populations, however? Do they tend to exhibit outlooks on Vietnam and conscription which are peculiarly characteristic of them as a "subculture" within Australian society?

The broad answer to the last question is "no," whether the comparison is made with young people of various educational levels and occupation, or with the general Australian population. In 1966, surveys were conducted at the Universities of Melbourne and Sydney. The Melbourne survey disclosed that about 80 per cent favored conscription for overseas service under one circumstance or another, and almost 70 per cent felt that Australia should have a combat presence in Vietnam. At Sydney, the question whether Australia should have conscription "at the present time" found 59 per cent in favor and 37 per cent opposed; the presence of Australian troops in Vietnam was supported by 68 per cent—almost identical to the Melbourne results. At both institutions, the proportion of those favoring conscript troops in Vietnam was much lower than support for the principle of troops serving there—20 per cent at Melbourne, 34 per cent at Sydney.[49]

A 1967 University of Sydney survey showed a decline in senti-ment favoring broad government policy, but not enough of a decline to give much comfort to the cause of opposition. Fifty-one per cent supported Australian participation in the war and 48 per cent were opposed; 49 per cent favored conscription for overseas service "at the present time," while 50 per cent opposed it.[50] A 1967 University of Tasmania survey was almost identical to Sydney's respecting atti-tudes toward Australia's commitment in Vietnam—50 per cent in favor and 46 per cent opposed. Furthermore, the Tasmanian students were virtually at one with their counterparts in the 1966 Melbourne and Sydney surveys on the question of the use of conscript troops in Vietnam; only 28 per cent favored the practice.[51] In 1967, more gen-eral university polls yielded comparable results. Three-quarters of the university student respondents in a Gallup Poll favored the con-tinuation of an Australian combat presence in Vietnam. On a question comparable to the one that had been asked at Sydney in 1966, where conscription had yielded a 59 per cent–37 per cent distribution, the Gallup organization's result was 54.5 per cent–42 per cent.[52]

Comparisons in these broad terms with young people generally have not revealed any marked deviations. The above-cited Gallup survey showed that among a nationwide group of young people aged 14–21, 56.8 per cent favored conscription per se and 67.8 per cent approved of a military commitment in Vietnam. A year later, in early 1968, nearly 70 per cent of the Australian 14–21 age group favored a continuation of the troop commitment in Vietnam. Almost identical responses were given by the university student members of the survey population.[53] Respondents aged 16–20 in a privately com-missioned survey[54] and young worker respondents aged 15–20 in a 1966–1967 Melbourne survey[55] were 36 per cent and 30 per cent, re-spectively, in favor of the presence of conscripts in Vietnam—com-pared, as has been indicated, with 20 per cent at the University of Melbourne and 34 per cent at the University of Sydney in 1966, and 28 per cent at the University of Tasmania in 1967.

Nor do university students constitute an exception to the rule of the Australian population generally. A November 1966 Gallup survey resulted in 63.3 per cent favoring conscription.[56] September 1966[57] and May 1967[58] surveys indicated that 60.6 per cent and 62.2 per cent, respectively, broadly supported the Vietnamese commitment so far as they were prepared to counsel the retention of Australian troops in Vietnam. The general population, like university students, has consistently fallen short of a majority favoring the use of *conscript* troops in Vietnam—38 per cent in May and July of 1966, 37 per cent in November 1966, then up to 42 per cent in July of 1967.[59]

On the question of approval or disapproval for conscription as such, students have tended to voice approval by a slightly larger margin than the general population. A Canberra survey gives hint of at least one, but an important, predisposing factor that might account for this. It was learned that from among the three categories of "supporters," "moderates," and "opponents" of conscription, those who were the best informed *factually* about past and prevailing conscription practices in Australia were disproportionately represented among the supporters of conscription. Among younger male respondents, the positive correlation between knowledge and support for conscription was especially dramatic.[60] Since it is a reasonable surmise that university students rank among the better informed sections of the population, their knowledge of conscription may be one of the contributing factors in their inclination to endorse conscription. Being a university student has therefore not served to "radicalize" people, if opposition to conscription in principle is defined as a radical rather than a moderate or conservative outlook when placed in political context. Additionally, the similar student and general population reactions to established Australian government policy are probably attributable to the essentially middle-class, generally non-ALP background and origins of students. Students do not frequently undergo a shift of party preferences from those their home and class environment have spawned. The University of Melbourne survey, for instance, indicated that student party preferences ran better than two to one L-CP and DLP as against the ALP, even though Labor collected 40 per cent of the national vote a few months later at the House of Representatives election.[61] In March 1967, a Gallup survey found only 13 per cent of the university-attending sample favoring the ALP.[62] By April 1968, this figure had risen to 25.6 per cent—still less than half of the support extended to the Liberals.[63] Admittedly, however, both surveys were based on extremely small samples.

But it should not be assumed that Australian university student political outlooks are as conventional as—if not more than—those distributed throughout the general population. The University of Melbourne survey concluded that "it would seem that students, are in

159

the main, a conservative middle class (ideologically) community within a conservative middle class society." But the investigators also remarked that a heartening feature of the survey results was "the relatively low proportion of students who would blindly follow the foreign policy of the party that they would vote for. It seems that students are still willing to examine and criticise the foreign policies of the major political parties." This was substantiated in such ways as the nonpartisan support which was accorded to economic aid to Vietnam, and the large number of L-CP supporters who objected to compulsory overseas service except in times of national emergency and who wanted to confine the troop commitment in Vietnam to volunteers.[64]

Some Trends Within the Australian University Student Community

This "selectivity" in foreign policy attitudes would seem to accord with other aspects of Australian university student outlook and behavior. The general support of conscription and of the troop commitment in Vietnam at the University of Melbourne, plus the fact that the vast majority of students are not formal political club members, did not preclude the rude demonstration against Holt when he spoke at the university in 1967. There probably were more student hooters and howlers in the audience than belonged to all Melbourne political clubs put together. After the fact, it was generally conceded that the demonstration had not been preplanned and organized. The year before Calwell had faced a similar disturbance at the university. Such outbursts seemed to be aimed at conventional politicians uttering conventional remarks. Certainly the one against Holt appeared to represent "an anti-political feeling rather than an anti-Government action."[65] The number of students at the principal public anti-Vietnam demonstrations has definitely been greater than the number of students who have been formally enrolled in militant university political clubs in the cities concerned, or who have counted themselves among NFL aid collectors (or donors) or among nonregistrants for National Service.

Australian university life is, even among the relative political apathetics, undergoing change. Students at large are assuming a growing interest in supporting such causes as civil liberties and the enhancement of underdeveloped peoples. Some of this is discernible in the strongly favorable opinion found in the universities for breaching the restricted migration policy or abolishing capital punishment in the several states. Some of it is expressed in donations to Aboriginal improvement campaigns, toward overseas aid programs such as those operated under the aegis of the World University Service, and through duty in such programs for emerging societies as Australian Volunteers Abroad and Community Aid Abroad.

Some of it has been expressed within Australia in quite tangible ways by followers of various political parties. One such instance has been the promotion of conscientious objection outlets for those unwilling to serve in war. Another occurred at the University of Queensland, a campus with a tradition of considerable conservatism. In October 1966 the Queensland police intervened in a demonstration which had been staged to oppose Vietnam and conscription, and a number of students were arrested for participating in an illegal procession. A civil liberties group was formed to rescind regulations which the state government was able to invoke quite capriciously against peacefully protesting people, or against causes to which it objected. Ultimately, students of various political persuasions marched by the thousands and otherwise protested against the government's proscriptions on peaceful dissent.[66] At Monash a mass student meeting voted overwhelmingly to condemn the vice-chancellor's rulings that had prohibited campus solicitation of funds for the NLF, and had otherwise clamped down on political activities which were inside the law within the community at large.[67] In May–June 1968, students of all political persuasions throughout the country demonstrated their unqualified opposition to the Gorton government's attempts to require universities to serve as informers vis-à-vis draft-eligible students.

Australian university students, similar to the public at large, have not supplied a large proportion of their numbers to the organized anti-Vietnam and anticonscription movement, and their opinions on these topics have broadly adhered to those of the general public. But a minority of the students has made an important contribution to the protest movement, both by virtue of participation per se, and by the dramatization of Vietnamese dissent far out of proportion to the number of students involved. Among those in the great majority who are not activists, quite apart from party preference, there is a distinguishable spirit of questioning and skepticism abroad in university student circles. It is a spirit directed against standard politicians grinding out allegedly vapid formulas, and against automatic acquiescence in any particular set of beliefs associated with a political party on such themes as Vietnam and Australia's appropriate role there. It is the reaction of nuance, not of gullibility and mindless imitation. The tenor of liberality, and concern and even aid for the underprivileged, is probably very much a part of the syndrome of middle- and educated-class behavior in developed societies, identified as "belief in 'noneconomic liberalism'—support for civil liberties, for unpopular minorities, internationalism, and so forth."[68] Even before the era of Vietnam and conscription, some evidence existed that among the Australian young (thirty years and under), the most powerful influence promoting "radicalism," even in this restricted sense, was exposure to university education.[69]

Vietnam and conscription for compulsory service overseas evoked particularly challenging questions, and it was immensely difficult to answer whether Australia's national interests were being served by a major investment of conscript troops and diplomatic capital in an unpleasantly ambiguous, seemingly stalemated, decimating and formally undeclared Asian war. University faculty members, to whom students were exposed, increasingly declaimed upon and debated Vietnam, and became engaged in various facets of organized Vietnam protest. The Students' Representative Councils and student newspapers became filled with comment on these issues. Student militants, despite their distinct minority status, helped to make the Vietnam controversy vivid, either by opposing the Australian commitment through a drumfire of comment and a wide assortment of tactics, or by becoming targets of counterreaction. The male students, even if deferred for their studies, remained conscriptable—in a country which never before, even in two world wars, had opted for conscription for unlimited overseas service, and which never before had found itself in a war as unsatisfying as Vietnam was almost from the beginning.[70]

Chapter 8. Some Observations on the Australian Political Process: Party Politics, Foreign Policy, and Civil Liberties

The Vietnam and conscription controversies have very substantially intruded into Australian political dialogue, and have elicited conspicuous public protest response. In degree, style, and intensity of expression these manifestations have rather markedly departed from the traditional sublimation of foreign and defense policy questions in Australian politics.

What remains is to synthesize these themes so as to appraise broader consequences for the Australian political process. In this chapter we shall consider the implications of Vietnam and conscription for organized politics and selected aspects of public policy, while the concluding chapter will address itself to these controversies' effect upon public awareness, outlook, and electoral behavior. Our immediate concern is with Vietnam-conscription's implications for party life, for the formulation and presentation of external policy, and for civil liberties.

Party Life, Foreign Policy, and Vietnam-Conscription

The Australian political tradition has been characterized by bruising and often personal party dialogue. During the protracted period of Labor isolation from national office, and especially since the advent of the DLP, this tendency has been magnified, with the bluntness of the discourse over Vietnam and conscription building upon rather than replacing established patterns of political conduct. Vietnam and conscription, however, because they have touched on fundamental, sensitive, and even personally charged themes, have endowed party politics with an exceptionally vivid and at times psychedelic coloration. The debate has certainly kept these issues prominently displayed before both political elites and the general public, but has tended to distort as much as to illuminate the options and arguments which have been proffered. As charges and countercharges of deceit, cupidity, inhumanity, and unpatriotism have been bandied about, the contagion has spread to aspects of the party battle not associated with the Vietnam debate. The chief personalities in the debate have had much to do with the force and style of the argument. Holt and

Calwell were less inhibited than Gorton and Whitlam, not only in the starkness of their substantive positions, but respecting the heat with which they excoriated their opponents. Whitlam's attribution of "debauchery" to Holt and Calwell in their conduct of the 1966 campaign may be understood in this context.

Being neither trivial nor passing controversies, Vietnam-conscription extended beyond the Holt and Calwell periods, and the parties and their leaders were afterward either unwilling or unable to shake off much of the partisan smoke and fire which had risen up before. Australia is a well aggregated and consensualized society, and one whose party system has generally reflected these qualities. Despite some conventional political rhetoric to the contrary, domestic affairs have not generated serious differences among the principal parties. There have not been conflicts over the very legitimacy of the state or the mode of political authority, nor conflicts generated by deep class, religious, or regional antagonisms. While foreign policy differences between the main party groups were in the past marked, they generally remained in the background. The vigor, length, and presentational sharpness of Vietnam-conscription have now raised external policy to prominence in the party debate and in electoral campaigns, and have infected party politics at large. The partisan dialogue has therefore become less adaptive and more strained, and interparty politics have presented an image of widened difference between the parties, between whom reconciliation is made more difficult.

The interparty dialogue has affected intraparty politics, particularly Labor's. The intractability of the Vietnam-conscription debate has had both hardening and mellowing effects upon the ALP. Those predisposed to principle became even more determined to exhibit the courage of their convictions as they became revolted by the kind of war being waged and the sacrifice of conscripted Australians there. Others, while not necessarily minimizing their disdain for Australia's Vietnamese policies, became distressed over the rigidities of authoritative party positions and the manner in which the lashings of political opponents were keeping the party out of power, and therefore barring it from reorienting prevailing Australian policy. The contest of persuasions in the ALP exposed conflicting philosophies of program, internal party decision-making procedures, and the role of leadership. While Vietnam and conscription played a conspicuous part in inducing self-re-examination in the party, they failed to settle the question of which persuasions would prevail. If anything, the dispute only reconfirmed Labor's seemingly incurable talent for open-air self-flagellation, obstructed any passage toward reconciliation with the DLP, and maintained the party's vulnerability to jibes of programmatic ambivalence and internal turmoil. The very credibility of the ALP as an alternative government was once again questioned, a condition to which Vietnam-conscription had measurably contributed.

The L-CP's ability to continue ringing up electoral victories was thereby facilitated, partially by default. Both in foreign policy and otherwise, as Whitlam made every effort to underscore in the 1967 Senate campaign, a tired, complacent, and callous government was bound to take too much for granted. Unchastened by any prospect or actual fact of defeat, it performed as if it owed its investiture to Divine Right.

The government was convinced that its policies on Vietnam and conscription were right and necessary for Australia. But it also was convinced that considerable political mileage could be gained by according massive publicity, sometimes presented in unctuous and hyperbolic terms, to the contrast between its own and Labor's position. It therefore became especially difficult for Australian policy to maintain a reserve force of flexibility which would allow accommodation to shifting circumstances in the international picture.

This nexus between foreign policy and domestic politics is illustrated by the rush of foreign events roughly between mid-1967 and mid-1968. It is well to remember the dominant features of Australia's conventional approach to Southeast Asia. The first has been to regard Southeast Asia as a kind of front line of defense, where local disturbances should be checked before they could widen into a general war and before Australia would find itself threatened. To assist in this task of regional containment, troop commitments, including in Vietnam, have been periodically undertaken by L-CP governments. The corollary of such a "forward" defense strategy has been that Australia, as a country of only modest military and diplomatic capacity, would act in concert with one or more considerably stronger allies.

But when the Wilson government in Britain quickened the implementation of standing plans to disengage East of Suez, and then

President Johnson announced his unconditional Vietnamese bombing reduction and earnest appeal for negotiations, Australian policy found itself spun around on its heels.

> The decision of the United Kingdom to accelerate its withdrawal from Asia was a calamitous one for the Holt Government which had quite literally undertaken no serious contingency planning despite the widely predicted likelihood of a U.K. withdrawal. The immediate response of the Holt Administration was to consider moving Australia's forward posture north from Malaysia and the British alliance to Vietnam, Thailand and the American alliance. Events have shown that this was an unsure assumption on which to base future policy.[1]

The Australian government was caught almost by total surprise by the President's announcement. Canberra was confronted by the *fait accompli* of a moderated American posture while until the very eve of Johnson's announcement it had been proclaiming a stiff-necked position which had approved of a reduction or suspension of interdiction against the North only if a tangible and convincing *quid pro quo* were proffered by the other side. Previous unease in Australian official circles that the United States, having had its fingers singed in Vietnam, might not again venture into another potentially nettlesome Asian commitment, now became more pronounced. Australian representations had failed to dissuade Britain from a precipitous disengagement in Asia. Now, American subscription to the dousing of future Asian disturbances had become distressingly problematical.

The L-CP government had its own reasoned views why a "forward" defense strategy, based on collaboration with major allies, was sound. But it indulged in almost clamorous reiteration that all was well, partially to score political points by enshrouding the government in a cloak of collective, anti-Communist respectability, while ridiculing the timorous, negative, nationally destructive opinions ascribed to Labor. In part, the government had become the victim of its own propaganda. When the Johnson announcement arrived, the government hedged; it hoped the President's gambit would work, but it was not unduly sanguine.

> As hawkish and as totally committed as the Australian Government appears, it would not deliberately try to abort any American initiative to end hostilities. It is just that in terms of internal politics the Government has left itself so far out on a limb on the

bombing policy that it doesn't like to see President Johnson, of all people, saw it neatly off. Nor does it like to have so crudely exposed the harsh reality that, in the scheme of things in Vietnam, Australia is a military and political insignificance.[2]

Gorton as prime minister has not fully shared Holt's ebullient enthusiasm for the "forward" defense concept and the concomitant and (under Holt) open-ended Australian troop commitment in Vietnam. But the L-CP government found itself unprepared to meet fresh exigencies, and politically stood rather embarrassingly undressed. First Britain's disengagement plans and then America's unexpected turn toward moderation in Vietnam, possibly signalling the last such American involvement in Asia, were announced. Had the force and spirit of the internal debate not driven the government to near-categorical assumptions and conduct, it might have enjoyed better foresight to plan and rearrange. This could have implied a somewhat modified foreign policy for Australia, but also a far better preparation of the general and interested-attentive publics for any surgery which might have needed performing on conventional policy.

As the preliminary talks in Paris between representatives of Hanoi and Washington were getting under way, Canberra was undertaking a sober and comprehensive review of its foreign and defense policies. There was no thought of dislocating the delicate negotiations in Paris, or of pulling troops out of Vietnam, or otherwise slackening in devotion to the line dominant at the moment in Washington. But there was a thinking-out-loud process, pre-eminently on Gorton's part, in which the forward defense strategy was reappraised, and with it the prospect of elaborate Australian pledges to enter Southeast Asian altercations when powerful assurance of American involvement could not be assumed. However, a number of government backbenchers and ministers alike, including Paul Hasluck, the external affairs minister, and Allen Fairhall, the defense minister, were skeptical about any abrupt reorientation.[3]

The implications of a possible movement away from the deployment of troops in Southeast Asian trouble spots and the substitution of a highly mobile force stationed in Australia, available for genuine emergencies at home or abroad, would be considerable. They would include a reversal of hallowed strategic premises, and, as some observers noticed, a sliding up to that aspect of Labor's own 1967 Adelaide conference position which called for strengthening defenses at home while dismantling the prevailing Southeast Asian garrison approach of the L-CP.[4] The implications of such a step would also be political. Much of the sting would now be gone from the paddle with which for so long the government has been swatting the ALP over foreign policy. Political considerations helped to fashion a stubborn and loudly broadcast foreign policy, of which Vietnam became the centerpiece. The policy was rather suddenly found to be unsteady.

It is hazardous to speculate as to what the new contours of government policy will be, what nuances will enter Labor policy, and how the dialogue over Vietnam and foreign policy more generally will develop. Late May and early June of 1968, for instance, became a period of intensive diplomacy and policy re-evaluation. Gorton traveled to America. There he conferred at length with President Johnson, members of the administration, and even some leading presidential aspirants of both parties. Familiar with the pressures Vietnam had generated, he arrived unsure of where America's Southeast Asian policies might head. When he left, he was considerably gratified. "The true paradox of the situation was that Gorton arrived in America fearing that America was retreating from Asia, only to find himself being reproached politely even for contemplating such a withdrawal on the part of Australia."[5] Conversations held immediately thereafter in Kuala Lumpur among Australia, New Zealand, Britain, Malaysia, and Singapore seemed to suggest that, despite Britain's disengagement and America's reluctance to underwrite formally any new defense arrangements in the area, Australia could feel reasonably safe about continuing with the essentials of a "forward" defense strategy even after the British were gone.[6]

The policy projections implicit in the above developments may or may not be borne out by time. The unfolding of the Vietnamese situation, the configuration of the Southeast Asian security scene generally, and the realities, as against the expectations, of a new administration in Washington could revive anxieties about adhering to established policy postulates. Politically, it is likely that there will be some shift of advantage to Labor which, with the benefit of hindsight, could make invidious comparisons between its own frequent admonitions and what was first the government's casual confidence, then a stumbling about in the face of new situations, and then an apparently fingers-crossed return to fairly traditional approaches. The politics of Vietnam and conscription lasted too long, and were too astringently conducted, to give much promise that in the foreseeable future foreign policy would not continue to be the plaything of politics. Foreign policy may also continue to be prominent in electoral campaigns, in part because of the appetizing opportunities which one or both political sides might uncover and proceed to exploit.

Australian Civil Liberties in Perspective

In talking about Vietnam-conscription's bearing on the conduct of party politics and the formulation of public policy it is instructive to weigh the effects of these controversies beyond the foreign policy realm. The theme of civil liberties serves this purpose well. It is a theme under which we can examine the level of equanimity at which Vietnam-conscription dissent has been handled by public authorities and how, in turn, the public has responded.

To set in context the treatment of civil liberties under the pressures of Vietnam and conscription, something needs to be said of Australian civil liberties traditions. There is a popularly shared notion that the Australian people, while caring for their own personal interests, have been disinterested in the principles underlying civil liberties, and disinterested in reacting to impositions which might befall others, especially those of heterodox beliefs. When "freedom of thought and speech are tolerated [it is] mainly because Australians 'couldn't care less.' "[7] While Australians are described as prepared to defend stoutly individuals who have had a "raw deal," as another observer has framed it, "protest and criticism is [sic] sporadic rather than continuous. So long as individuals are not obviously adversely affected, Australians show little concern about matters of principle. 'She'll be right' is a well used and familiar phrase revealing an attitude which implies: 'Why bother, why fuss; it will all turn out right in the end.' "[8]

In support of this characterization stands the tone of Australian society at large. There is no bill of rights in the Australian Constitution to serve as a symbolic magnet or a legal hook for the defense of individual freedoms, and the states themselves are almost equally bereft of basic law provisions of this order. The Australian political culture was shaped without bitter political conflicts, but with a reliance in the radical tradition on the element of coercion. It was shaped by an educational system which over the generations failed to produce a sizable, viable intellectual leadership, and it was a system which extolled "practicality" rather than principle.[9] People came to live in a fairly affluent though rather prosaic atmosphere. Life, liberty, and the pursuit of happiness were reinterpreted for Australian conditions. "Life" became an amalgam of a wish to be left alone, a distrust of the police who were the visible, meddling agents of authority, and of a special, proud, yet singularly insular Australian nationalism. "Pursuit of happiness" became the pursuit of property, in the sense that personal socioeconomic interest dominated. Jobs, adequate wages, claims upon welfare benefits, were the measures of this interest. "Liberty," however, was neglected, or at least relegated to the position described above.

The actual course of governmental restrictions on politically related liberties can also be interpreted to imply that there has been a tradition of disrespect for them. The First World War was notorious because of the extent of controls imposed on the civilian population, but especially for the severe and often arbitrary fashion in which Prime Minister Hughes enforced censorship.[10] In the twenties, a great many political tracts, most of them Communist or anarchist in inspiration, were banned from entry into Australia. At the opening of World War II, not only was the Communist party outlawed, but so were a host of related left-wing organizations. The war itself occasioned fresh public security regulations, including stringent censorship, though the employment of powers was decidedly more circumspect than it had been in the war of a generation earlier.[11] The post-World War II period occasioned major legislative efforts whose net effect was the curtailment of liberties. The Labor government in the late forties considerably strengthened the Crimes Act, allowing wide latitude of interpretation for prosecutions in security matters. L-CP governments attempted to outlaw the Communist party, which had been relegitimized after the Soviet Union had become an ally, and in the sixties brought before Parliament an even wider extension of the Crimes Act in respect to the scope of treason, espionage, and breach of official secrets, and proposed new offenses as well.

The point of these illustrations is that Australian governments have compiled a record, both in and out of wartime emergencies, of imposing laws and regulations and indulging in practices not consonant with the scrupulous defense of politically related civil liberties. In a society not temperamentally and otherwise acclimated to championing civil protections, such a tradition was easier to perpetuate. The public grumbled when personally affected, but saw little importance in the long-term implications of the erosion of civil liberties. If the price of liberty was eternal vigilance, Australians, according to this interpretation, were unprepared to pay it, and

> no one who has studied Australian politics at close quarters can deny that there is a taint of intolerance among the Left and Right, a contempt for individual freedom, which makes Fascism or National Socialism always credible. Perhaps [D. H.] Lawrence got closest to the truth [respecting Australia] when he wrote: "Great freedom in the air. Yet, if you got into the wrong stream on the pavement you felt they'd tread you down almost unseeing. You just *musn't* get in the wrong stream—Liberty!"[12]

But there is another side to the argument. According to one celebrated Australian historian, "our profound suspicion of authority and pretentiousness provides some safeguard against the main danger of our time: dictatorship from either the right or the left. . . . it is probably harder to imagine a Hitler, a Stalin or even a Perón flourishing here than in any other country on earth, including England itself."[13] On the side of governmental restraints on personal liberties, here too a more balanced picture can be derived. Political censorship tapered off in the thirties. There was considerably more circumspection in World War II than in World War I in the employment of sweeping powers which were at the disposal of the government. Much of the post-World War II power available to the authorities has been kept in abeyance. There has been very slight recourse to the intimidation of persons or groups holding politically deviant opinions, and censorship has concentrated on sex rather than security. Legal remedies for the accused have been plentiful. One distinguished constitutional lawyer has concluded that "in general, Australian law adequately protects security of the person, and in practice allows a very wide liberty of expression and association."[14] Another prominent student of the subject, while uneasy over the excesses previously committed by Australian governments, concludes that the politically related civil liberties situation is not in conspicuous disrepair. The main remaining abuses are not really derived from considered public policy, but abuses fathered by official secrecy, excessive legislative delegation, inadequate political review, and the like. They are abuses which are brought on by the administrative state, and against which countervailing safeguards are not presently sufficient.[15]

But what of the public response to civil liberties? The Second World War gave a certain amount of impetus to public concern over the various abridgements inherent in wartime regulations. Particularly in the early stages of the war, not only the Australian Council for Civil Liberties, admittedly a collection of intellectual and professional types, but trade union organizations as well, were very watchful, and were not hesitant to draw excesses to the government's attention.[16] The 1951 constitutional referendum on outlawing the Communist party failed to carry, either in a majority of the states or in the country at large. The referendum was clouded by all kinds of extraneous considerations, but the Labor opposition placed heavy reliance on attacking its provision on onus of proof; an individual about to be declared a Communist would be regarded as one unless *he* could prove he wasn't one. In the preceding year, a Gallup survey had found that 56 per cent of the public felt that the government should carry the burden of proof, and only 34 per cent felt that the onus should fall on the individual.[17] Throughout the fifties and sixties organized activity developed against such disparate yet "civil liberties"—connected practices as indifference toward Aboriginal welfare, the White Australia policy, capital punishment, South African apartheid, restrictive drinking laws, and censorship of allegedly obscene literature. Most of this opposition was articulated by small minorities. But the postwar period had brought broadened educational opportunities and an unbending of curricular emphases, an extension of the force of varied media, a rise in serious journalism, and an overall cosmopolitanization of the society.

If available survey research data are a reliable index, then the more disparaging formulations of public perceptions on freedoms and liberties require readjustment. The evidence that exists admittedly derives from attitudes toward essentially nonpolitical matters, but it is reasonable to infer that it is representative of civil liberties thinking in the large.

Aggregatively, the public is no longer (if it ever markedly was) blatantly intolerant of the privileges of others, careless about the administration of justice, and apt to regard policemen not as a constructive force in the community but rather as a "son-of-a-bitch copper" symbol of meddling authority. In the postwar period, sentiment on behalf of capital punishment for crimes of murder steadily declined. In 1953, 69 per cent favored the death penalty and 24 per cent opposed it. In 1967, 42 per cent favored death while 45 per cent recommended imprisonment.[18] In late 1967 the public was asked about telephone tapping by the police. The question was very much loaded in favor of an "allow" rather than "ban" response, since "ban" was defined in unqualified terms, excluding even security cases, while "allow" was defined as permissible only in special circumstances and if authorized by a judge, i.e., under very careful safeguards. While nearly two-thirds opted to "allow," fully a quarter were opposed without qualification. In the context of the question, this appears to have been a significant expression of civil libertarian sentiment.[19]

While a 1965 survey revealed considerable support for an ombudsman in each Australian state,[20] recent attitudes toward the police cannot be construed as openly denigratory. A survey of occupational status conducted in the early sixties did not reveal a particularly high status attribution to policemen. As contrasted with other skilled workers, policemen ranked relatively high. All told, however, while they stood ahead of stenographers, government clerks, and wage-earning electricians, they ranked behind air hostesses, bank tellers, and plumbers with their own businesses.[21] More significant are recent Gallup findings. In 1965, 56 per cent believed that police interrogation methods were fair and only 16 per cent explicitly thought the contrary.[22] The general point being argued here was sustained in a poll undertaken two years later. Seventy-two per cent had a great deal of respect for the police, 23 per cent had some respect, and only 4 per cent had "hardly any" respect.[23]

While there are discernible trends that the public has moved to a more balanced position on rights, toleration, and the place of police and various agencies of public authority, the editors of a major Australian sociological study have concluded, however, that the rise of libertarian concern "is fairly sharply checked by the almost equal indifference, if not equal culpability, of the existing parties."[24] We now need to examine the presence of "indifference" or "culpability" in Australian politics and public agencies respecting Vietnam and conscription, issues which have become dominant at a time when the entire tenor of civil liberties, both officially and in public regard, had appeared to be settling at a reasonably relaxed and accommodationist level.

Vietnam-Conscription and the Civil Liberties Record: 1

Our discussion of Vietnam-conscription's impact on civil liberties might profitably be so organized as to lead upward from comment

173

on the tenor of administration to major areas of public policy relevant to the subject. Although we shall be primarily concerned with the operations of the federal authorities, the behavior of state governments will necessarily be included.

Australian opposition to the Vietnamese involvement and to conscription has come to involve frequent, sometimes well-attended, at times noisy demonstrations, and there have been inevitable encounters with security personnel, primarily state police. If a judgment must be made, it would probably be that crowd control and the arrests which have intermittently occurred have been handled with reasonable circumspection. The major exceptions, if indeed they literally are exceptions, have arisen when there have been demonstrations against noteworthy persons, sometimes members of the government but more directly as when visiting dignitaries have been paraded. Thus there were serious commotions when Johnson visited Australia. The police, in all likelihood alive to the need to insure the safety of such figures, have in those circumstances behaved more roughly than usual. A university student booklet, emphasizing experiences in Melbourne, was published shortly after Johnson's visit. It contained a number of testimonials by persons who experienced or directly observed instances of police excesses. Its conclusion was that "it is pretty poor when the police force whose job it is (among others) to protect a civilian's rights, is actually used to suppress them."[25] As the police have gained in experience in dealing with demonstrators, the result has been a quicker, more efficient, though not necessarily more "brutal" approach, though more ingenious tactics by demonstrators have probably toughened police reactions. The apparent increase in charges of police brutality results from this toughness, from the rising determination of protesters not to be cowed, from their occasional determination to invite arrest, and from their frankly political motive of gaining sympathy for the cause of protest and discrediting the authorities by pointing accusing fingers at the police.

A second area of civil liberties concern relates to the methods of police investigation and intelligence gathering. There seems to be evidence of fitful harassment of protesters, spread out over a considerable period of time, and later of increased resort to intrusive and information gathering techniques as anti-Vietnamese and conscription protest has widened. There is the case of a Sydney man who wrote anti-Vietnam, anticonscription slogans across the envelopes he posted in the mail. The man's mother was visited by Commonwealth officials and told that severe action might be forthcoming against her son. The man himself was phoned at work. He was asked to desist from his graffitic pastime. A Commonwealth Police postal investigator made vague threats of repercussions if the man persisted, but there was no straight answer to what law or regulation was being violated.[26] Then there is the case of a visitation by Commonwealth police to the AICD offices in Sydney. The AICD reports that the callers said they were under instructions to question officials of the AICD and fraternal bodies. "The police officers were subsequently invited to make an appointment to attend at the A.I.C.D. rooms but cancelled the engagement when they learned that press and TV journalists and cameramen had assembled to witness the interrogation."[27]

There are also spreading indications that the Australian Security Intelligence Organization (ASIO), an investigatory body which works under a considerable shroud of secrecy, has become a diligent, though at times amateurish, inquirer into the affairs of people and bodies connected with protest activity. A Monash student of known progressive views disclosed that an attempt had been made by an ASIO agent to recruit him for membership in the Communist party, from which vantage point names and operational information could be reported. Apologetically, it was explained that the ASIO could only afford to pay expenses, not a retainer fee. However, the ASIO would guarantee clearance in any future employment where Communist party membership might otherwise create embarrassment.[28] In 1968, it was reported that a student at the University of Western Australia, on leave from the Commonwealth public service, had been approached by the ASIO to give information about a "Vietnam Information Week" which had been held at the university.[29] As of time of writing, disclosures are being made by James Cairns that some Commonwealth security body—possibly the ASIO but more likely military intelligence—had not only "bugged" a conversation he held in his own home with a conscientious objector, but that security personnel had tapped telephone conversations between conscientious objectors and representatives of the press, radio, and television.[30]

Reports of ASIO attempts to recruit informers at universities and to eavesdrop bring to mind the general theme of possible interference in higher education where Vietnam-conscription protest has been concerned. The federal record in this area will be touched upon later, when we discuss government efforts to convert the universities into informers against draft-eligible men. In general, the Australian state record has been good, but Victoria is something of an exception, in part because Monash and Melbourne universities have been among the most militant seats of protest activity. This state activity has taken the form of the rhetoric of political indignation, of attempts to pry into university affairs, and of special uses of police authority.

Late in 1966, for example, we notice a rash of condemnatory speeches in the Victorian Parliament. Victorian university student protesters were denounced as hooligans and scabs, living off the taxpayers' money while engaging in destructive behavior. The government should carefully examine their conduct, and the university should be told to get rid of them.[31] Unless the behavior of university students improved, university appropriations should be cut off—"In future, no discipline, no dough!"[32] As for the vice-chancellor of the University of Melbourne, Sir George Paton, he was a brilliant scholar, but hopelessly naive as an administrator. "Professor Paton is a pipsqueak. He is a step-down from a Walt Disney comic strip. Professor Paton is not the man to control the university."[33] Faculty members in Victorian universities were using "political, subversive and unobjective tactics" in presenting material, an especially horrid phenomenon, since such presentations were designed to inculcate "a particular political line, which is opposed to the Government line."[34]

In 1967 came the aid to the NLF blowup at Monash and Melbourne. The state Council of the Victorian Liberal party responded by resolving (almost unanimously, among a group of 250 delegates) that students contemplating the distribution of such assistance should be sent to Vietnam to witness the war at first hand.[35] Although the Victorian minister for education promised that the Victorian Liberal government would allow the universities to handle the matter in their own way,[36] his promise was not exactly kept. Victorian detectives followed, harassed, and in various ways invaded the privacy of Monash students who were involved in the fund collections, even though no "crime" was involved.[37] As legislation to check the fund collections was being brought before the federal Parliament, Victorian Premier Sir Henry Bolte expressed his apprehension that Victorian tax money was being used to subsidize the fund-collecting students. The matter was brought before the Victorian Cabinet, which ordered an accounting from the vice-chancellors of Melbourne and Monash as to which students were doing what in this respect, and what the university authorities thought of it.[38] There were no tangible reprisals from the state government against the universities; new federal legislation in the form of the Defense Forces Protection Act and a certain amount of disciplinary action in the universities apparently was sufficient mollification of the critics in the Bolte government. Still, the Victorian experience, although not typical of the remainder of the country, does suggest the extent to which Vietnam and conscription in Australia, even at the state level, have insinuated themselves into extra-foreign policy questions, in this instance university affairs.

The record respecting censorship of published materials, both at the state and federal levels, has been very good, despite a fair amount of static that has been raised in parliamentary bodies, often for purpose of scoring political points, about the unfair, inflammatory, or otherwise allegedly despicable nature of protest propaganda. This leniency has prevailed even in Victoria, a state with an outlandish record for banning the sale of ostensibly salacious materials. There the vice squad confiscated copies of the pamphlet *American Atrocities in Vietnam*, on grounds that it seemed to violate state obscenity law, since it contained illustrations of gross cruelty. The complaint was not proceeded with, and the pamphlet continued to circulate freely.[39] A South Australian informant reports that in his state, which admittedly was until early 1968 led by a Labor, not a Liberal, government during the bulk of the Vietnam controversy period—a Labor government which initiated the first "bill of rights" in Australian state history—there was no official harassment or censorship. "Censorship" in South Australia has, as in other parts of Australia, been indirect and private—occasional denial of privately owned meeting halls to protest groups and successful pressure by Liberal politicians to bar protest group spokesmen from appearing before fraternal and other organizations.

The federal record on censorship has been commendable. The federal authorities possess power to ban the entry of undesirable materials into the country, and to control seditious materials circulating internally. The only significant instance of restriction occurred in 1965, when a Peking-produced film on Vietnam entitled *Hit the U.S. Aggression* was stopped by censors under regulations which prohibit material "likely to be offensive to the people of a friendly nation or to the people of a part of the Queen's dominion" or, more broadly, which bar "any matter the exhibition of which is undesirable to the public interest."[40] Otherwise, all varieties of political material have been allowed to circulate, although at point of writing the government was investigating for possible action a "how to do it" pamphlet on draft dodging. When a number of CSIRO scientists signed the anti-Vietnamese petition which was published in the *Australian Journal of Science*, Gorton, then minister for education and science, said rather gratuitously that while he thought their views were completely wrong, they were entitled to express such views, since they were employees of a statutory authority and not of the public service.[41]

As the war ground on, as the Australian press displayed growing doubts about government policy and protest activity maintained its momentum, signs appeared that the practice of permissiveness might have to change. In 1968 various Liberal backbenchers began to express openly what had been troubling them for some time. War news emanating from Vietnam being publicized in Australian media might undermine Australian troop morale; it might be improperly influencing Australian thinking because of its sensational and/or distorted qualities. Advocacy of censorship of Vietnamese military operations on security grounds is one thing. But a broader censorship has been raised in these calls for tightening up. One senior Cabinet minister was reported to have commented that it was "reprehensible" for the press to question the tactics and strategy of Australian forces in Vietnam.[42] Gorton himself became irritable and peevish. He remarked in Parliament that the Australian press "very largely does not support as much as it might the efforts of Australians and others in [Vietnam]."[43] Not long afterward, at a Gorton press conference in Saigon, an Australian correspondent asserted that North Vietnamese forces were better equipped than Australian units. Gorton is a seasoned politician and occupies the highest and most sensitive position in the land, but he retorted, "I would like to make it perfectly clear that the progress of the Australian military forces will not be questioned in my presence. At least I will not accept this." On that note he broke off the press conference.[44] On the occasion of this same Vietnamese visit, Gorton told Australian troops in the field that they should take no notice of "any nut who carries placards or sits in the middle of the road in Australia," while he cautioned them not to build hopes on "things that are called peace talks in Paris."[45]

So far, no formal censorship has been imposed. Nor do snappish remarks by ministers against the alleged partiality of the press constitute an informal censorship. But the greater the evidence that the war was inconclusive, the sharper the dissent in mass media, the less restrained the protests, the more there has been a mood of government frustration, of an impulse in counterpunch. It is a departure from loftier perches of another time when the government and its supporters were convinced that Vietnam could be satisfactorily resolved, most press opinion was with the government, and little was lost by being more decorous.

Vietnam-Conscription and the Civil Liberties Record: 2

We now pass to a consideration of some main themes of public policy, starting with the federal government's attitude toward Australian contacts or dealings with the "enemy" in the Vietnamese conflict. Respecting freedom of movement, namely the ability of Australians to travel to North Vietnam, the government has been lenient, despite certain formal reservations to the contrary. This approach is consistent with past practice regarding travel to China and other Communist countries. Prior to 1964, Australian passports contained a statement that they were valid for travel anywhere except to all Communist countries, which were itemized by name. Persons wishing to travel to any of these countries were asked to prepare a written application stating where and why they wished to go. In practice, permission was given *pro forma* regardless of what reasons were submitted, with the intended countries of call being scratched out on the passport. There was a fine for falsifying applications, but no effort was made to check on the application's authenticity. Given total official permissiveness, there was little if any reason for an applicant to lie.

In 1964, all mention of prohibited countries was deleted from Australian passports, though it was still theoretically possible to withhold or confiscate a passport. This was the situation when the Vietnamese war developed. The government made a partial return to the pre-1964 practice, insofar as of May 1965 it began to enter "Not Available for Travel to North Vietnam" on all passports. It has also tightened earlier practice by denying requests that this prohibition be waived. This has been so even when the requests have come from prominent and obviously non-Communist persons, among them James Cairns, who expressed a wish to go in 1966, and Kenneth W. Thomas, an Australian Reform Movement Senate candidate, who wished to go the following year.

When Cairns was denied an exception, he did not press his case further. Thomas, however, persisted. Although he was told by Minister for Immigration Billy Snedden that no exceptions had ever been made on the North Vietnamese travel rule and none would be made for him, the admission came that "travel to a country for which a passport is not valid does not constitute an offence against Australian law."[46] *De facto*, an Australian traveling to North Vietnam without official permission simply surrenders his rights and privileges to a passport while there, but is not subject to penalties for having gone without permission, or a forfeiture of his passport for future purposes. The main deterrant to visiting North Vietnam has not been the law, but the unwillingness of the North Vietnamese to admit petitioners for entry, as Thomas himself discovered.

We are already familiar with the official restrictions on aid to the NLF and to North Vietnam. The fact that the government decided, be it for political considerations or otherwise, to impose penalties for the collection and distribution of such moneys can, of course, in itself be construed as an expression of official illiberality, and fresh regulations were later announced in order to seal off loopholes.

Even so, the government's performance requires some qualification. The government was reluctant to apply the extremely stringent legal apparatus already on hand, namely the Crimes Act. There were some doubts about the precise applicability of the Crimes Act, since it defined as illegal assistance of any sort which was rendered to an enemy, but with "enemy" being proclaimed as such by parliamentary action or by a formal declaration of war.[47] Assuming that there was genuine legal doubt whether the fund collectors could be prosecuted under the Crimes Act without an appropriate proclamation/declaration, the government was hesitant to undertake the appropriate steps. But beyond this technical consideration, a submission by the attorney general, Nigel Bowen, persuaded the government that the Crimes Act, with its criminal categories of "treason" and "treachery" and its draconic punitive provisions of life imprisonment and even execution, was much too strong medicine. Since it was inappropriate to "use a sledge-hammer to crack a nut," a combination of the new Defense Forces Protection Act and controls over the disbursement of funds under the supervision of the Reserve Bank of Australia was decided upon.[48] In sum, the government might have chosen to move more drastically than it in fact did.

The enforcement of the Defense Forces Protection Act is itself a matter of policy choice. After the act's passage, attempts at collecting and donating funds subsided, but did not disappear. The government did close several loopholes, but was reticent to ferret out and prosecute those few individuals who were pressing ahead. The government no doubt hoped that donations would eventually peter out, and that there would not be a need to risk the embarrassment of bad publicity, the creation of martyrs, or the fueling of the Vietnamese protest movement in general by prosecuting a handful of university students.

But in March 1968 a group of students at Melbourne and Monash mailed a circular to students around the country. Recipients of the circular were being requested to contribute funds to the London-based Medical Aid Committee for Vietnam, for distribution to the NLF and within North Vietnam. The contributors would deliberately have their names made public, and the complete roster would be presented to the Commonwealth attorney general.

The purpose of this appeal was to undermine the Defense Forces Protection Act. As the circular argued, if a hundred or more persons throughout the country participated in the project,

> the Government would be placed in a very difficult position. They would have to prosecute all 100 or none at all. In launching prosecution they would be providing the people concerned with an opportunity to publicly explain their reasons for supporting the N.L.F. and opposing the war. Although considerable pressure for conviction would be mounted by the mass media it is quite possible some jury member would have enough honesty and courage to hold out for an acquittal. Even if the 100 were found guilty it would be very difficult for a court to impose gaol sentences without some sort of public outcry (and the existence of more than 100 political prisoners in Australian gaols would have international repercussions).[49]

Furthermore, "As the war escalates with more casualties and more opposition at home, the Government will resort to more repressive measures in order to protect the morale of our troops. We therefore believe it is essential to give them a sharp rebuff at this stage."[50] At point of writing, the Commonwealth government was investigating the matter. It is not known what action, if any, will be taken, although, as the sponsors have clearly indicated, they wish to provoke the government into prosecutions. Perhaps the government will welcome the opportunity, since by mid-1968 it had become generally more aggressive in acting against its critics.

Australia's experience with conscription during the period of the Vietnamese war supplies another opportunity to glance at the observance of civil liberties. Conscription was formally begun early in 1965. After a three-year review of the operation of the National Service Act, the record seemed to indicate that the government was neither fanatical nor vindictive in dealing with those who broke one aspect of the law or another, nor was it averse to making adjustments and some liberalizations in the interpretation of call-up procedures and even in the treatment of conscientious objectors.

For instance, the law came to provide that if a draft card were willfully burned, a hundred-dollar fine could be imposed. If it were otherwise lost or destroyed, its holder faced a twenty-dollar fine unless he notified the Department of Labor and National Service. These regulations were, however, very feebly enforced, even when there was a suspicion that the card had been destroyed as an act of political defiance. The principal purpose of draft cards was to prove National Service registration to an employer, for presentation at times of National Service medical examinations, and for presentation at induction centers at time of call-up. An employer faced a heavy fine for each day he employed a person without first checking his draft card. However, as one well-placed informant advised the author,

I know of about a dozen non-registrants. All but one have gone about . . . [their] employment or studies quite unmolested. One was supposed to register in the first ballot three years ago. The only one to have had any action taken against him should have registered a year ago. He has been summoned to appear in court next month. The only explanation as to why he was summoned is that a week before he received the summons he made an application for a passport. No action has been taken against his employer.

Moreover, the government did not harass groups seeking to assist potential or actual conscientious objectors, and was helpful in advising young men of their rights when conscientious objection exemption was being sought. Although it was not prepared to provide for "selective," i.e. anti-Vietnamese-war, conscientious objection, it failed to appeal a strategic 1967 case in which conscientious objection had been given very broad construction by a court. After some awkward handling of prominent conscientious objection cases, notably that of one William White, it liberalized some of its administrative procedures. In response to various queries, notably from the National Union of Australian University Students, it refined and made more equitable the categories of and terms under which students would be subject to call-up.[51]

In May of 1968, however, the Gorton government introduced legislation designed to close loopholes and otherwise to strengthen the punitive provisions of the National Service Act. Fines for such offenses as failure to register, making false statements and burning of draft cards were increased, most being doubled. Draft dodgers would not be tried by juries, and if convicted would serve two years in prison. Airline and shipping companies operating out of Australia were to be subject to fines if they issued tickets to draft-eligible men who could not present a certificate from the Department of Labor and National Service. "Any person"—including employers, educators, parents, clergymen, and others—could be subject to a fine of two hundred dollars for failure to provide information, on request, on men liable for call-up, and institutions such as schools, universities, hospitals, and unions could also be required to cooperate.[52]

The ALP opposition quickly responded, taunting the government for Gestapo tactics and the encouragement of pimping. It determined to oppose the measure unless wholesale amendments were incorporated, notably amendments removing the onus of providing information and "tattling" from various persons and institutions, and guaranteeing trial by jury for those charged with evasion of service.[53]

The government's own reaction was that a noisy minority was trying to subvert the National Service Act, that obligations to serve had to be met under the law, and that the most efficient and persuasive methods for insuring compliance were required. Lacking a majority in either chamber of Parliament, Labor could not alone have hoped to loosen the government's position. But a number of the government's own followers were anxious about the bill's sweeping provisions, and the DLP, controlling the balance of power in the Senate, insisted on some alterations. Wishing to protect the bill's passage, bit by bit the government capitulated to some of the criticisms. Families would not be penalized for refusing to disclose information on the whereabouts of men eligible for service. Doctors, attorneys, and clergymen would not be required to violate professional confidences. Even educational institutions in their corporate capacity would not be required to supply information about draft-eligible men.[54] The government had given in, though not comprehensively, and not out of a sense of civil libertarian propriety but because it was loath to jeopardize the bill, and because articulate public reaction was overwhelmingly hostile to the bill's earlier versions. In its way, the bill had been symptomatic of the times. After accumulating a respectable record on the Vietnam and conscription-related dimensions of civil liberties observance, the government had become more arrogant, intrusive, intolerant, and harsh.

Vietnam-Conscription and the State of Civil Liberties: Political and Societal Implications

As the government was introducing its controversial legislation to strengthen the enforcement of the National Service Act, it presented to Parliament a background statement on protest activities in Australia. Two themes were braided into the statement. First, the majority of demonstrations were not spontaneous, but carefully prearranged. Second, much of the prearranging was under the thumb of organizations which could be traced back to Communist influence. The AICD, for instance, was instrumental in the formation of certain more specialized protest groups in 1965 and 1966. But AICD maintained links with the World Peace Council, and the World Peace Council was under Communist domination. Gullible, unsuspecting people were getting caught up in what in the last analysis was a Communist conspiracy to defeat the Vietnamese war effort.[55]

This was only one in a long series of attacks and innuendoes by government ministers against the protest movement and its allegedly sinister sponsorship. Even while civil liberties, including the rights of active protesters, were being reasonably respected, there developed an almost routinized ministerial defamation of the protest movement. In June 1965 Menzies flatly declared, "There hasn't been a peace rally in my country for years that wasn't organized by the Communists."[56] Later in the year, Gordon Freeth, minister for shipping, told a teach-in audience in Perth that "Communist attitudes will be heard here without the slightest chance of being exposed. I do not brand everyone who disagrees with me as a Communist. Why have teach-ins become a craze? No matter how powerful the views and arguments advanced here, they will have no influence on Chinese and Russian policies."[57] In March of 1966, Allen Fairhall, minister for defense, said that protest demonstrations in Australia, carried out by a noisy minority of "sign painters and card burners," were confusing the Australian public mind and indirectly aiding Hanoi.[58] Later in the month, Leslie Bury, minister for labor and national service, told Parliament that those who actively resisted the draft in Australia were under the sway of sinister influences; "we are engaged in serious political warfare of a very complicated character and have the enemy conducting it in our midst."[59] In 1967, J. M. Fraser, minister for the army, told an audience at the University of Adelaide that there was a campaign in Australia, heavily affected by Communists, to undermine what Australia was doing in Vietnam by creating "moral doubt and confusion."[60]

Such continuous, sneering, and half-truth remarks from highly placed ministers, although interspersed with genuflections toward the principles of freedom of speech and assembly, have been complementary to the turgid, emotionally charged climate of the entire Vietnam-conscription debate. Such assaults against the protest movement have actually sharpened the edge of the party debate. Labor has been opposed to many of the premises and practices of the government's foreign policy, and has been hypersensitive to the flood of abuse that the L-CP has piled on it. It has therefore reacted with voluble counterattack whenever it has perceived an opportunity to expose what it claims is the government's use of political motive to clamp down on basic liberties. This it did in the debate on the Defense Forces Protection Bill, and then again in 1968 when legislation was brought in to curtail draft evasion. When Whitlam intervened in this debate, his speech was purple with indignation. The government's foreign policy now lay in ruins, he insisted. Divisions over where and how to move next had racked the government benches. To paper over the cracks, the government had resorted to the "one thing that will always unite their ranks, and that is an easy show of crude patriotism here at home." The bill insulted the traditions of justice and fair play. Labor not only opposed the substantive features of the bill, but "its whole spirit, its harsh, intolerant, inquisitorial spirit." Anticonscription demonstrations would not decrease as the result of the bill. The government would encourage the very thing it claimed it wished to avoid—it was legislating to incite lawbreaking.[61]

The government parties have on their part characterized Labor's positions, not as brilliant and inspired defenses of public liberties, but as lame diversions from the ALP's own internal schisms and bankrupt policies, as evasions of patriotic responsibility, and as screens for the presence of Labor people in such obnoxious, Communist-directed bodies as AICD. Thus the debate over Vietnam and conscription has been intensified, and the parties driven farther apart, both by the substance of what the government has done in the civil liberties area, and by the mutual imputations of deceit, transparent opportunism, and just plain un-Australianism.

When the government began to evince an edginess over the progress of its foreign and defense policies, with voiced thoughts that perhaps the press was disloyal to Australian interests, that some censorship might be in order, and that the conscription law would need to be administered far more vigorously, not just the ALP but the press and various sectors of the community began to react. In part for political gain, the government had almost to the point of second nature broadcast its disdain for those who organized themselves to oppose government policies; it now became simple to indict *it* for playing shoddy politics with Australian liberties. Intimations that the government might censor Vietnamese news available for Australian distribution did not go unchallenged. "Such [doctored] reports could all too easily become influential in Australian domestic policies," reasoned the *Canberra Times*, "by 'proving' Government policies to have been correct. The issue of censorship in this war is not simply of press freedom; it is one which raises the spectre of government manipulation of public opinion."[62] Nor did the timing of the bill to strengthen draft evasion regulations and the statement on Communist influence on protest groups go unnoticed. The government had presented controversial and imprudent measures by which to judge and punish offenders against the conscription program, immediately followed by the "revelations" of the symbiosis between Communism and protest. For the Melbourne *Age*, it was "hard to avoid the suspicion that it was no mere coincidence" that the statement on demonstrations "came so soon after reasoned criticism of the Government's ugly and clumsy attempt to catch up with a few youths who try to evade the call-up. The speech has the air of a 'mood piece,' an attempt to create in the public mind the notion that questioning the Government's behavior is tantamount to disloyalty to Australia's best interests."[63]

Suspicion that the government was swinging around to playing politics with civil rights *and* exacerbating rather than taming public feelings have not been confined to the Labor party and the press. The government's 1968 proposals to impose heavy penalties on draft evaders by summary jurisdiction and to use employers, teachers, and perhaps even parents as informers were attacked by such disparate groups as the Australian Council of Churches, the metropolitan press, pacifist organizations, and the DLP. The *Age* crystallized the issue at stake by editorializing that there had been little evidence of serious and irresponsible draft evasion. Now the government was introducing legislation which was unnecessary, abhorrent to numerous sectors of the community, and corrosive of elementary privileges and liberties. "The dogmatic coercion of conformity will only create new divisions in a community which, so far, has responded to the demands of national security with comparative calm and considerable responsibility."[64]

What can be said of the association between Vietnam-conscription and civil liberties in its impact on the Australian community? Vietnam and conscription have touched on various features of civil rights at both the state and federal levels, and have been publicized in political debate. Not since the 1950–1951 dispute over the Communist party ban has there been such intense political clash over a civil liberties issue, and the controversy generated by Vietnam-conscription has lasted considerably longer and has become more immediately felt by the general population. The debate in 1950–1951 over the rights of a tiny minority of people who were or might have been alleged to be Communists, however significant in principle, was after all somewhat academic to most Australians. Vietnam and conscription, however, have developed civil liberties overtones which have spread to students, academics, assorted protesters, draft-eligible men, and those whom in May 1968 the government tried to make accountable for young men with whom they were in family, educational, occupational, or other contact. The media have carried substantial reports and commentaries on these developments, and the civil liberties aspects of Vietnam-conscription have served to increase public interest both in Vietnam-conscription as public policy questions, and in civil liberties as such.

One of the predictable derivations of this heightened public interest has been the appearance of alignments. On the one side, there have been numerous reports of disgust being expressed by Australian servicemen in or recently returned from Vietnam who have wanted to "take a poke" at demonstrators or to "send them to Vietnam to fight Charlie."[65] There have been incidents of condemnation and ostracism of activists or presumed activists by the civilian population. Hitchhiking Monash students have been refused rides by motorists who somehow felt that all who attended the "little red schoolhouse" were tainted by NLF collections and other licentious behavior. Protest groups have been denied the use of private meeting halls. Letters to the editors of newspapers have often appealed to honor and patriotism while excoriating the more conspicuous exhibitors of dissent.

On the other side, perceived civil rights violations have excited far more interest and even solidarity among groups which, historically, have been only sporadically or nominally concerned. This has been especially true among the better educated, professional, and generally attentive-elite sectors of the community. Churchmen and church bodies have become visibly concerned with matters of conscience and military service and the equitable treatment of conscientious objectors. Newspaper editors and writers have been quick to point up shortcomings in civil liberties observance, and especially to denounce politically inspired or rationalized intrusions on rights. University students and academics, regardless of their opinions on the merits of Vietnam and conscription, have closed ranks in the face of attempts at official intimidation and prying. The government's 1968 proposal to require universities to serve as informers against draft-eligible students drew especially severe censure from student bodies, staff associations, and even normally conservative vice-chancellors across Australia. Had the government persisted in requiring universities to serve as informers, it would likely have encountered massive noncompliance. Even with the government's legislation amended, *individual* university officers such as registrars will not readily cooperate when student records are subpoenaed.

This has been part of something approaching a chain reaction. Civil liberties interest traceable to Vietnam-conscription has induced interest in civil liberties more widely, raised the attention level at which Vietnam and conscription per se are being regarded, and stimulated organization and activism as such among persons and groups not previously disposed to become involved. These are tendencies which have paralleled such general Australian trends as more frequent and more sophisticated public issue treatment in the media, greater opportunities for tertiary education, renovations in educational approaches at various levels, and a diffusion of cosmopolitan outlook.

The Labor party, sensing a need for and growing public interest in civil rights protections, has become very forthright in espousing individual liberty, and has even proposed a formal constitutionally implanted "bill of rights."[66] Vietnam and conscription did not produce a whole new case on behalf of civil rights observance, nor did they suddenly move people from indifference to concern in this area. But despite the frequently exaggerated fault ascribed to the authorities and the political rhetoric which has blurred a fair part of the debate, Vietnam and conscription did become a catalyst of real significance.

The general Australian public appears over the years to have shifted from a position of indifference or cynicism about civil liberties to a more concerned and tolerant position, and toward a more balanced outlook on the relationship governing rights, the law, and the place of police authorities. It would also appear that governments, both state and federal, had gradually become more circumspect in their own approach to both procedural and substantive due process, especially where political connotations were involved. Disputes about the observance of civil rights proprieties in the context of Vietnam-conscription have surely accentuated popular level interest in the subject. But such disputes, often presented in a highly animated manner, have appeared at a time when the public had only recently, and perhaps tentatively, acquired its more tolerant and balanced civil liberties outlook, therefore putting the public and its newly acquired outlook to a severe test.

The one available opinion survey on a Vietnam-related civil rights issue[67] supports the cause of moderation. In September of 1967, the public was asked whether people should be allowed to send money to the Viet Cong by means other than the Red Cross. The vast majority—85.3 per cent—were opposed, 9.8 per cent were in favor, and 4.8 per cent stood undecided. Among those who opposed such donations, however, very little vindictiveness was apparent. Those favoring severe penalties were in a distinct minority. A regrouping of the relevant survey data suggests that no more, and quite possibly less, than 25 per cent of those opposing collections were for as much or stronger punitive action against convicted offenders than the government itself had legislated just a few weeks earlier. Another rather illuminating result of the survey was that willingness to allow donations steadily *declined with each progressively older age group.* Persons twenty-one to twenty-nine years of age were clearly the most inclined to permit collections. Since this age group has tended to be the most "hawkish" on questions of general Vietnamese policy, it is plausible to conclude that, quite apart from feelings about Vietnam, the Australian public is indeed becoming increasingly tolerant/permissive regarding civil liberties.

Still, as the ALP and the press have come to suggest, divisiveness may be being encouraged by official actions portrayed as encroachments on privileges and protections, especially for "reasons of state" or politics. Vietnam and conscription as public policy issues have hardly encouraged neutrality of opinion, nor have their civil liberties facets. Nor can long-standing public attitudes of low regard for politicians and the profession of politics be excluded from the equation. A society traditionally skeptical of its political leaders and of the agents of authority will not have its estimate of them enhanced in an atmosphere of recrimination where civil rights become a political football. The choice in the party debate is made to appear as one between two devils. It becomes difficult to choose between a party which is accused of trampling rights beneath the jackboot of cheap political expediency, and a party which is accused of failing to meet its responsibilities to national security and to the deterrence, apprehension, and punishment of those who would flaunt their country's interests.

Chapter 9. The Australian Public and Vietnam-Conscription: Some Measures of Interest, Opinion, and Electoral Behavior

This study has illustrated the multifaceted and vigorous manner in which the Vietnam and conscription controversies have been played out in Australia. It has been repeatedly suggested that these forces have carried influence for socializing the public into an awareness of and politically relevant reaction to Vietnam and conscription, and external affairs more generally. The preceding chapter contained an interpretation of the broad impact of Vietnam-conscription's political uses and substantive formulations and of public reception in connection with civil liberties. The present concluding chapter raises three related questions: (1) Have there been conclusive signs of awareness and interest in Vietnam and conscription? (2) What attitudes toward the various dimensions of these issues has the public adopted? (3) Has electoral behavior been seriously conditioned by Vietnam-conscription, and if so, in what manner and to which party group's advantage?

The Salience of Vietnam-Conscription for the Australian Public

The first of our three questions cannot be answered by an absolute standard, but in relation to previous patterns of public interest in external subjects. The situation prior to 1964–1965, as recounted in Chapter I, was that the public took slight interest in foreign affairs, was in no noticeable way affected by foreign policy when asked to judge which issues were shaping up to be, or had been, critical during the conduct of electoral campaigns, and was not influenced by foreign policy in the act of voting.

As far as interest as such is concerned, there are some striking Gallup data available from a survey conducted in December of 1967, after Vietnam-conscription had been before the public for some time. Respondents were given a list of eleven assorted topics frequently covered in the news media, and were asked which one, two, or three of these interested them most. In first place stood the Vietnamese war (53.1 per cent). In second place stood "international affairs and the U.N." (47.1 per cent). Third place was occupied by "Australian politics" (41.9 per cent). Sports, social events, crime, and other items trailed well behind. The two foreign subjects picked first and second were chosen most often by young people twenty-one to twenty-nine years of age in respect to age groups, by upper classes in respect to economic classification, and by professionals in respect to occupation, revealing a clear association between education and interest in foreign policy.[1]

We can now examine the three nationwide elections which are relevant to our purpose—the Senate election of November 1964, the House election of November 1966, and the Senate election of November 1967.

The 1964 Senate election was conducted within weeks of the Menzies government's decision to conscript for unrestricted overseas service. The major parties made conscription the key issue in the campaign. Although there was no Vietnam issue at that time, the government's conscription announcement, because it was precedent shattering, gave considerable color to the debate. Two weeks before the election, with the party battle lines already drawn, 30 per cent of the electorate felt that conscription would be the foremost issue, and 27 per cent identified "defense." Other replies ranked far, far behind, though there was a very sizable group—34 per cent—who had "no idea."[2]

By the 1966 House election, conscription had been instituted, conscripts were among those who had been committed to combat in Vietnam, and both issues were being fiercely contested by the parties. Data drawn from several sources substantiate the importance assigned to these subjects by the voting public. Respecting the Holt and Calwell policy speeches, a nationwide sample of slightly over a thousand was asked: "What do you feel were the three most important things Mr. Holt/Mr. Calwell talked about?" For Holt, the top two items recalled were foreign policy (43 per cent) and defense (21 per cent). For Calwell, defense and the economy tied for first place (28 per cent), and foreign policy was a strong runner-up (26 per cent).[3]

Secondly, we can consult a survey conducted in Isaacs, an inner Melbourne suburb composed of fairly heterogeneous ethnic, economic, religious, and educational groups. Two surveys were conducted, the first six weeks before polling and the second the weekend immediately before polling. The question in the first poll was "What do you think will be the most important issue in this election?" The second survey asked "What do you think will be the issue that will decide this election?" The results are shown in Table 2. While the

Table 2. *Major Election Issues in Isaacs Survey (percentage)*

	First survey	Second survey
Mentioned Vietnam, conscription, defense, etc., as chief issue	66	72
Mentioned only domestic issues	19	20
Identified no issues	15	7

sample was small, "that between two-thirds and three-quarters of the respondents saw foreign policy-cum-defence as a deciding issue is remarkably high."[4]

Gallup polling in September and again in November 1966 showed less startling results, but nonetheless results disclosing far more external policy interest than had obtained prior to 1964. Respondents were asked to list one, two, or three issues which would, to them, be important in casting their votes. In September, 23.2 per cent listed conscription and 20.9 per cent named Vietnam.[5] In November, the two themes were listed by 23.1 per cent and 21.2 per cent of the respondents, respectively.[6]

In the 1967 Senate election, by which time conscription per se had lost some of its steam but Vietnam was even more dominant in public controversy than before, the same question resulted in 16.7 per cent opting for conscription and 26.8 per cent for Vietnam.[7] The 1966 and 1967 Gallup data on issue salience are wholly complementary to the data on general subject-matter interest noticed above, and further testify to the importance of external affairs for young, upper-economic-class and professional people. In November 1966 and November 1967 these three categories of voters invariably led all other categories included within their respective age, economic status, and occupational groupings as to the importance assigned to Vietnam.

Public Attitudes toward Vietnam and Conscription

The preceding evidence establishes that contemporary public interest in Vietnam and conscription is considerably stronger than was the interest and importance assigned to external topics in earlier times. We now proceed to the substance of public attitudes, where our task is threefold. We will wish to notice aggregate opinion on major questions relating to Vietnam and conscription. We will examine the distribution by party support, of agreement or disagreement with particular policy options. We will follow, both for the population at large and for particular party supporters, any significant swings toward or away from clusterings of opinion manifested early in the history of these two controversies. The object will be to link these factors to provide a reasonably clear picture of Australian sentiments, and to lay a basis for the later assaying of electoral behavior.

The Australian Gallup organization has over time inquired about five public attitude themes: (1) Opinion on conscription for overseas service, without regard to any Vietnamese overtones. (2) Opinion, on an after-the-fact basis, on whether conscript troops should have been dispatched to Vietnam. (3) Opinion on whether the Australian military commitment in Vietnam should be continued or all the forces be withdrawn. (4) Opinion on whether the Australian troop commitment should be enlarged. (5) Opinion on the conduct of the war generally. Data from these and other surveys utilized in this study were available through the middle of 1968.

The Menzies government's decision late in 1964 was taken in the face of a presumably deep Australian public hostility toward compulsion for overseas duty, and of the reluctance of parties since the First World War to violate this assumption. Furthermore, from the time that the new conscription program was announced, there has been no major war entanglement such as in 1939–1945, and one could surmise that the public would have been less rather than more interested in putting aside the antioverseas tradition. But the public attitudes toward recent conscription have proved to be something of a surprise. From November 1964 onward, the public has evinced a powerful and quite steady preference for the new system. In November 1964, 71 per cent supported it, 25 per cent were opposed, and 4 per cent undecided. Three years later, the figures were 70 per cent—25 per cent—5 per cent. At no point has explicit support sagged beneath 63 per cent, nor explicit opposition risen over 31 per cent. In other words, at least a two-to-one margin on behalf of conscription for unlimited overseas service has continuously existed.[8]

The second opinion theme has entailed questions on the assignment of troops to Vietnam. When the question was first put in early and mid-1965, it simply asked whether there was approval for shipping combat troops there. The question did not include reference to conscripts, and in fact there as yet were no conscripts assigned to Vietnam. Approval was reasonably strong: 52 per cent–37 per cent –11 per cent (approve, disapprove, undecided) in May, and 59 per cent–27 per cent–14 per cent in July.[9] Once conscripts were stationed in Vietnam, the question was amended to read whether the public approved, *post hoc*, of the decision that had sent them there. The three available polls, conducted between mid-1966 and mid-1967, reveal a different story. In each instance the above figures on approval of troops for Vietnam were nearly reversed. In no poll was there a majority in favor of having sent conscripts to Vietnam. The least support came in November 1966 (37 per cent–52 per cent–11 per cent), and the most in July 1967 (42 per cent–49 per cent–8 per cent).[10]

It would have been interesting had Gallup surveys asked whether the return of *conscripts only* from Vietnam was favored, but they did not. Instead, the question whether there was approval for retaining the forces or returning them (all of them) from Vietnam was asked several times. The public responded favorably to continuation, sometimes by two-to-one margins. There was a peak approval point of 62 per cent and a low approval point of 57 per cent. The "undecided" category, however, was always considerable, averaging about 13 per cent.[11]

Although the public was reluctant to withdraw the troops from Vietnam once they were there, it was, as revealed by February 1966 and November 1967 polls, reluctant to sanction an *increase* in the Australian military commitment. In February 1966, only a simple majority approved an increase (48 per cent–35 per cent–17 per cent).[12] In November 1967, the opponents of an increased commitment dominated–37 per cent in favor of an increase, 46 per cent against, and 17 per cent undecided.[13] Again we find considerable numbers of undecided respondents.

The question categories above seem to add up to certain trends. The public has favored the principle of conscription for overseas service, but has been uncomfortable that conscripts have been ordered to fight in Vietnam. It has not been prepared to "pull the rug" out from under the Australian commitment by unceremoniously returning all troops, but has been skeptical about increased allocations of troops. On this basis, the public mood can be termed generally moderate.

This mood of moderation is especially well highlighted through an analysis of public reactions to how the Vietnamese war ought to be prosecuted. Early in 1965, when the war was young and optimistic thoughts were being articulated that, with modestly intensified pressure, the conflict could be steered to a fairly early conclusion, 53 per cent approved the American bombing of the North, 29 per cent disapproved, and 18 per cent were undecided.[14] Two and a half years later, in November 1967, on a question which offered options of continuing the bombing or halting it *unconditionally* (i.e., without promised reciprocity by the North), it was a virtual draw: 39.8 per cent —38.4 per cent—21.8 per cent.[15] Two months earlier, without the qualification of an unconditional halt, more wanted to stop (43.4 per cent) than to continue the bombing (39.2 per cent).[16] By June 1968, following Johnson's announcement of an unconditional bombing reduction of the North but with the Paris conversations in an altogether inconclusive state, public attitudes mellowed further. Those interested in resuming interdiction of the North at large had declined to 31.7 per cent. There was a clear majority on behalf of accommodation: 12.4 per cent were content with the bombing of limited sectors of the North, and fully 40 per cent opposed any bombardment of the North.[17]

So far as general guidelines of escalation/obdurateness are concerned, again the evidence points toward conciliation. Between September 1966 and September 1967, on similar questions of allied intensification, maintenance of status quo, or a start at withdrawal from Vietnam, the "hawks" were in a distinct minority. The September 1966 figures were 24.0 per cent, 42.7 per cent, and 20.8 per cent, respectively, with 12.5 per cent undecided.[18] A year later, the figures for these options were 37.2 per cent, 17.5 per cent, 28.6 per cent, and 16.8 per cent undecided[19] and in February of 1968 basically the same distribution held[20]—reflecting, by the shrinkage of the status quo position and the size of the undecided response, the frustrations being felt about how to proceed. In February 1967, on the options of complete victory or a compromise solution in Vietnam, only 26.5 per cent agreed with the former course; 62 per cent were for compromise, and 11.5 per cent were undecided.[21]

Public feeling about policy alternatives in Vietnam has moved toward and remained at a position of moderation, with a considerable body of opinion—three or four times as many as on conscription for overseas service—undecided as to appropriate allied policy. The political relevance of these data is fairly plain. The old Calwellian stress on battling against conscription in the 1964 Senate and 1966 House elections missed the dominant mood of Australian opinion by a wide margin. Likewise, Calwell's insistence on "bringing home the boys" once they had been planted in Vietnam was unattractive. Whitlam did not thunder about conscription as such, and he rapidly—both before and after the 1967 Adelaide conference—stepped away from urging the rapid removal of forces from Vietnam. But Australian opinion has not favored sabre-rattling, either. It first mildly supported and then opposed troop increases, and in this sense has run less with the L-CP and more with Labor. Opinion has also decidedly been averse to trigger-happiness and diplomatic intractability in Vietnam. Since losing its early majority for bombing the North, it has flowed with Labor and against the government in what were for long key government postulates. It is these points—halting the bombing of the North, avoiding further escalation on the ground, and settling for a compromise formula, that have been pressed by Whitlam. From what has been said so far, Calwell missed and Whitlam struck the modal or at least developing qualities of Australian public opinion respecting Vietnam and conscription. Even among Labor voters, there was a majority favoring conscription for overseas service, and more Labor supporters favored rather than opposed the retention of the established force in Vietnam.

It is now proposed to spin out some variations on the above material, especially by inspecting opinion in some of its party-political rather than aggregate dimensions. First, consider Table 3, in which salience of conscription and Vietnam as issues of personally felt electoral importance is related to party preference during the 1966 House and 1967 Senate elections.[22]

Table 3. *Salience of Vietnam and Conscription in 1966 and 1967 Senate Elections (percentage)*

Issues at elections	National proportion assigning salience	Proportion of electors assigning salience, by party affiliation		
		ALP	DLP	L-CP
Conscription 1966	23.1	25.9	20.4	22.4
Vietnam 1966	21.2	15.8	31.2	24.5
Conscription 1967	16.7	20.8	19.1	13.7
Vietnam 1967	26.8	24.4	28.4	30.0

Inferences drawn from the data in Table 3 suggest the following: (1) In terms of campaign emphasis, Calwell's stress on conscription as above the Vietnam policy ingredient of the controversy at large was somewhat misplaced. Fewer DLP and L-CP voters, whom presumably Labor would wish to detach from their normal party loyalties, ascribed salience to conscription than did ALP voters or the public at large. Conversely, more DLP and L-CP voters than ALP supporters or the national average focused on Vietnam. (2) In 1967, the salience of conscription had faded and Vietnam's importance to voters had increased, which accorded with Whitlam's own emphasis in the Senate campaign, and the DLP and L-CP assignment of salience to Vietnam was, as in 1966, greater than for ALP supporters or for the nation. Hence, as a matter of recovering votes lost in 1966, Whitlam was stressing the proper facet of the controversy, and a position which was substantially compatible with general national feelings.

Another way to scrutinize the electoral appropriateness of Calwell's campaign emphasis is to look at women electors. Calwell not only emphasized conscription as an issue in 1964 and 1966, but made a special appeal to women, feeling that as mothers or grandmothers or mothers-to-be they would be particularly sensitive about having their sons or grandsons dragooned into military service and sent off to fight and perhaps die in stupid wars.

On this point, Calwell can be shown to have misread female sentiment. Just before the 1964 Senate balloting, when the new conscription plan was set before a Gallup audience, men and women were about equal in their responses, when the overall figures stood at 71 per cent in favor and only 25 per cent explicitly opposed.[23] In polls taken in 1966, overall opposition to conscription increased slightly, owing to the actual engagement of conscript troops in the Vietnamese war. Still, the proportion of explicit male-female opposition was not measurably disparate. In July, 24.6 per cent of the men and 28.0 per cent of the women were opposed.[24] In November, at the heat of the Calwell-ALP campaign against conscription and the open appeal for women's votes, 30.8 per cent of the males and 34.2 per cent of the females were against conscription.[25] By late 1967, with conscription no longer an electorally burning issue, the scale of male-female opposition was 25.8 per cent and 25.0 per cent, respectively.[26] In other words, women were not as a group especially beguiled by Calwell's appeal. To make matters worse for the Calwell strategy, we find that, at the 1966 election, women *less* than men (21.1 per cent as against 25.2 per cent) considered conscription to be an important issue in determining their electoral choice.[27]

Finally, attention is called to Table 4.[28] Here an attempt is made to demonstrate, according to three population categories, the connection between electoral preferences and salience assigned to Vietnam and conscription as important electoral issues. The three population categories are indicated by economic class, occupation, and age. Respecting occupation, only four of the divisions from among a number of others listed in Gallup surveys are presented, but they represent the lowest and the highest divisions of nonrural Labor strength. These comparisons suggest with striking regularity that Labor's electoral support in the 1966 and 1967 elections was highest among those groups of people who ascribed the *least* salience to conscription and Vietnam, and *weakest* among those who assigned them the strongest salience.

Irrespective of how firmly Labor supporters may have agreed with Labor policy on Vietnam and conscription, *electorally* it made little difference that this was the case, since they were the weakest ascribers of electoral importance to foreign policy questions. It was rather among those who supported Labor least that foreign and defense policy counted for most. In this sense, it can be judged that Calwell's overpowering emphasis on external affairs, and especially conscription, in 1966 was not helpful to the ALP, while Whitlam's quite successful effort to avert a direct confrontation with the government over external affairs in 1967 was more sensible.

Apart from differences between Calwell and Whitlam in intensity of emphasis on external affairs, there was also a considerable qualitative difference. To the extent that he propounded external policy positions in 1967, Whitlam was less categorical and, as it were, more "constructive" than Calwell, having moved closer to the government's own position. Here data from the surveys on public reactions to general questions on Vietnamese policy can be reintroduced. Groups attributing the greatest salience to external questions, as has just been shown, have also been the most strongly anti-Labor, and poll by poll they have been the most conservative or "hawkish" on general policy questions. Whitlam's half-turn to the right on foreign and defense policy was also a turn toward these groups; to the extent that Whitlam advertised a Labor external policy, it was a policy considerably more congenial than Calwell's had been vis-à-vis

Table 4: Voting Intention and Issue Salience by Population Categories (percentage)

1966

Category	ALP Voting intention				Salience of conscription				Salience of Vietnam			
	1	2	3	4	1	2	3	4	1	2	3	4
Economic class	19.2	40.4	49.5		24.9	23.1	17.3		26.5	19.4	13.6	
Occupation	14.0	11.8	47.2	61.8	31.3	20.9	21.5	18.8	42.2	28.3	14.4	10.9
Age	31.6	36.6	32.4	32.1	25.9	23.8	20.0	24.5	30.6	19.5	18.9	20.3

1967

Category	ALP Voting intention				Salience of conscription				Salience of Vietnam			
	1	2	3	4	1	2	3	4	1	2	3	4
Economic class	30.0	48.4	61.3		16.7	17.4	12.7		32.3	24.3	13.0	
Occupation	25.0	19.4	53.2	66.8	25.0	23.1	18.5	15.6	44.8	36.0	18.3	17.0
Age	38.5	43.1	42.3	39.0	17.6	18.5	15.0	10.5	35.4	27.8	21.8	20.1

Key to categories: Economic Class: (1) upper, (2) artisan, (3) lower
Occupation: (1) professional, (2) managerial, (3) semiskilled, (4) unskilled
Age: (1) 21–29, (2) 30–49, (3) 50–69, (4) 70 and over

those groups which placed especially strong importance on external issues. Electorally, for Labor's traditional support groups, foreign-defense policy did not matter much anyway.

We have been making frequent allusions to Calwell-Whitlam differences about their handling of Vietnam-conscription. In general, the verdict has been that Whitlam's approach was more attuned to national feeling, and potentially more profitable electorally. Before explicit formulations on electoral behavior are advanced, a brief venture into the subject of public acceptance of the two men becomes germane.

Political party leaders do or do not command confidence for a variety of reasons which are extremely difficult to disentangle or isolate. Their programmatic posture, style, vigor, and the rest all merge to create a public image. In Australia, by the time Vietnam-conscription had become serious public questions, comparisons were already being made between Calwell and Whitlam, his heir apparent. In early 1966, before Calwell announced that he would relinquish the leadership unless Labor won the next election and before Whitlam had differentiated himself from Calwell on Vietnam, Calwell had lost popularity with the public. A Gallup survey showed that among *non*-ALP voters 40 per cent preferred Whitlam and only 14 per cent leaned toward Calwell for the ALP leadership; most others had no opinion on any particular man.[29] Another, less rigorous and locally conducted poll, had Calwell, Whitlam, and a local Sydney political figure running about even.[30] In September 1966, L-CP respondents to a Gallup survey supported Whitlam over Calwell by better than two to one. More dramatic was the revelation that of those non-ALP respondents who felt they might shift from their present allegiances to Labor's side at the forthcoming election, Whitlam was preferred over Calwell by a four-to-one margin[31]—at a time when Whitlam had already moved to carve out a personal view on foreign policy.

Here was clear indication that a Labor electoral success predicated on prying voters out of the anti- and into the pro-Labor camp was related to who led the ALP. Even among Labor supporters, Calwell enjoyed only a fractional lead over Whitlam. Once Whitlam had succeeded to the leadership, he was the overwhelming favorite for the position among electors of all partisan affiliations. Not even Cairns received anything beyond desultory support. This, at least, was the situation in July of 1967.[32]

It is tempting to introduce the results of a survey conducted in June of 1968, just as Whitlam was feuding with portions of the ALP and shortly after Cairns had narrowly missed assuming the parliamentary leadership. The public was asked: "If the ALP split into a group led by Dr. Cairns, and a group led by Mr. Whitlam, and the *DLP* joined Mr. Whitlam's group—which of these groups [Cairns Labor, Whitlam Labor, L-CP, etc] would you then vote for?" Retabulated figures which excluded the 7.5 per cent who gave no answer revealed three times as much strength for a Whitlam party as for a Cairns party (47.1 per cent vs. 16.4 per cent). Furthermore, the Whitlam party strength was impressively greater than the combined Liberal and Country party vote (34.8 per cent). Under such a hypothetical party rearrangement, it was found that only 2.4 per cent of the previous ALP vote and 6.4 per cent of the DLP would gravitate to the L-CP. On the other hand, 28.6 per cent of the standard L-CP vote and 81 per cent of the normal DLP vote would now align itself with a Whitlam party.[33]

These data do not allow a judgment that Calwell was or Cairns is necessarily unpreferred and Whitlam preferred because of their respective Vietnam-conscription attitudes. Tentatively, however, it can be surmised that Whitlam's sense of political balance, as illustrated by the content and emphasis of his Vietnam-conscription position and his style of their presentation, fit well with the general public's impression of him as the more agreeable, and therefore more electorally supportable, Labor leader.

Vietnam-Conscription and Electoral Behavior

The material above has indicated that, respecting Vietnam-conscription, the Australian public (1) became seriously interested, (2) assigned considerable salience to such issues in elections, (3) assumed a generally moderate outlook, and (4) was disposed to oppose the emphases and substance of these issues as propounded by Calwell and more nearly to accept Whitlam's approach. The next undertaking is an analysis of whether elections have in fact been influenced by Vietnam-conscription, and if so, to which party's benefit.

The first step will be to appraise these questions by relating issue salience to those persons who were "swing" or weakly committed voters, and to those persons who, regardless of their previous partisan anchoring, contemplated a change in allegiance. These, of course, are the kinds of people whose electoral behavior wins or loses elections, since the bulk of the electorate remains fixed to its traditional party ties. The second step will entail the presentation of two case studies, which should provide a fruitful basis for checking on the importance and direction of foreign policy in recent Australian electoral politics.

We begin by citing an aspect of the 1966 Isaacs survey already mentioned. The question put was "Have these particular issues [i.e., Vietnam and conscription] affected your vote?" The survey population was small, but the results, as shown in Table 5, have signifi-

Table 5. *Degree of Effect of Vietnam and Conscription in Isaacs Survey*

Party connection and number of respondents	Percentage of affirmative replies
Solid ALP (22)	14
Solid Liberal (30)	17
Solid DLP (4)	25
Swing ALP/Liberal/DLP (27)	36
Refused, can't remember, new voters (24)	40

cance.[34] From among those respondents expressing a party association or preference, those most affected by foreign policy were swing voters and people not firmly set in their voting habits. The salience of Vietnam-conscription was twice as great for this key group as for the settled supporters of the major parties.

This theme can be further concretized by reference to Gallup data.[35] It will be remembered that just prior to the 1966 House and 1967 Senate elections the public was asked to list one, two, or three issues which were felt to be important in determining the individual's own forthcoming vote. There were ten such options in 1966 and eleven in 1967; Vietnam and conscription appeared in each survey. The Gallup organization surveyed the same national sample on whether there might be a change from original voting intention to some other party by the time the balloting actually occurred. Table 6 telescopes Vietnam-conscription salience and voting change variables for the 1966 and 1967 elections. It indicates the extent to which Vietnam and conscription were regarded as electorally salient issues among those who thought they might change their vote, those who said they might change to the ALP, to the DLP, and to the L-CP, and to those who were certain they were not going to change their vote.

Table 6. *Salience of Vietnam and Conscription in Changing Votes (percentage)*

Issue	Might change vote	Might change to ALP	Might change to DPL	Might change to L-CP	Won't change vote
1966 House election					
Conscription	27.7	20.8	58.2	24.1	22.9
Vietnam	36.1	28.1	42.1	42.2	20.6
1967 Senate election					
Conscription	18.2	19.6	14.7	18.9	16.6
Vietnam	39.7	43.1	50.5	29.4	25.9

It should be stressed that among those who indicated that they might change their vote Vietnam was by far the most saliently construed issue from among the ten listed in 1966 and the eleven listed in 1967. In 1966, 21.2 per cent of the general population selected Vietnam as an issue of personally regarded electoral importance, but 36.1 per cent of those indicating a possibility of voting change picked Vietnam. In 1967, Vietnam was selected by 26.8 per cent of the general public, but it was selected by 39.7 per cent of those considering a voting switch. For the wavering, electorally strategic target voters, those people who would be tipping the scales in the voting outcome, Vietnam was inordinately important.

Confirmation of the importance of external policy issues is gained by a glance at the preceding tables. We find that in both 1966 and 1967 those electors indicating a possible voting switch were above the general public in their assignment of salience to Vietnam and conscription, while electors definitely not considering a voting change were consistently below the national average in salience ascription on these issues. These data are thereby complementary to the Isaacs survey findings on swing voters.

Further reference to the tables indicates toward which party group the prospective vote changers leaned. In 1966, these electors were inclined to move toward the L-CP and the DLP rather than toward the ALP, clearly suggesting the unpopularity of the Calwellian position on Vietnam-conscription and foreshadowing Labor's electoral defeat. In 1967, persons considering a voting shift were far more inclined to select Labor than the L-CP. The proportion considering a move to the DLP remained very high, and in fact the DLP did well in the forthcoming Senate election, advancing from a 1966 House performance of 7.3 per cent of the formal vote to 9.7 per cent in 1967. The DLP's 1967 improvement was mainly scored in Victoria and Queensland, not nationwide, suggesting that local rather than all-Australian considerations, such as foreign policy, contributed to the gain. Also, the place of the Senate as a house of review was very much in prominence in the Senate election. The Senate had on several occasions acted as the "conscience of the public," and the DLP made much of the fact that it controlled the balance of power there, and asked the public to keep it so. Indeed, even in Victoria and Queensland, the ALP vote managed to rise, not fall, as the DLP improved. In Victoria Labor was up by 5.3 per cent, and in Queensland by 3.4 per cent. It was the government, not the ALP, that was harmed most by DLP advances.

Labor recorded an excellent improvement between 1966 and 1967, moving from 39.8 per cent to 45.0 per cent of the vote. Had the same voting distribution applied in a House election, the government's majority would have been reduced from its prevailing forty to about ten, and the L-CP could probably have retained office only on the strength of DLP preferences.[36] Both Whitlam and Calwell felt that the vote represented a repudiation of government foreign policy.[37] While there were assorted issues in the 1967 campaign, the data given above, when considered in combination with the various material presented earlier in this chapter, make it quite plain that electoral behavior was influenced by external policy issues, and that the beneficiary was Labor. Foreign policy had also influenced the 1966 House election, but in that instance the beneficiary had been the L-CP.

The two promised case studies, both concerned with the 1966 election, would seem to verify the electoral salience of foreign policy and Calwellian Labor's detriment from it. First we look to the performance of the Liberal Reform Group, as it was known in 1966. The LRG was founded as an almost strictly one-issue party, namely to oppose the government's Vietnamese policy. It was a brand new party, without traditions or an established body of voting loyalists, and was built and run by political amateurs. Its aggregate vote was unimpressive—1.96 per cent in Victoria, 1.31 per cent in New South Wales, and 1.03 per cent in the country at large. But in the ten Victorian seats it did contest it drew 4.4 per cent of the vote and 4.8 per cent in the dozen contested New South Wales seats. Its New South Wales figure was higher than what the established DLP polled, either in the state at large or in the constituencies where both the LRG and the DLP were present.

The LRG's foreign policy position differed from the government's, and in that sense its vote was an antigovernment vote. But an analysis of electoral data suggests that the LRG extracted as many if not more normally ALP as government party first preferences. Within the twelve New South Wales seats, the government drew 8.4 per cent *more* of the vote than in the other New South Wales seats not contested by the LRG, while the ALP did 11.2 per cent *worse* in LRG-contested seats than elsewhere in the state. Compared to 1963, the previous House election when there was no LRG, the government in these twelve seats raised its vote by 4.2 per cent, while the ALP declined by 5.4 per cent.

The Victorian results are not nearly as startling, but are still impressive. In the ten Victorian seats, the government vote was only fractionally lower in 1966 than in 1963—0.2 per cent—but the Labor vote was 9.4 per cent lower than in 1963. Part of this Labor decline in Victoria could be traced to the presence of serious independent candidates, as in the seat of Batman. But the DLP vote in these ten constituencies was virtually unchanged, having next to no effect on lowering the Labor total from its 1963 level.

The mere fact of a strong LRG showing in both states suggests the importance of Vietnam as an issue, and the movement of many ALP, not just Liberal, voters to the LRG suggests the mood of the public at the time. There was some dissatisfaction among Liberal voters with government policy which a specialized anti-Vietnam party such as the LRG could exploit, since Labor was not regarded as a tasteful voting alternative under Calwell. Among Labor adherents, the LRG offered a refuge for those who disagreed with government policy but could not accept the Calwellian version and approach to Vietnam-conscription. In either case, it could be argued that Labor was the loser. The LRG pulled a number of Laborites from their moorings, despite the proximity of its and Labor's external policy. The reorientation in foreign policy which Whitlam brought to Labor in 1967 carried votes to Labor. The decline of LRG–Australian Reform Movement strength in the Senate election is entirely understandable in light of the above analysis. The ARM Senate slate won 2.36 per cent of the statewide vote in New South

Wales, and only 0.67 per cent of the vote in Victoria. To be critical of government policy in 1967 no longer implied being forced to support a party which, at least in terms of the exposition provided by its leader, was out of touch with broad public sentiment and which presented its case in an inordinately extravagant manner.

The second illustration concerns the case of Sam Benson, the man who was forced out of the ALP in the second half of 1966 because of his split with standing party policy on Vietnam and conscription. Benson had narrowly won the Victorian seat of Batman in 1963 by 703 preference votes. Demographic changes in Batman between 1963 and 1966 were to Labor's disadvantage. Also, it would have been plausible to assume that had Benson contested Batman in 1966 as an accredited Laborite he would have lost because, in Victoria at large, the swing against Labor in 1966 was about 4 per cent.

But Benson decided to contest the seat in 1966 as an independent—ordinarily a thankless undertaking. He came in a poor second in first preferences to the new, authorized ALP candidate. However, since no candidate achieved an absolute majority of the vote, further preferences were distributed, and on the basis of their distribution he won by 6,021 votes over the ALP entry. This he accomplished by almost astonishingly gaining approximately 95 per cent of the second preferences of both the Liberal and DLP candidates. Although considerations such as Benson's personal popularity and martyr's role no doubt counted toward his victory, the single, most significant variable appeared to have been his foreign policy stance. It was the theme on which he had, in a blaze of publicity, left the ALP, and it was the theme he stressed in his campaign; he had *not* taken exception to Labor's domestic policies. In Batman, the local LRG candidate did poorly. Out of ten Victorian seats contested by the LRG, its Batman vote was third from the bottom—2.8 per cent—in comparison to a composite 4.4 per cent output in the ten seats. Once again, as in the 1967 Senate election at large, the availability of a nonrabid yet not uncritical alternative to government external policy seemed to have undercut the viability of the LRG-ARM.

The Public and Vietnam-Conscription: A Concluding Note

Vietnam and conscription have created a climate of external policy interest in Australia for a number of reasons. The issues themselves have been extremely basic and even intimately felt down to the rank and file of the population. They have been argued out for a considerable period of time. When they have been argued by the parties, the alternatives expressed have often been blunt and extravagant. The style of political debate has been biting. The Labor party has undergone publicly displayed turmoil over Vietnam and conscription. Vietnam and conscription have created the phenomenon of an organized protest movement which, while limited to a small minority, has embraced people from various faiths, backgrounds, and walks of life. The protest movement has been accorded considerable publicity, and has occasioned the spilling over of Vietnam and conscription from the strict area of external affairs into other concerns of public policy and behavior, such as civil liberties. The issues have been reported and interpreted and reinterpreted time and again in the news media and in special settings such as teach-ins.

These have been factors which have conditioned a fresh public interest in and political response to foreign policy, traditionally a subject of little popular concern, an awakening which has permeated both the mass public and the attentive-interested sectors of the public. Transformations in Australian society have also made their contribution to a heightened awareness of foreign policy questions. Previous Australian voting studies indicated not only the insignificance of foreign policy but also the only incidental role played by public policy issues *qua* issues when electors have proceeded to make choices at the polling stations. The dominant impulses have been class identification, general perceptions of party credibility/reliability, images of party elites, and so on.[38] Vietnam and conscription have not reversed this pattern, but they have amended it. Both the 1966 House and 1967 Senate elections were, with different results, affected by the external policy dialogue. This conclusion stands even when it is admitted that the personalities who led parties, the style with which they operated, the general tenor or "image" that was cast by leaders and parties alike, and various domestic policy questions became mixed with foreign policy issues as issues in their own right.

Judgments cannot be final, but it would appear that the ability of Vietnam and conscription to intrude in strength into organized politics and into the public's thinking will prove to be an agent for raising foreign policy to a more visible plane in future, and possibly to make the public generally more keenly policy-issue conscious. Perhaps these are developments which in the natural course of events would have come anyway, but Vietnam and conscription should be regarded as having speeded up the process.

Vietnam and conscription have generated deep disagreements and have opened some wounds in the Australian body politic. It has been a controversy which has not been acted upon or reacted to with decorum and equanimity. These destabilizing contributions of the Vietnam-conscription controversy should not be belittled. The foreign policy dialogue has injected a new, or at least newly advertised, ideological dimension into a well-aggregated society which, despite a colorful political climate, has been averse to ideological disputation.

It is unknown whether the legacy of Vietnam and conscription will impose a heavy strain on this traditional pragmatism, but one clue points opposite. Despite the fulminations of politicians, protesters, and irate citizens, the public has shown itself to be moderate in its conclusions about the foreign policy issues which have been controverted around it. Attitude surveys and electoral data alike suggest that the public has not been driven into hostile camps of opinion. By and large, the evidence indicates that the "vital center" has not been emptied. There is frustration and uneasiness aplenty over where and how Australian and allied policy ought to proceed, but the mood has remained rather characteristically Australian—adaptive, resilient, and suspicious of bottled formulas.

Notes

Chapter 1. The Australian Public and the Salience of External Affairs: A Perspective

1. For a good summary of this phenomenon, see Richard N. Rosecrance, "The Radical Culture in Australia," in Louis Hartz, ed., *The Founding of New Societies* (New York: Harcourt, Brace and World, 1964), esp. pp. 291–298.
2. Werner Levi, *Australia's Outlook on Asia* (Sydney: Angus and Robertson, 1958), p. 8.
3. Ronald Taft and Kenneth F. Walker, "Australia," in Arnold M. Rose, ed., *The Institutions of Advanced Societies* (Minneapolis: University of Minnesota Press, 1958), p. 145.
4. See the commentary by P. D. Phillips, "The Pacific through Australian Eyes," *Austral-Asiatic Bulletin,* VI (March 1945), 14.
5. Sir Granville Ryrie, *Commonwealth Parliamentary Debates (CPD),* House of Representatives (HR), April 3, 1924, p. 344.
6. Kim E. Beazley, "Labour and Foreign Policy," *Australian Outlook,* XX (Aug. 1966), 126.
7. Paul Hasluck, *The Government and the People 1939–1941* (Canberra: Australian War Memorial, 1952), p. 29.
8. For the comparison, see *Report[s] of the Department of External Affairs* (Canberra: Department of External Affairs, 1939; 1940), and *Annual Report 1 July 1966–30 June 1967* (Canberra: Department of External Affairs, 1967). Also see comments on the development of the Department in Alan Watt, *The Evolution of Australian Foreign Policy 1938–65* (Cambridge: Cambridge University Press, 1967), *passim.*
9. See William Macmahon Ball, ed., *Press, Radio and World Affairs* (Melbourne: Melbourne University Press for the Victorian Branch, Institute of Pacific Relations, 1938), *passim,* and Jack Shepherd, *Australia's Interests and Policies in the Far East* (New York: Institute of Pacific Relations, 1940), pp. 72–76.
10. John Douglas Pringle, *Australian Accent* (London: Chatto and Windus, 1958), p. 165.
11. Sam Lipski in *Bulletin* (Sydney), Feb. 19, 1966.
12. For supporting commentary, see James Plimsoll, "Asian Issues in the Australian Press," *Current Notes on International Affairs,* XXXVI (Nov. 1965), 745–757, and Derek McDougall, "The Australian Press Coverage of the Vietnam War in 1965," *Australian Outlook,* XX (Dec. 1966), 303–310.
13. Henry Mayer, *The Press in Australia* (Melbourne: Lansdowne Press, 1964), pp. 233–237.
14. J. S. Western and Colin A. Hughes, "The Mass Media in Australia: A Preliminary Report," *Politics,* II (Nov. 1967), 193–196.
15. Data taken from *ibid.,* pp. 194–195.
16. Summarized in *Australian Gallup Polls (AGP),* Nos. 690–699, June–July 1950, and Nos. 960–974, Nov.–Dec. 1953.
17. Western and Hughes, *op. cit.,* p. 198.
18. For a discussion of public affairs television broadcasting, see Mungo McCallum, "Reporting TV Reporting," *Quadrant,* X (July–Aug. 1966), 41–48.

19. Patrick Tennison in *Australian* (Canberra), Oct. 26, 1967. Also see Leonard Radic in Melbourne *Age*, Oct. 25, 1967.
20. Australian Broadcasting Commission, *Thirty-fifth Annual Report 1966–67*, p. 28.
21. See the account in *Sydney Sun-Herald*, April 24, 1966.
22. Western and Hughes, *op. cit.*, pp. 192, 194.
23. Watt, *op. cit.*, p. 298.
24. See *ibid.*, pp. 297–298; Fred Alexander, "The Australian People and the World," in George Caiger, ed., *The Australian Way of Life* (New York: Columbia University Press, 1953), pp. 156–157; Gordon Greenwood, "Foreign Policy and the Community," Seventeenth Roy Milne Memorial Lecture (Melbourne: AIIA, 1966), pp. 30–31.
25. New South Wales Department of Education, *Syllabus in Asian Social Studies, Advanced and Ordinary Courses, Forms II–IV* (Sydney, 1967).
26. See remarks by J. M. Fraser, minister for education and science, *Sydney Morning Herald*, April 9, 1968.
27. For reviews of Asian language instruction in various states, see *Australian*, March 19, 20, and 23, 1968.
28. *Ibid.*, March 21, 1968.
29. Namely, Levi, *op. cit.*; Richard N. Rosecrance, *Australian Diplomacy and Japan, 1945–1951* (Melbourne: Melbourne University Press for the Australian National University, 1962); Henry S. Albinski, *Australian Policies and Attitudes toward China* (Princeton: Princeton University Press, 1965).
30. For a report on the achievements of students in Asian civilization at the ANU, see H. H. E. Loofs, "Australian Awareness of Southeast Asia: An Assessment of Its Development," *Australian Outlook*, XXI (Dec. 1967), 347–358.
31. Mayer, *op. cit.*, p. 267.
32. *Ibid.*, pp. 230–231.
33. Colin A. Hughes and John S. Western, *The Prime Minister's Policy Speech* (Canberra: Australian National University Press, 1966), p. 146.
34. *Canberra Times*, Aug. 1, 1967.
35. Paul Lafitte, *Social Structure and Personality in the Factory* (London: Routledge and Kegan Paul, 1958), p. 116.
36. Henry Mayer, Peter Loveday, and Peter Westerway, "Images of Politics: An Analysis of Letters to the Press on the Richardson Report," *Australian Journal of Politics and History*, VI (Nov. 1960), 153–175.
37. Western and Hughes, *op. cit.*, p. 198.
38. See the comments of S. Encel, "Power," in Peter Coleman, ed., *Australian Civilization* (Melbourne: F. W. Cheshire, 1962), pp. 208–210.
39. Data on sittings are found in "Backbenchers," *Current Affairs Bulletin*, XXXVII (April 18, 1966), 167.
40. See Don Aitkin in *Nation* (Sydney), Jan. 28, 1967.
41. L. F. Crisp, *Australian National Government* (Melbourne: Longmans, Green, 1965), p. 128. Various data on Parliamentarians are also found in S. Encel, "The Political *Elite* in Australia," *Political Studies*, IX (Feb. 1961), 16–36, and in L. F. Crisp, *The Australian Federal Labour Party 1901–1951* (London: Longmans, Green, 1955), pp. 327–329.
42. H. B. Turner, "The Foreign Affairs Committee of the Australian Parliament," *Australian Outlook*, XX (April 1966), 25.
43. B. D. Beddie, "Some Internal Political Problems," in John Wilkes, ed., *Australia's Defense and Foreign Policy* (Sydney: Angus and Robertson for the Australian Institute of Political Science, 1964), p. 143. Also see H. B. Turner, "The Reform of Parliament," *Australian Quarterly*, XXXVII (Dec. 1965),

56–64; Greenwood, *op. cit.*, pp. 13–18; *Sydney Morning Herald,* April 18, 1967.

44. The special foreign policy nature of the 1937 election is examined in George Fairbanks, "Isolationism vs. Imperialism: The 1937 Election," *Politics,* II (Nov. 1967), 245–255. Also see Hasluck, *op. cit.,* pp. 84–86.

45. See Leicester Webb, *Communism and Democracy in Australia* (Melbourne: F. W. Cheshire for the Australian National University, 1954), pp. 10–15; Albinski, *op. cit.,* pp. 34–37.

46. *AGP,* Nos. 756–774, May–June 1951.

47. *Ibid.,* Nos. 999–1005, April 1954.

48. *Ibid.,* Nos. 1006–1021, May–June, 1954.

49. *Ibid.,* Nos. 1592–1604, March–April 1962.

50. Creighton Burns, *Parties and People* (Melbourne: Melbourne University Press, 1961), p. 133.

51. Hughes and Western, *op. cit.,* p. 69.

52. *Ibid.,* p. 166. Also see p. 169.

Chapter 2. The Clash of Party Positions on Vietnam-Conscription

1. *Sydney Morning Herald,* Nov. 8, 1966.

2. *CPD,* HR, April 30, 1968, p. 950.

3. Seymour Martin Lipset, *The First New Nation* (New York: Basic Books, 1963), p. 255.

4. See especially R. S. Parker, "Power in Australia," *Australian and New Zealand Journal of Sociology,* I (Oct. 1965), 85–96.

5. J. E. Pagan, Melbourne *Age,* Oct. 11, 1966.

6. "Labor Speaks" column in Melbourne *Herald,* Aug. 12, 1967.

7. J. D. B. Miller, "Party Traditions," in *Australia and Foreign Policy* (ABC Boyer Lectures, 1963), p. 49.

8. Australian Labor party, *Official Proceedings of the 22nd Commonwealth Conference,* Brisbane, March 1957, p. 95.

9. Kim E. Beazley, "Labour and Foreign Policy," *Australian Outlook,* XX (Aug. 1966), 129.

10. *Canberra Times,* Sept. 5, 1967. For convenient summaries of the government's appraisal of the Vietnamese conflict, see *Viet Nam: Recent Statements of Australian Policy* (Canberra: Issued under the Authority of the Minister for External Affairs, 1965); *Viet Nam: Questions and Answers* (Canberra: Issued under the Authority of the Minister for External Affairs, 1966); *Vietnam: Efforts for Peace* (Canberra: Issued under the Authority of the Minister for External Affairs, 1967). For an analysis of the government's Vietnamese policy in wider foreign policy perspective, see Henry S. Albinski, "Australia's Foreign Policy: The Lessons of Vietnam," in Richard A. Preston, ed., *Contemporary Australia* (Durham, N. C.: Duke University Press, 1969), and Amry and Mary Belle Vanderbosh, *Australia Faces Southeast Asia* (Lexington: University of Kentucky Press, 1967), pp. 108–129.

11. *Sydney Morning Herald,* Feb. 6, 1968.

12. Melbourne *Age,* May 29, 1967.

13. For Calwell's development of this theme, see *CPD,* HR, May 4, 1965, pp. 1102–1103; Australian Labor party, *Official Report of the Proceedings of the 26th Commonwealth Conference,* Sydney, Aug. 1965, pp. 250–251; Melbourne *Age,* May 17, 1966; and Melbourne *Herald,* Jan. 23, 1968. Also see Whitlam, *Canberra Times,* April 1, 1968.

14. *Sydney Morning Herald*, April 16, 1966.
15. *A.L.P. Journal* (Sydney), June 1965.
16. *CPD*, HR, Nov. 10, 1964, pp. 2715–2724.
17. For a discussion of the World War Two decision, see K. S. Inglis, "Conscription in Peace and War, 1911–1945," *Teaching History*, II (Oct. 1967), 30–41.
18. See in particular Calwell's reply, *CPD*, HR, Nov. 12, 1964, pp. 2920–2928.
19. *Sydney Morning Herald*, March 14 and 26, 1968.
20. *Ibid.*, Nov. 12, 1966.
21. *Ibid.*, Nov. 22, 1966.
22. Gorton, *Canberra Times*, April 8, 1968. Also see the analysis of Jonathan Gaul in *ibid.*, April 2, 1968.
23. Australian Labor party, *Speakers Notes*, No. 8/66 (May 20, 1966), pp. 115–116.
24. *Sydney Morning Herald*, Nov. 22 and 23, 1966.
25. *Ibid.*, Feb. 27, 1967.
26. Australian Labor party, *Platform, Constitution and Rules, 27th Commonwealth Conference*, Adelaide, Aug. 1967, pp. 32–34.
27. ABC television interview, in *Australian*, March 7, 1968.
28. *Melbourne Age*, May 10, 1966.
29. *Sydney Morning Herald*, April 14, 1966.
30. See Whitlam, *CPD*, HR, Aug. 22, 1967, p. 298, and Whitlam and Senator Arthur Poyser, *Canberra Times*, Oct. 23, 1967.
31. For discussions of Australia's overseas aid program, see Paul Hasluck, *CPD*, HR, Sept. 5, 1967, pp. 760–765; *Australian International Aid* (Canberra: Department of External Affairs, 1967); "Australian Aid Abroad," *Current Affairs Bulletin*, XL (Nov. 20, 1967), 195–207; Peter Robinson in *Australian Financial Review*, Sept. 27, 1967; Douglas Brass in *Australian*, Dec. 6, 1967.
32. *Canberra Times*, Jan. 31, 1968. For a broadly ranging Whitlam criticism of official civil aid efforts, see Melbourne *Age*, March 18, 1968.
33. Calwell, *Sydney Morning Herald*, May 24, 1965.
34. Hasluck, *CPD*, HR, March 10, 1966, p. 176.
35. *Canberra Times*, April 1, 1968.
36. William McMahon, Treasurer, *Australian*, Nov. 20, 1967.
37. Gorton, *Sydney Morning Herald*, Feb. 14, 1968; Jonathan Gaul in *Canberra Times*, April 2, 1968.
38. Gorton, *CPD*, HR, April 2, 1968, pp. 641–642.
39. *CPD*, HR, May 2, 1968, p. 1074.
40. *Ibid.*, March 26, 1968, p. 462.
41. *Australian*, March 3, 1966.
42. *CPD*, HR, April 6, 1965, p. 621.
43. For example, see Calwell, *A.L.P. News* (Sydney), July 5, 1965, and July 11, 1966; Whitlam, *Sydney Morning Herald*, July 13, 1967, Melbourne *Age*, Nov. 17, 1967, and *Canberra Times*, Nov. 24, 1967.
44. Whitlam, *CPD*, HR, Aug. 17, 1967, p. 224.
45. See *News Weekly* (Melbourne), July 6, 1966.
46. Melbourne *Age*, Jan. 2, 1968.
47. *Australian*, Nov. 22, 1967.
48. For instance, J. F. Cairns, *Sydney Morning Herald*, Feb. 7, 1966, and Melbourne *Age*, Aug. 14, 1967; Whitlam, *CPD*, HR, Feb. 28, 1967, p. 206, *Australian*, Nov. 14, 1967, *Sydney Morning Herald*, Feb. 15, 1968, and *Canberra Times*, March 25, 1968.
49. Melbourne *Age*, July 15, 1967.

50. Calwell, *CPD*, HR, March 23, 1965, p. 241.
51. Whitlam, Melbourne *Age*, April 2, 1968, and *CPD*, HR, April 2, 1968, p. 645.
52. *Sydney Morning Herald*, Nov. 15, 1967.
53. Hasluck, *ibid.*, Sept. 21, 1964.
54. Holt, Melbourne *Age*, Nov. 15, 1966.
55. *Canberra Times*, Nov. 21, 1967.
56. For a statistical review of DLP foreign and defense policy emphasis, see James Spigelman, "D.L.P. Policy: Content and Subject Matter," *Politics*, I (Nov. 1966), 107–121.
57. Senator Vincent Gair, Melbourne *Age*, Nov. 14, 1966.
58. See exposition of DLP foreign and defense policy in *Focus* (Sydney), Nov. 1967; *Sydney Morning Herald*, Nov. 8, 1966; *Canberra Times*, Oct. 23, 1967. Also see B. A. Santamaria, "The Holt Stereotype," *Quadrant*, XI (July–Aug. 1967), 54–63.
59. For expositions of the Movement's policies, see Gordon Barton in *Sydney Morning Herald*, Nov. 16, 1966, and Feb. 10, 1968, and party advertisements in *ibid.*, Nov. 12, 1966, and Nov. 8, 1967.

Chapter 3. Stylistic Characteristics of the Party Dialogue over Vietnam and Conscription

1. On Holt's social commitment to Asia, see his remarks in *Current Notes on International Affairs*, XXXVIII (Jan. 1967), 8, and Alan Reid's interpretation in *Bulletin*, Jan. 21, 1967.
2. For some commentaries on contrasts between the two prime ministers, see Sir Alan Watt, "Australians at War in Vietnam," *Round Table*, No. 224 (Oct. 1966), pp. 358–359, and Donald Horne in *Bulletin*, Dec. 23, 1967.
3. Bruce Grant, Melbourne *Age*, Dec. 22, 1967.
4. "Observer" in *Bulletin*, Dec. 30, 1967.
5. Melbourne *Age*, March 31, 1966.
6. For instance, *ibid.*, Nov. 10, 17, and 24, 1966, and Nov. 23, 1967.
7. J. B. Keefe, *CPD*, Senate, Sept. 7, 1967, p. 612. For a news account of the event, see *Sydney Morning Herald*, Aug. 18, 1967.
8. *Canberra Times*, Feb. 7, 1968. For comparable opinion, see Peter Hastings in *Australian*, Nov. 26, 1966, Jonathan Gaul in *Canberra Times*, Nov. 20, 1967, and Bruce Grant in Melbourne *Age*, Jan. 24, 1968.
9. *Sydney Morning Herald*, Feb. 15, 1968.
10. J. F. Cairns, *CPD*, HR, Nov. 17, 1964, pp. 3098–3099. Also see Calwell, *ibid.*, pp. 3006–3007.
11. Calwell, Melbourne *Age*, May 23, 1966, *Sydney Morning Herald*, May 24 and Nov. 12, 1966, and *CPD*, HR, Oct. 28, 1966, pp. 2382–2383.
12. *CPD*, HR, Oct. 18, 1967, p. 1937.
13. *Australian*, April 13, 1968.
14. Holt, Melbourne *Age*, Nov. 12, 1966.
15. Donald Chipp, *CPD*, HR, Nov. 16, 1964, p. 3048.
16. Statement by Allan Fraser, Labor MHR, in Melbourne *Age*, June 24, 1966.
17. For instance, L. J. Reynolds, *CPD*, HR, Dec. 2, 1965, pp. 3567–3569; Calwell and Menzies, *ibid.*, Dec. 3, 1965, p. 3585; answer to question on notice, *ibid.*, Sept. 22, 1966, p. 1249; J. B. Keefe, *CPD*, Senate, Sept. 20, 1967, p. 781.
18. *Sydney Morning Herald*, Oct. 7, 1966.

19. Melbourne *Age*, Oct. 10, 1966.
20. *Ibid.*, Oct. 8, 1966, and *Sydney Morning Herald*, Oct. 13, 1966.
21. Melbourne *Age*, Oct. 24, 1966.
22. *Canberra Times*, Aug. 1, 1967.
23. *CPD*, HR, Nov. 12, 1964, p. 2928.
24. Melbourne *Age*, May 16, 1966.
25. *Ibid.*, Oct. 24, 1966.
26. *Ibid.*, Nov. 18, 1966.
27. *Sydney Morning Herald*, April 16, 1966.
28. Australian Labor party, *Vietnam and Conscription*, Speakers Notes, No. 19/66 (Oct. 21, 1966).
29. The character and politics of Australia's trade with China have been treated in Henry S. Albinski, *Australia's Policies and Attitudes toward China* (Princeton: Princeton University Press, 1965), pp. 249–348. Also see Albinski, "Australia and the Chinese Strategic Embargo," *Australian Outlook*, XIX (Aug. 1965), 117–128.
30. The debate is found in *CPD*, Senate, Aug. 29, 1967, pp. 281–318.
31. *CPD*, HR, Aug. 17, 1967, p. 218.
32. Hartley Cant, *CPD*, *Senate*, Aug. 29, 1967, p. 291.
33. Melbourne *Age*, Oct. 12, 1966.
34. A. W. Jones, *CPD*, HR, Aug. 24, 1966, p. 386.
35. Francis McManus, *CPD*, Senate, March 30, 1966, p. 362.
36. *Canberra Times*, Nov. 10, 1967.
37. *Australian*, Nov. 21, 1967.
38. *CPD*, HR, Aug. 31, 1966, p. 623.
39. See a review of the Australian Students' Labor Federation position in Andrew Clark, Melbourne *Age*, July 27, 1967.
40. *Ibid.*, Aug. 11, 1967, and *Canberra Times*, Aug. 12, 1967.
41. *CPD*, HR, Aug. 16, 1967, pp. 108–109.
42. *Canberra Times*, Aug. 21, 1967.
43. See various Labor comments during the debate in *CPD*, HR, Aug. 31, 1967, pp. 673–737, and *CPD*, Senate, Aug. 16, 1967, pp. 38–69, Sept. 6, 1967, pp. 535–589, and Sept. 7, 1967, pp. 607–646, 655–670.
44. *CPD*, Senate, Sept. 7, 1967, pp. 617–618.

Chapter 4. Vietnam and Conscription as Reflections of Labor's Internal Problems

1. For a good résumé of the government parties' propaganda against the ALP's decision-making process relating to Vietnam, see *The Stake Is Freedom* (Canberra: Federal Secretariat, Liberal party of Australia, 1966), section on "The A.L.P. and External Security." For a recent commentary on the ALP's vulnerability to criticisms over organizational problems on another public policy issue, see Henry S. Albinski, *The Australian Labor Party and the Aid to Parochial Schools Controversy* (University Park, Pa.: Penn State Studies Series, 1966). A well balanced account of Labor's programmatic and decision-making traditions may be found in D. W. Rawson, *Labor in Vain?* (Melbourne: Longmans, 1966).
2. For illustrations of the government's public comparison of Calwell, Whitlam, and official party positions on Vietnam-conscription, see Holt, Melbourne *Age*, Nov. 17, 1967, and *Canberra Times*, Nov. 24, 1967.

3. See Melbourne *Age*, Aug. 25, 1966, and John Bennetts in *ibid.*, Nov. 24, 1966; Peter Samuel in *Bulletin*, Sept. 10, 1966.
4. Melbourne *Age*, Sept. 10, 1966, and *Sydney Morning Herald*, Jan. 14, 1967.
5. *Outlook* (Sydney), X (Oct. 1966), 3–4.
6. For instance, see Brian Buckley in *Bulletin*, Sept. 3, 1966, and John Bennetts, Melbourne *Age*, Nov. 28, 1966.
7. See Ian Fitchett, *Sydney Morning Herald*, Nov. 30, Dec. 7 and 8, 1966, and John Bennetts, Melbourne *Age*, Dec. 6, 1966.
8. *Sydney Morning Herald*, Dec. 24, 1966, and Jan. 10 and 19, 1967.
9. *Australian*, Jan. 10, 1967.
10. See an analysis in depth of Whitlam's victory in Brian Johns, *Sydney Morning Herald*, Feb. 11, 1967.
11. *Ibid.*, Feb. 27, 1967.
12. *Australian*, March 2, 1967.
13. *Ibid.*, April 21 and May 11, 1967.
14. Melbourne *Age*, June 16, 1967.
15. Ian Fitchett, *Sydney Morning Herald*, July 24, 1967.
16. See accounts in *Australian*, March 2 and 4, 1967; Melbourne *Age*, March 10, 1967; Alan Reid in *Bulletin*, March 11, 1967.
17. *A.L.P. News*, March 25, 1967; *Outlook*, XI (April 1967), 19.
18. *Sydney Morning Herald*, March 31, 1967; Erich Walsh in *Nation*, April 8, 1967; *Bulletin*, April 8, 1967.
19. *Sydney Morning Herald*, May 27 and June 2 and 8, 1967; Melbourne *Age*, June 2, 1967.
20. Melbourne *Age*, June 3, 1967.
21. *Ibid.*, June 9, 1967.
22. See a résumé of Whitlam's reorganization plans in Jonathan Gaul, *Canberra Times*, Aug. 8, 1967.
23. His speeches before the Victorian, South Australian, and New South Wales conferences are reproduced in *Towards a National Party with a National Purpose: Let Us Begin Now!*, 1967.
24. See Michelle Grattan, "The Benson Affair," *Australian Quarterly*, XXXIX (Sept. 1967), 20–37.
25. For some comments on the Whitlam-Victorian confrontation, see Geoffrey Barker, Melbourne *Age*, June 13, 1967, and Ian Fitchett, *Sydney Morning Herald*, June 15, 1967.
26. Adelaide *Advertiser*, Aug. 2, 1967. For an excellent summary of the conference forces which contended over party reorganization, see Brian Johns, *Clarion* (Sydney), Aug. 9, 1967.
27. For illustrations of these party trends, see remarks of returning ALP Vietnam visitors in Melbourne *Age*, July 18 and Aug. 18, 1966, and Len Reynolds, *A.L.P. News*, Aug. 23, 1966. Also see the interpretation by Alan Reid, *Bulletin*, Aug. 13, 1966.
28. For instance, *Australian*, Nov. 29 and Dec. 6, 1966, and *Australian Worker*, Nov. 30, 1966.
29. Tom Truman, *Ideological Groups in the Australian Labor Party and Their Attitudes* (Brisbane: University of Queensland Press, 1965), University of Queensland Papers, Department of History and Political Science, I, No. 2, 70–72.
30. *Australian*, July 29, 1967.
31. Letter to *Bulletin*, June 17, 1967, from various Victorians.
32. *Sydney Morning Herald*, June 17, 1967, and *Canberra Times*, July 29, 1967.
33. Melbourne *Age*, Aug. 4, 1967.

34. *Ibid.*, and Brisbane *Courier-Mail*, Aug. 4, 1967.
35. *Canberra Times*, Aug. 24, 1967.
36. See Colin A. Hughes, "The Capricornia By-Election," *Australian Quarterly*, XXXIX (Dec. 1967), 7–20.
37. *Sydney Morning Herald*, Nov. 24, 1967.
38. For instance, *Canberra Times*, Feb. 8 and 9, 1968, and Melbourne *Age*, Feb. 15, 1968.
39. *Australian*, Feb. 9, 1968.
40. *Canberra Times*, Feb. 19, 1968.
41. For some interpretations of this view, see Alan Reid in *Bulletin*, Oct. 28 and Dec. 9, 1967, and Jonathan Gaul, *Canberra Times*, Nov. 20, 1967.
42. *Sydney Morning Herald*, Dec. 2, 1967, and Melbourne *Age*, Jan. 2 and Feb. 15, 1968.
43. See *Australian*, Feb. 20 and April 11, 1968.
44. *Ibid.*, Oct. 16, 1967.
45. Melbourne *Age*, Feb. 13, 1968.
46. *Ibid.*, March 25, 1968.
47. *Canberra Times*, April 20, 1968.
48. See Whitlam's explanation of his position in a letter addressed to all ALP federal caucus members, *ibid.*, April 25, 1968.
49. See Cairns's letter to all ALP federal caucus members, *ibid.*, April 27, 1968.
50. Melbourne *Age*, March 7, 1968.
51. *Canberra Times*, April 4, 1968.
52. Alan Ramsey, *Australian*, April 24, 1968. Also see Melbourne *Age*, March 27, 1968; David Solomon in *Australian*, April 20, 1968; Jonathan Gaul in *Canberra Times*, April 30, 1968.
53. *Australian*, May 4 and 8, 1968.

Chapter 5. Organized Public Protest Activity: General Characteristics

1. For background material and commentaries on the Peace Council–Peace Congress movement, see Harold Crouch, *The Melbourne Peace Movement* (Melbourne: *Dissent* Pamphlet, 1963); Denis Strangman, "The Peace Movement," *Social Survey*, XIII (Oct. 1964), 261–263, XIII (Nov. 1964), 293–295, and XIV (Feb. 1965), 21–23; Billy Snedden (attorney general), *CPD*, HR, Sept. 3, 1964, pp. 969–972; *Bulletin*, Nov. 7, 1964.
2. *Statement of Aims of S.O.S.*, mimeographed.
3. AICD (N.S.W.) *Constitution*, p. ii.
4. AICD (N.S.W.), *Vietnam: How Can This Agony Be Ended*, 1966.
5. *News Weekly*, July 12, 1967.
6. See editorial, *Vietnam Action*, I (July 1967), 2.
7. Advertisement in *Australian*, April 4, 1968. Similarly, see Vietnam Mobilization Committee (Sydney), *World Mobilisation . . . to End the War in Vietnam*, April 18, 1968, mimeographed.
8. Campaign for Peace in Vietnam brochure, no title (1967), p. 4.
9. *Canberra Times*, Feb. 8, 1968.
10. For examples of Australian materials, see University Study Group on Vietnam, *Vietnam and Australia* (Gladesville, N.S.W.: University Study Group on Vietnam, 1966); Peace in Vietnam Association, *Vietnam: Points of View* (1967); Harold Levien, *Vietnam: Myth and Reality* (Rose Bay, N.S.W.: Published by the author, 1967).
11. Alma Scaysbrook, *A Mother Speaks*, mimeographed.
12. *Canberra Times*, Feb. 14, 1968.

13. For a highly entertaining account of the mood of the 1967 October Mobilization Rally, see Claire Wagner in *Nation*, Nov. 4, 1967.
14. AICD *News Letter*, Dec. 1966.
15. *Viet Protest News* (Vietnam Day Committee, Victoria), Vol. I, No. 10.
16. AICD *News Letter*, May 1967.
17. AICD (N.S.W.), *Secretary's Report to Annual General Meeting*, June 1967, pp. 3–4, mimeographed.
18. For recent exposition of the CPA's orientation and popular front tactics, see Fred Wells, "The Left Coalition," *Quadrant*, XI (May–June 1967), 57–62; Rex Mortimer, "Communists and the Australian Left," *New Left Review*, No. 4 (Nov.–Dec. 1967), pp. 45–53; " 'New Look' C.P.A.," *Current Affairs Bulletin*, XL (Sept. 25, 1967), 131–144.
19. Richard Dixon, "Issues in Labor Conflict," *Australian Left Review* (Feb.–March 1967), pp. 38, 39.
20. Campaign for Peace in Vietnam, *The Campaign Needs Money!*, mimeographed.
21. AICD *News Letter*, Dec. 1967.
22. Brian Johns, *Sydney Morning Herald*, April 15, 1966. For a similar conclusion, see *Bulletin*, March 26, 1966.
23. *AGP*, No. 188, Feb. 4, 1967.
24. *Ibid.*, Nos. 1981–2002, June–Nov. 1967.
25. *Ibid.*, No. 190, May 19, 1967.
26. *Ibid.*, No. 194, Nov. 18, 1967.
27. *Ibid.*, No. 192, Sept. 22, 1967.
28. AICD *News Letter*, Dec. 1967.
29. *Ibid.*
30. K. J. Morris, *CPD*, Senate, March 30, 1966, p. 340.
31. For instance, see comments on ARM organization in Peter Samuel, *Bulletin*, Dec. 2, 1967; Brisbane *Courier-Mail*, Sept. 11, 1967.
32. *AGP*, No. 187, Nov. 18, 1966.
33. *Sydney Morning Herald*, Oct. 31, 1967.
34. AICD *News Letter*, Dec. 1967.

Chapter 6. The Churches, Veterans, and Vietnam-Conscription

1. Australian Quaker Peace Committee, *Possible Solution to Vietnam* (n.d.). Also see letter to prime minister of April 21, 1967, signed by Mrs. Jean Richards, convener, and statement of January 8, 1968, mimeographed.
2. Fellowship of Reconciliation—Sydney Branch, *The Federal Elections and Christian Conscience*, 1966. Also see press conference statement of March 7, 1968, mimeographed.
3. Bishop G. F. Cranswick, Hobart *Mercury*, Aug. 21, 1966.
4. Bishop K. J. Clements, *Canberra Times*, Aug. 7, 1967.
5. Archbishop George Appleton, *Australian*, April 11, 1966.
6. Archbishop Phillip Strong, *ibid.*, April 17, 1967.
7. C. F. Gribble, William Young, A. W. Stephenson, and Phillip Strong, respectively, *Sydney Morning Herald*, June 9, 1967.
8. *Vietnam: Exchange of Letters between the Prime Minister . . . and the Rt. Rev. J. S. Moyes . . . and Certain Archbishops and Bishops* (Canberra: Prime Minister's Department, 1965).
9. Melbourne *Age*, Oct. 13, 1967.
10. *Ibid.*, Oct. 18, 1967.
11. *Sydney Morning Herald*, Oct. 13, 1967.

12. *Ibid.*
13. *Australian,* Oct. 4, 1967.
14. *Sydney Morning Herald,* April 22, 1966.
15. Melbourne *Age,* Oct. 23, 1967.
16. Graham Williams in *Australian,* Feb. 19, 1968; Melbourne *Age,* March 9, 1968.
17. *AGP,* No. 185, Sept. 17, 1966.
18. *Ibid.,* No. 188, Feb. 4, 1967.
19. *Ibid.,* No. 194, Nov. 18, 1967.
20. *Sydney Morning Herald,* Nov. 21, 1958.
21. *News Weekly,* April 22, 1959.
22. Melbourne *Age,* Nov. 17, 1966. For a discussion of Fox's remarks, see *Catholic Worker* (Melbourne), Dec. 1966–Jan. 1967.
23. M. J. Charlesworth, Melbourne *Age,* April 14, 1967.
24. Catholics for Peace (N.S.W.), *Statement of Name, Objects, Methods, By-Laws and Other Terms,* mimeographed.
25. *Pax Newsletter* (Victoria), July 1967. Also see *Australian,* Dec. 21, 1966.
26. See "Marxist-Christian Dialogue," by various authors, *Australian Left Review,* No. 6 (Dec. 1967), pp. 7–27; *Bulletin,* Nov. 4, 1967.
27. *Catholic Worker,* Aug. 1967.
28. See Brian Johns, *Sydney Morning Herald,* Aug. 23, 1967.
29. For a critique of Catholic radicalism, see Patrick Morgan, "Varieties of Political Catholicism," *Quadrant,* XI (Sept.–Oct. 1967), 41–54.
30. Ian Moffitt and Graham Williams, *Australian,* Sept. 19, 1967.
31. For instance, Dennis Kenny, "A Moral Estimate of the U.S. and Australian Commitment in Vietnam," Roger Pryke, "Catholics and War," and John Burnheim, "The Morality of Conscientious Objection," in *Catholics for Peace,* speeches delivered at St. John's College, University of Sydney, at the Forum on Catholics–War–Vietnam, June 18, 1967, mimeographed; Dennis Kenny, "Catholics and War," *Catholic Worker,* April 1967.
32. Brian Johns, *Sydney Morning Herald,* Aug. 23, 1967; *Australian,* Nov. 29, 1967.
33. See an account of the proceedings in "Religion Today" column, *Australian,* April 17, 1967. For the text of the bishops' statement, see *Catholic Weekly* (Sydney), April 13, 1967.
34. For example, Fox, *Advocate* (Melbourne), Dec. 7, 1967.
35. *Bulletin,* Nov. 4, 1967.
36. Allan Barnes, Melbourne *Age,* Oct. 9, 1967.
37. For recent expressions, see *Catholic Weekly,* Oct. 26, 1967, and *Advocate,* Feb. 8, 1968.
38. *AGP,* No. 188, Feb. 4, 1967.
39. *Ibid.,* No. 190, May 19, 1967.
40. *Ibid.,* No. 194, Nov. 18, 1967.
41. *Ibid.,* No. 198, June 22, 1968.
42. Denis P. Altman, "Foreign Policy and the Elections," *Politics,* II (May 1967), 64–65.
43. *AGP,* No. 187, Nov. 18, 1966.
44. *Ibid.,* No. 194, Nov. 18, 1967.
45. *The Record* (Perth), Jan. 4, 1968.
46. *Australian,* July 28, 1967.
47. For a discussion of ACFOA activities and a listing and description of Australian private aid organizations, see Australian Council for Overseas Aid, *Not by Governments Alone* (Melbourne: ACFOA, 1967). Vietnamese aid

activities are described in ACFOA, *Aid to South Vietnam* (1968?).

48. Wire from Harvey Perkins, secretary of Inter-Church Aid, *Canberra Times,* Sept. 4, 1967. Also see *ibid.,* Aug. 28 and Sept. 28, 1967; *Australian,* Aug. 28, 1967.
49. Melbourne *Age,* Feb. 20, 1968.
50. *Sydney Morning Herald,* March 9, 1968.
51. For general treatments of the RSL, see G. L. Kristianson, *The Politics of Patriotism* (Canberra: Australian National University Press, 1966), and "The 'R.S.L.,'" *Current Affairs Bulletin,* XXXV (April 26, 1965), 178–191.
52. Returned Services League, *50th Annual Report* (Canberra: RSL National Executive, 1966), p. 27.
53. For recent expressions, see Sir Arthur Lee, national president, *Sydney Morning Herald,* Aug. 23, 1967; Sir William Yeo, New South Wales president, *Australian,* Oct. 25, 1967.
54. Returned Services League, *51st Annual Report* (Canberra: RSL National Executive, 1967), p. 21.
55. Returned Services League, *National President's Interim Report,* Appendix G, 1967, mimeographed, pp. 7–8.
56. *Canberra Times,* Feb. 14, 1968.
57. For a review of the situation, see *Sydney Morning Herald,* June 3, 1967; *Bulletin,* June 17, 1967.
58. *Canberra Times,* Aug. 17, 1967.
59. *Ibid.,* Aug. 18, 1967.

Chapter 7. Vietnamese Protest among Academics, Artists, and University Students

1. Vincent Buckley, "Intellectuals," in Peter Coleman, ed., *Australian Civilization* (Melbourne: F. W. Cheshire, 1962), p. 99.
2. Donald Horne, *The Lucky Country* (Baltimore: Penguin Books, 1965), p. 195.
3. Craig McGregor, *Profile of Australia* (Chicago: Henry Regnery, 1967), p. 277.
4. For a general statement about the place of intellectuals in political life, see "Intellectuals—and Politics," *Current Affairs Bulletin,* XL (Aug. 28, 1967), 99–110. For general reflections on changes in Australian university life, see P. H. Partridge, "The University System" and "The State of the Universities," in E. L. French, ed., *Melbourne Studies in Education 1960–61* (Melbourne: Melbourne University Press, 1962), pp. 51–71 and 72–94, respectively. At least some of Partridge's remarks are aimed at redressing the quite uncomplimentary picture of Australian universities painted by A. P. Rowe, *If the Gown Fits* (Melbourne: Melbourne University Press, 1960).
5. Australian Council for Overseas Aid, *Aid to South Vietnam.*
6. *Sydney Morning Herald,* Aug. 19, 1967; *Catholic Worker,* Sept. 1967.
7. "Statement on the War in Vietnam by Australian Scientists," *Australian Journal of Science,* XXX (Nov. 1967), xlvi–xlvii. Also see *Canberra Times,* Nov. 28, 1967.
8. Melbourne *Herald,* Oct. 5, 1966.
9. *Australian,* Nov. 10, 1966.
10. Tasmania University Union, *Survey of Student and Staff Opinion on the Issues of Vietnam and Conscription,* 1967.
11. See *Sydney Morning Herald,* Oct. 14, 1967. For a comparable expression by

artists in another state, see Queensland Peace Committee for International Co-operation and Disarmament *Newsletter*, Nov. 1967.

12. *Australian*, Nov. 18, 1967; Melbourne *Age*, Dec. 2, 1967; *Peacemaker* (Melbourne), Federal Pacifist Council of Australia, Jan. 1968.
13. For a description, see Melbourne *Age*, Nov. 11, 1967.
14. See Keith Thomas in *Nation*, Feb. 17, 1968; Ian Morrison in *Outlook*, XII (April 1968), 23.
15. From Campaign for Peace in Vietnam, Royal South Australian Society of Arts exhibition, Dec. 1967–Jan. 1968, "Artists on War."
16. Patrick McCaughey, Melbourne *Age*, Oct. 25, 1967.
17. Brisbane *Courier-Mail*, Sept. 9, 1967.
18. *Australian*, April 1, 1968.
19. Melbourne *Age*, Sept. 9 and 19, 1967.
20. For a review of cases heard where Vietnam opposition was claimed as a basis for conscientious objection, see *Peacemaker*, Jan. 1968.
21. *Australian*, Oct. 18, 1967, and Ian Moffitt in *ibid.*, Feb. 28, 1968.
22. Melbourne *Age*, Oct. 6, 1966.
23. National Union of Australian University Students, *Report of the National Affairs Committee to National Council—February 1968*; *Canberra Times*, Feb. 14, 1968.
24. See *Woroni* (Australian National University Students' Representative Council newspaper), April 4, 1968.
25. See Francis James's own account in *Nation*, Sept. 9, 1967.
26. Melbourne *Age*, Aug. 1, 1967; *Canberra Times*, Aug. 3, 1967; Don Hewett in *Australian*, Aug. 19, 1967.
27. *Australian*, Oct. 19 and Nov. 18, 1967.
28. *Canberra Times*, Aug. 15, 1967.
29. Melbourne *Age*, Sept. 7 and 9, 1967.
30. Hasluck, *Current Notes on International Affairs*, XXXVIII (Sept. 1967), 388, and *CPD, HR*, Sept. 19, 1967, p. 1032.
31. *Canberra Times*, Feb. 19, 1968. Also see *Bulletin*, Feb. 17, 1968.
32. C. N. and F. M. Katz, "Changes in Students at University," *Vestes*, VIII (March 1965), 14.
33. Tony Staley, "Student Activists: Rebels and Alfs," *Politics*, II (Nov. 1967), 157–158.
34. University of Sydney Students' Representative Council, *S.R.C. Student Opinion Survey 1967*.
35. Ian Moffitt in *Australian*, Feb. 26, 1968.
36. See letters from J. B. Sissons and George Brzotowski to *Canberra Times*, Aug. 8 and 10, 1967, respectively.
37. Alan Jarman, *CPD, HR*, Oct. 4 and 5, 1967, p. 1729. For other votes in the Monash Labor Club on the aid issue, see Melbourne *Age*, Aug. 1, 1967.
38. Warren Osmond, "Shock Therapy," *Dissent* (Spring 1967), p. 31.
39. See *Woroni*, June 22, 1967; *National U* (National Union of Australian University Students newspaper), June 30, 1967; *Bulletin*, June 24, 1967. For an exchange on the appropriateness of NUAUS spokesmanship on Vietnam-conscription, see Patrick Morgan and John Bannon, *National U*, April 1, 1968. For some general remarks about student politics and political interests, see "The University Student '67," *Current Affairs Bulletin*, XXXIX (March 13, 1967), esp. 125–127.
40. Staley, *op. cit.*, p. 158.
41. Michael Hyde and others, from "Which Way Treason?" *Vietnam Action*, I (Nov. 1967), 3.

42. ANU Labor Club Manifesto, in *Woroni*, Aug. 3, 1967.
43. Ian Moffitt in *Australian*, Feb. 26, 1968.
44. *Student Guerrilla* (University of Queensland, Society for Democratic Action), April 16, 1968.
45. Students for a Democratic Society, University of Sydney, *Students for a Democratic Society—Year II—1968*, mimeographed.
46. *National U*, June 10, 1968.
47. Terry Counihan, "The Student Pseudo-Left," *National U*, July 28, 1967.
48. Helen Hall, "Problems of the Student Left," *ibid.*, Sept. 4, 1967.
49. The Melbourne and Sydney results are contained in University of Melbourne, Students' Representative Council, Student Action Council, *Student Opinion on National Service—A Conscription Referendum*, 1966. Cited hereafter as *Conscription Referendum*.
50. University of Sydney, Students' Representative Council, *S.R.C. Student Opinion Survey 1967*.
51. Tasmania University Union, *Survey of Student and Staff Opinion on the Issues of Vietnam and Conscription*, 1967.
52. *AGP*, No. 189, March 17, 1967.
53. *Ibid.*, No. 197, April 1968.
54. *Conscription Referendum*.
55. Jocelyn Clarke, "Young Workers and Politics," *Politics*, II (Nov. 1967), 171.
56. *AGP*, No. 187, Nov. 18, 1966.
57. *Ibid.*, No. 185, Sept. 17, 1966.
58. *Ibid.*, No. 190, May 19, 1967.
59. *Ibid.*, Nos. 1981–2002, June–Nov. 1967, and No. 187, Nov. 18, 1966.
60. J. S. Western and P. R. Wilson, "Attitudes to Conscription," *Politics*, II (May 1967), 54.
61. *Conscription Referendum*.
62. *AGP*, No. 189, March 17, 1967.
63. *Ibid.*, No. 197, April 1968.
64. *Conscription Referendum*.
65. Melbourne *Age*, Aug. 2, 1967.
66. For summaries, see *Semper Floreat* (University of Queensland newspaper), Sept. 15, 1967; *National U*, Sept. 29, 1967; *Nation*, Sept. 23 and Nov. 4, 1967. For a general review of the problem, see Colin Hughes, "Marching Rule in Brisbane," *Quadrant*, XI (Nov.–Dec. 1967), 29–34.
67. Melbourne *Age*, Sept. 19, 1967.
68. Seymour Martin Lipset, "Students and Politics in Comparative Perspective," *Daedalus*, XCVIII (Winter 1968), 4.
69. Colin A. Hughes and John S. Western, *The Prime Minister's Policy Speech* (Canberra: Australian National University Press, 1966), pp. 114–115.
70. On developments among Australian university students generally, see the set of articles by John Hallows, *Australian*, June 13, 14, and 15, 1968.

Chapter 8. Some Observations on the Australian Political Process: Party Politics, Foreign Policy, and Civil Liberties

1. Maximilian Walsh, *Australian Financial Review*, May 10, 1968.
2. Alan Ramsey, *Australian*, April 3, 1968.
3. For reviews of this reassessment, see Jonathan Gaul, *Canberra Times*, May 11, 1968; Hugh Armfield, Melbourne *Age*, May 11, 1968; Alan Ramsey, *Australian*, May 13, 1968.

4. For instance, Wallace Brown, Brisbane *Courier-Mail*, May 11, 1968, and Herschel Hurst, Melbourne *Sun*, May 15, 1968.
5. Alan Reid, *Bulletin*, June 8, 1968. For Gorton's own impressions of the American trip, see *Canberra Times*, June 3, 1968.
6. *New York Times*, June 12, 1968; Melbourne *Age*, June 12, 1968.
7. Douglas McCallum, "The State of Liberty," in Peter Coleman, ed., *Australian Civilization* (Melbourne: F. W. Cheshire, 1962), p. 29.
8. Jeanne MacKenzie, *Australian Paradox* (London: MacGibbon and Kee, 1962), p. 154.
9. A. G. L. Shaw, "The Old Tradition," in Coleman, ed., *op. cit.*, pp. 23–24, and McCallum, "The State of Liberty," *ibid.*, pp. 45–46.
10. See Ernest Scott, *Australia during the War* (Sydney: Angus and Robertson, 1938), esp. pp. 57–104.
11. See Paul Hasluck, *The Government and the People 1939–1941* (Canberra: Australian War Memorial, 1952), pp. 174–187.
12. John Douglas Pringle, *Australian Accent* (London: Chatto and Windus, 1958), pp. 43–44.
13. Russel Ward, *The Australian Legend* (Melbourne: Oxford University Press, 1958), p. 239.
14. Geoffrey Sawer, *Australian Government Today* (Melbourne: Melbourne University Press, 1964), pp. 108–109.
15. Enid Campbell, "Australian Democracy and Political Opposition," in Richard A. Preston, ed., *Contemporary Australia* (Durham, N. C.: Duke University Press, 1969). The most comprehensive survey of the law and civil liberties generally is contained in Enid Campbell and Harry Whitmore, *Freedom in Australia* (Sydney: Sydney University Press, 1966).
16. Hasluck, *op. cit.*, pp. 177–178.
17. *AGP*, Nos. 690–699, June–July 1950.
18. *Ibid.*, Nos.1872–1883, Dec. 1965–Jan. 1966, and No. 188, Feb. 4, 1967.
19. *Ibid.*, No. 194, Nov. 18, 1967.
20. *Ibid.*, Nos. 1804–1819, Feb.–March 1965.
21. Athol A. Congalton, *Occupational Status in Australia*, University of New South Wales *Studies in Sociology*, No. 3 (Kensington, N.S.W.: School of Sociology, University of New South Wales, 1963).
22. *AGP*, Nos. 1852–1871, Sept.–Dec. 1965.
23. *Ibid.*, No. 193, Nov. 4, 1967.
24. A. F. Davies and S. Encel, "Politics," in Davies and Encel, eds., *Australian Society* (Melbourne: F. W. Cheshire, 1965), p. 109.
25. Monash University Students Representative Council, *Facts About the Anti LBJ Demonstration* (1966?), p. 2.
26. YCAC *News Letter*, Sept. 1966.
27. AICD *News Letter*, April 1966.
28. Alf Dowsley in *National U*, Sept. 29, 1967.
29. Melbourne *Age*, May 7, 1968.
30. *Canberra Times*, May 31, 1968, and Jonathan Gaul in *ibid.*, June 4, 1968; *Australian*, June 8, 1968.
31. Denis Lovegrove, *Victorian Parliamentary Debates*, Legislative Assembly, Dec. 1, 1966, pp. 2508–2509.
32. T. W. Mitchell, *ibid.*, Dec. 7, 1966, p. 2801.
33. *Ibid.*, p. 2800.
34. B. J. Dixon, *ibid.*, Dec. 6, 1966, pp. 2649, 2650.
35. Melbourne *Age*, July 28, 1967.
36. L. Thompson, *Canberra Times*, July 28, 1967.

37. Melbourne *Age*, July 29 and Aug. 4 and 9, 1967.
38. *Canberra Times*, Aug. 17 and 22, 1967.
39. For a review of the problem, see *Victorian Parliamentary Debates*, Legislative Assembly, esp. Sept. 7, 1966, pp. 95–98, and Sept. 13, 1966, pp. 150–165; Melbourne *Age*, Sept. 5, 10, and 20, 1966.
40. For an account, see *Nation*, Oct. 21, 1967.
41. *Canberra Times*, Nov. 28, 1967.
42. Christopher Forsyth in *Australian*, March 30, 1968. Also see *Sydney Morning Herald*, March 14, 1968.
43. *CPD*, HR, May 15, 1968, p. 1433.
44. *New York Times*, June 11, 1968.
45. *Canberra Times*, June 10, 1968.
46. Australian, Oct. 28, 1967. Also *ibid.*, Nov. 10, 1967. For an earlier and similar explanation by Snedden, see *CPD*, HR, March 1, 1967, p. 220.
47. For a succinct review of the legal inconveniences of applying the Crimes Act, see John Wheeldon, *CPD*, Senate, Aug. 16, 1967, pp. 50–51.
48. See the report in Sydney *Daily Telegraph*, Aug. 23, 1967.
49. See Richard L'Estrange in *Nation*, March 30, 1968.
50. Melbourne *Age*, March 19, 1968.
51. For an illustration of the dialogue between NUAUS and the government on National Service provisions and practices, see National Union of Australian University Students, *Report of the National Affairs Officer to Annual Council—February 1968, passim.*
52. Leslie Bury, minister for labor and national service, *CPD*, HR, May 1, 1968.
53. For typical Labor commentaries, see Whitlam, *ibid.*, May 15, 1968, pp. 1461–1466; Barnard, *ibid.*, May 15, 1968, pp. 1440–1448.
54. Melbourne *Age*, May 16 and 23, 1968; *Bulletin*, June 8, 1968.
55. Nigel Bowen, attorney general, *CPD*, HR, May 14, 1968, pp. 1386–1388.
56. *Sydney Morning Herald*, June 30, 1965.
57. *Nation*, Aug. 21, 1965.
58. *CPD*, HR, March 15, 1966, p. 246.
59. *Ibid.*, March 31, 1966, p. 797.
60. *Canberra Times*, Oct. 11, 1967.
61. *CPD*, HR, May 15, 1968, pp. 1461–1466.
62. *Canberra Times*, April 29, 1968.
63. Melbourne *Age*, May 16, 1968.
64. *Ibid.*, May 9, 1968.
65. For illustrations of servicemen's reactions to student collections on behalf of the NLF, see Adelaide *Advertiser*, Aug. 11 and 15, 1967.
66. For instance, see remarks by Lionel Murphy, ALP Senate leader, Melbourne *Age*, Aug. 3, 1967, and by Sam Cohen, deputy Senate leader, *Canberra Times*, Sept. 18, 1967. Also see "Tipping Talking" column in Melbourne *Herald*, Aug. 5, 1967.
67. *AGP*, No. 192, Sept. 22, 1967.

Chapter 9. The Australian Public and Vietnam-Conscription: Some Measures of Interest, Opinion, and Electoral Behavior

1. *AGP*, No. 195, Dec. 23, 1967.
2. *Ibid.*, Nos. 1789–1803, Oct.–Nov. 1964.
3. J. S. Western and Colin A. Hughes, "The Mass Media: A Preliminary Report," *Politics*, II (Nov. 1967), 198.

4. Denis P. Altman, "Foreign Policy and the Elections," *Politics*, II (May 1967), 63–64.
5. *AGP*, No. 185, Sept. 17, 1966.
6. *Ibid.*, No. 187, Nov. 18, 1966.
7. *Ibid.*, No. 194, Nov. 18, 1967.
8. For relevant data, see *ibid.*, Nos. 1789–1803, Oct.–Nov. 1964; Nos. 1900–1915, May–July 1966; No. 184, July 16, 1966; No. 187, Nov. 18, 1966; No. 194, Nov. 18, 1967. For further elaborations on conscription opinion, see J. S. Western and P. R. Wilson, "Attitudes to Conscription," *Politics*, II (May 1967), 48–56. Some of the categories of Vietnam and conscription opinion data have been grouped by Robert Cooksey, "Australian Opinion and Vietnam Policy," *Dissent*, No. 22 (Autumn 1968), pp. 5–11.
9. *AGP*, Nos. 1820–1835, March–June 1965, and Nos. 1836–1851, July–Sept. 1965.
10. *Ibid.*, No. 184, July 16, 1966; No. 187, Nov. 18, 1966; No. 191, July 29, 1967.
11. *Ibid.*, Nos. 1900–1905, May–July 1966; No. 185, Sept. 17, 1966; No. 190, May 19, 1967.
12. *Ibid.*, Nos. 1884–1899, Feb.–April 1966.
13. *Ibid.*, No. 193, Nov. 4, 1967.
14. *Ibid.*, Nos. 1820–1835, March–June 1965.
15. *Ibid.*, No. 193, Nov. 4, 1967.
16. *Ibid.*, No. 192, Sept. 22, 1967.
17. *Ibid.*, No. 198, June 22, 1968.
18. *Ibid.*, No. 185, Sept. 17, 1966.
19. *Ibid.*, No. 192, Sept. 22, 1967.
20. *Ibid.*, No. 196, Feb. 17, 1968.
21. *Ibid.*, No. 188, Feb. 4, 1967.
22. Drawn from *ibid.*, No. 187, Nov. 18, 1966, and No. 194, Nov. 18, 1967. Comparable results respecting general public support of government policy in 1966 were obtained in special polls commissioned by Labor occupants of the federal Queensland seats of Dawson and Capricornia. See *News Weekly*, June 22 and Oct. 26, 1966.
23. *AGP*, Nos. 1789–1803, Oct.–Nov. 1964.
24. *Ibid.*, No. 184, July 16, 1966.
25. *Ibid.*, No. 187, Nov. 18, 1966.
26. *Ibid.*, No. 194, Nov. 18, 1967.
27. *Ibid.*, No. 187, Nov. 18, 1966.
28. Drawn from *ibid.*, No. 187, Nov. 18, 1966, and No. 194, Nov. 18, 1967.
29. *Ibid.*, Nos. 1884–1899, Feb.–April 1966.
30. Maxwell Newton in *Nation*, May 28, 1966.
31. *AGP*, No. 185, Sept. 17, 1966.
32. *Ibid.*, No. 191, July 29, 1967.
33. *Ibid.*, No. 198, June 22, 1968.
34. Altman, *op. cit.*, p. 65.
35. Drawn from *AGP*, No. 187, Nov. 18, 1966, and No. 194, Nov. 18, 1967.
36. For illustrative analyses of the Senate election, see Alan Ramsey, *Australian*, Nov. 27, 1967, and Rohan Rivett, *Canberra Times*, Nov. 29, 1967.
37. See their remarks in Melbourne *Age*, Nov. 27, 1967.
38. For instance, D. W. Rawson, *Australia Votes* (Melbourne: Melbourne University Press, 1961); Creighton Burns, *Parties and People* (Melbourne: Melbourne University Press, 1961); Robert Alford, *Party and Society* (Chicago: Rand McNally, 1963), pp. 172–218.

Index

Aborigines: assisted by students, 161; civil libertarian concern, 172
Academics: conscription and Vietnam opinion, 146–48; conscription and Vietnam involvement, 145–46; general characteristics, 142–45; political outlook, 143–44; relief aid to Vietnam, 145
Adelaide, University of, scene of mock war crimes tribunal, 149
Advocate (Melbourne), Vietnamese position, 133
Asian studies in universities, 17
American Atrocities in Vietnam, confiscation of in Victoria, 177
American Friends Service Committee declaration endorsed by Australian Quakers, 122
Anglican Church: general Vietnamese views, 126; New South Wales Synod, Vietnamese views, 124; protest manifestations, 123; Victoria Synod, Vietnamese views, 124
ANZAC Pact, 8
ANZUS, 9; defended by ALP, 95
Archives, accessibility of, 21
Artists, Vietnam protest involvement, 148–49
Asia: coverage in press, 12–13; study of in schools and universities, 16–17
Asian languages, study of, 16–17
Asians, Australian contacts with, 10
Association for International Cooperation and Disarmament: assessment of composition, 112; ALP membership dispute, 85–86, 106; electoral involvement, 111–12; general characteristics, 85; L-CP accusation of Communist ties, 184; objectives, 105–6; relation to CPA, 114; report on policy inquiry, 175; as sponsor of peace groups, 107; sponsor of research facilities, 108
Australia-China Society: as foreign policy lobby, 102; as publicist, 16
Australia–Free China Association as publicist, 16
Australia–New Zealand Peace Congress as protagonist of peace causes, 103
Australian (Canberra): criticism of L-CP Vietnam policy, 47; quality newspaper, 12
Australian-American Association as publicist, 16
Australian Association for the United Nations as publicist, 16
Australian Broadcasting Commission: overseas representation, 12; parliamentary broadcasts, 14; television broadcasts, 14–15
Australian Care for Refugees, interdenominational efforts, 136, 137
Australian Catholic Relief, participation in Vietnamese relief, 136–37
Australian Committee of Responsibility for Children of Vietnam, 136; sponsorship of *Childermas,* 148
Australian Congress for International Cooperation and Disarmament as protagonist of peace causes, 103
Australian Council for Civil Liberties, World War II role, 172
Australian Council for Overseas Aid, 135–36
Australian Council of Churches: conscription and Vietnamese views, 124; cooperation in Vietnamese relief, 136–37; reaction to conscription violation regulations, 187
Australian Council of Trade Unions, denunciation of ship ban, 84
Australian Friends of Vietnam, pro-Vietnam position, 138–39
Australian Institute of International Affairs as publicist, 15–16

Australian Institute of Political Science as publicist, 16
Australian Journal of Science, source of academic protest petition, 146, 178
Australian Labor party: accused of unpatriotism, 72–73; accused of unfair electoral tactics, 60–61; affected by Vietnam-conscription, 164–65; aid to parochial schools difficulties, 27; attacked by L-CP for Vietnamese troop policy, 51–53; attacks on L-CP conscription violation regulations, 185; bill of rights advocacy, 188–89; bipartisanship in foreign policy, 34; Catholic Church relations, 127–28, 132; Catholic opinion presence, 126–27, 133, 134; civil aid to Vietnam assessment, 44; civil liberties record, 170, 172; consequences for of electoral behavior, 203–7; conscript troops in Vietnam outlook, 42–43; conscription attitudes, 6–7, 90–91, 93; conscription issue during World War I, 22–23; criticisms of conscription violation procedures, 182; criticisms of decision-making structure, 78; criticized by L-CP for conscription violation outlook, 185–86; criticized by L-CP for playing politics with Vietnam, 64; criticized for peace movement involvement, 118; electoral criticisms of from 1949, 26–27; external Communism attitudes, 35; L-CP Vietnamese policy criticism, 44–45; Malayan troop commitment attitude, 35; Mannix's criticisms, 128; opposition to revising Vietnam policy, 92; overseas service conscription outlook, 40; as part of CPA peace tactics, 114; peace group membership supplier, 116–18; postwar domestic policies, 24; postwar international outlook, 9; potential for support if reconstructed, 202; public reception of Vietnam-conscription policy, 198–99, 201; reaction to Foreign Affairs Committee, 21–22; reactions to handling of Chinese trade, 69, 70–72; rebukes L-CP for playing politics with Vietnam, 62–68; relationship to academics, 143–44; split, 26; supporters' Vietnam-conscription attitudes, 200; supporters' view of leaders, 201; Tasmanian academic opinion of policies, 147–48; traditional policy orientations, 6; United States alliance outlook, 49–50; as vehicle for instituting Vietnam policy change, 111, 113; Vietnam policy, 90, 93; Vietnamese conflict assessment, 37–39, 44; Vietnamese settlement outlook, 46–50; view of politicians, 19; views on domestic impact of Vietnam, 44; wartime external policies, 8–9
——External Affairs and Defense Committee: composition, 83; recommendations for policy alterations, 92–93
——Federal Conference: general characteristics, 77–78; structural reforms, 90; *1955,* party split, 26; *1957,* SEATO declaration, 35; *1959,* SEATO declaration, 35–36; *1963,* SEATO declaration, 36; *1967,* conscription policy, 42–43, 93; *1967,* defense policies, 167–68; *1967,* organizational alterations, 90; *1967,* Vietnam policy, 74, 93
——federal executive: clash with Whitlam, 97, 98; general characteristics, 78; structural alterations, 90; threat of use against Whitlam, 81
——New South Wales branch: AICD dispute, 85–86, 106, 118; fear of breakoff from ALP, 81; position on ALP reform, 89, 90
——Queensland branch: position on ALP reform, 89; elite conscription views, 91
——South Australian branch: position on ALP reform, 89
——Tasmanian branch: position on ALP reform, 89, 90
——Victorian branch: position on ALP reform, 89–90; attacks on Whitlam's revisionism, 97–98, 100; Vietnam position, 89
——Western Australian branch, position on ALP reform, 89, 90
Australian National University, Asian and Pacific studies, 17; student Vietnamese position, 154; support for NLF collections, 153
Australian National University Labor Club, news of conventional politics, 155–56
Australian Peace Council, as foreign policy lobby, 103

Australian Red Cross, conveyor of aid to NLF, 73
Australian Reform Movement. *See* Liberal Reform Group
Australian security, threats to, public opinion, 116–17
Australian Security Intelligence Organization, investigations, 175
Australian Student Christian Movement, Vietnam and conscription positions, 151
Australian Students' Labor Federation, aid to NLF decision, 73
Australian Television Network, 15
Australian Volunteers Abroad, nature of, 135; student participation in, 161

Baptists, Vietnamese views, 126
Barnard, Lance, AICD issue position, 86; assumes defense responsibility, 83; elected deputy leader, 82; Vietnamese trip report, 86–87
Barnes, Charles, imputes unpatriotism to ALP, 72–73
Barton, Gordon, on businessmen in LRG, 119; Vietnamese appraisal, 32
Barwick, Sir Garfield, as External Affairs Minister, 25
Batman (Victoria), Benson campaign, 207
Bennetts, John, political assessment of Johnson's Australian visit, 66
Benson, Sam, denounced by Victorian ALP branch, 89; electoral campaign in 1966, 207
Bill of rights, absence of, 169; advocated by ALP, 188–89
Bolte, Sir Henry, concern over NLF fund collections, 176
Boonaroo dispute, 84–86
Bowen, Nigel, on use of Crimes Act against NLF fund collectors, 180
Britain, Australian reliance upon before World War II, 5–6; disengagement from Asia, 165–66, 167, 168
Bulletin, quality magazine, 13
Bundy, William, meets Whitlam, 83
Burnheim, John, conscription position, 131
Bury, Leslie, denunciation of conscription opponents, 185

Cairns, James, allegations against ASIO, 175; attack on party revisionists, 80–81; contests leadership against Whitlam, 98–99; criticism of Johnson's visit to Australia, 66; defeated by Whitlam for leadership, 82; intention to visit North Vietnam, 179–80; Ky visit reaction, 82; opinion on as potential leader, 201; potential support for reconstituted ALP under his direction, 202; Victorian executive membership, 86; Vietnamese position, 98–99
Caldwell, Arthur, appraisal of 1967 Senate election, 205; attack on Ky, 81–82, 116; attack on L-CP conscription policy, 67; attacked by Whitlam for 1966 election behavior, 96; attacks Whitlam's revisionism, 97; attempt to embarrass Whitlam over Ky visit, 82; attempted assassination of, 61; Australian peacemaking mission to Hanoi proposal, 48; conscription opinions, 79; criticism of ALP decision-making during his leadership, 78; criticism of electorate's behavior, 92; criticized for playing politics with Vietnam, 64; demonstrated against at Melbourne, 160; electoral emphasis on Vietnam-conscription, 197–99, 201; federal executive confrontation with Whitlam, 98; object of Whitlam's criticism, 79–80; opinion on as leader, 201; personal attacks on L-CP, 67; political style on Vietnam-conscription, 164; preoccupation with Vietnamese conflict, 49; public recollection of external affairs remarks, 192; response to Johnson's Australian visit, 66; says L-CP would countenance nuclear arms in Vietnam, 72; on use of conscript troops in Vietnam, 42, 43; Victorian executive membership, 86; Vietnamese conflict assessment, 38
Cambodia, sought as conduit for NLF fund collections, 151–52

Foreign investment, 11
Foreign policy: bipartisan aspects, 34; electoral salience, 203–7; parliamentary treatment, 59; public awareness of, 191–93, 208; Vietnam's impact, 165–69
Fox, Bishop Arthur, political position, 128, 132
Fraser, J. M.: Communist ties with peace movement allegation, 185; criticized for impropriety, 65; imputes unpatriotism to ALP, 72; Vietnam debate participation, 15
Freeth, Gordon, denunciation of Communists, 184
Fulbright, William, cited by peace groups, 108; meets Whitlam, 83

Geneva Conference, proposed by ALP for Vietnamese settlement, 48
Gilroy, Norman Cardinal: relations with N.S.W. ALP, 127; sanctions Catholic peace activities, 131
Gorton, John: attack on Whitlam's Vietnamese policy, 52–53; criticism of ALP Vietnam policy, 42; CSIRO members' petition reaction, 178; foreign policy outlook, 167; Higgins by-election role, 95; impatient with dissent, 178; on importance of Vietnam, 37; jeered at electoral meeting, 109–10; on need to persevere in Vietnam, 45; political style on Vietnam-conscription, 164; rebuked for playing politics with Vietnam, 62; size of military commitment in Vietnam views, 41; United States de-escalation policy reaction, 46; visit to United States, 168

Hannaford, D. C., criticism of L-CP handling of aid to NLF issue, 76
Harriman, Averell, meets Whitlam, 83
Hartley, W. H., criticized by Whitlam, 97
Hasluck, Sir Paul: Cambodia-NLF fund collections reactions, 152; as external affairs minister, 25; foreign policy views, 167
Hendrickson, Albion, Vietnamese conflict assessment, 37
Higgins (Victoria) by-election (1968), 95–96, 97
Hit the U.S. Aggression, film subjected to censorship, 177
Hobart Mercury readers' poll, 13
Holt, Harold: attack on Labor Clubs over aid to NLF, 74–75; attacked by Whitlam for 1966 election behavior, 96; Australian Council of Churches request recipient, 124; Corio by-election appraisal, 84; criticism of ALP Vietnam policy, 42; criticized by Calwell for warmongering, 79; criticized by churches for aid to NLF legislation, 137; death of, 95; demonstrated against at Melbourne, 149, 160; demonstrated against at Monash, 149–50; electoral meetings reception, 60; foreign policy outlook, 167; implored to de-escalate Vietnam war, 109; on importance of Vietnam, 37; personally attacked by Calwell, 67; political style on Vietnam-conscription, 163–64; public recollection of external policy remarks, 192; as publicist of Vietnamese conflict, 61; role in 1967 Senate election, 95; on status of politicians, 18; temperamental qualities and projection of Vietnam, 57–59; troop withdrawal from Vietnam objection, 51; unpatriotism charges against ALP, 72; United States policy ties expression, 47; view of Calwell as ALP leader, 79–80
Hughes, William Morris: censorship imposition in World War I, 170; conscription controversy role, 6–7; German New Guinea policy, 6
Hungarian Revolution, object of Protestant protest, 123

Ideology, Australian, 4–5, 33–34; effect of Vietnam-conscription on, 208–9; role of politics, 164
Immigration: policy, 10; Vietnamese children to Australia, 58
Indochinese Crisis: Australian interest in, 9; as electoral issue, 28

Indonesia, independence support from waterside workers, 102
Inter-Church Aid, objection to legislation barring NLF and North Vietnam aid, 137
Inter-Parliamentary Union, parliamentary attendance at, 21
Isaacs (Victoria) opinion survey, 192–93, 203
Isolationism, 7

James, Francis, NLF collections, 151
Japanese Peace Treaty, Australian interest in, 9
Jeparit dispute, 84–86
John XXIII (pope), views endorsed by progressive Catholics, 129
Johnson, Lyndon: bombing halt announcement, 46, 166, 167; bombing halt announcement impact on Australian politics, 53; bombing halt attacked by Vietnam Action Campaign, 106; meeting with Gorton, 168; meets Whitlam, 83; object of demonstrations, 110; promulgates "San Antonio formula," 46; visit to Australia, 65–66, 174
Jones, C. H., views on conventional politics, 156

Keefe, J. B., criticism of Johnson's Australian visit, 65–66
Kennedy, Robert, meets Whitlam, 83
Knox, Archbishop James: audience with Whitlam, 132; position on priests in protest movement, 132
Kooyong (Victoria) by-election (1966), 60
Korean War, Australian involvement in, 9
Ky, Nguyen Cao: visit to Australia, 81–82, 110; public reactions to Australian visit, 116

Labor clubs, aid to NLF controversy, 73–75; merger plans, 157; political outlooks, 155–57
LaTrobe (Victoria) by-election (1960), 28
Lawrence, D. H., on freedom in Australia, 171
Lee Kuan-yew, Vietnamese views, 91
Lee, Sir Arthur, Australian Friends of Vietnam membership, 138–39
Liberal-Country parties: affected by Vietnam-conscription, 165; ALP accusations of demeaning tactics, 60–61; attempts to strengthen conscription legislation, 183–84; bipartisanship in foreign policy, 34; campaign emphases, 25–26; censorship advocacy manifestations, 178; Chinese role in Vietnamese conflict assessment, 41; Chinese trade defense, 69; civil liberties record, 170; consequences for of electoral behavior, 203–7; criticism of ALP for conscription violation outlook, 185–86; criticism of ALP for playing politics with Vietnam, 64; criticism of ALP postwar foreign policy, 24; criticism of ALP Vietnam assessments, 42; criticized by ALP for slavishness to United States policy, 47–48, 50–51; criticized for approach to protest activity, 186–87; criticized for playing politics with Vietnam, 62–68; external Communism outlook, 34; on need to persevere in Vietnam, 51–53; overseas service conscription justification, 39–40; potential support for if ALP reconstituted, 202; protest demonstration views, 184–85; Tasmanian academic opinion of policies, 147–48; unpatriotism imputation to ALP, 72–73; Vietnamese conflict assessment, 36–37, 38–39, 41–42, 45–46
Liberal Reform Group: composition, 119; electoral participation, 111; electoral support for on external affairs issues, 205–7; foreign and defense policy outlook, 55–56; general characteristics, 54–55, 118–19; Vietnamese conflict assessment, 55; Vietnamese conflict interest, 31–32

McMahon, William, expression of ties with United States policy, 47
McManus, Francis, on aid to NLF, 73–74
Malayan Emergency, Australian involvement in, 9
Malayan troop commitment, ALP attitude toward, 35
Malaysian troop commitment, as electoral issue, 29
Malaysian Borneo, Australian troop commitment, 41
Mannix, Archbishop Daniel: anti-ALP activity, 127–28; conscription attitudes, 22–23
Mansfield, Mike, meets Whitlam, 83
Melbourne *Age*: grade of readership, 18; on need to protect civil liberties, 187; on propriety of L-CP behavior, 186; readers' poll, 13; Vietnamese relief drive, 136
Melbourne Labor Club, NLF fund collection controversy, 152
Melbourne, University of: demonstration against Calwell, 160; demonstration against Holt, 149, 160; conscription and Vietnam student survey, 157–58; object of state government concern, 176–77; student activist survey, 154–55; student circumvention of NLF collection ban, 181–82; student partisan preferences, 159, 160
Menzies, Sir Robert: Communist ties with peace movements allegation, 184; international affairs approach, 25; overseas service conscription justification, 39–40; political style, 25; recipient of protest letter from Protestant clergymen, 123; temperamental qualities and projection of Vietnam, 57; on Vietnamese negotiations, 47
Methodist church: as foreign policy lobby, 102; general Vietnamese views, 125–26; New South Wales conference, Vietnamese views, 124; Victoria conference, Vietnamese views, 124
Monash Labor Club: membership, 153–54; NLF fund collection controversy, 151–52, 156; outlook toward ALP, 155
Monash University: NLF fund collections, 73; object of state government concern, 176–77; ostracism of students of, 188; protests against Holt, 149–50; student circumvention of NLF collection ban, 181–82; student civil liberty protests, 161; student protests, 150
Moomba Festival as occasion for peace demonstrations, 110

Nation, quality magazine, 13
National Civic Council: as conservative Catholic organization: 127, 129; supported by Mannix, 128
National Liberation Front: attempts to circumvent law on collections for, 181–82; fund collection, 73–76, 150, 151–53, 157; fund collection controversy in Victoria, 176–77; public opinion on aid to, 117, 189–90; regulations against collections for, 180–82; Tasmanian academic opinion on aid to, 147
National Union of Australian University Students: appeals for conscription law liberalization, 183; Vietnamese position, 151, 154
Nationalism, Australian, 3, 170
New England, University of, student activist survey, 153
New South Wales, University of, setting for Vietnam Objectors Group, 150
News Weekly: conservative Catholic organ, 127; distribution in Victoria, 128
Nolan, B., Victorian executive membership, 86
North Vietnam: Australian attempts to visit, 179–80; public view of as threat, 117, 126; recipient of Australian aid, 73–76, 137
North-West Cape signal station: as electoral issue, 27; object of peace group protests, 103
Nuclear-free zone: as electoral issue, 27; support from peace groups, 103

Seamen's Union, *Boonaroo* and *Jeparit* disputes, 84–86
SEATO, 9; ALP attitude, 35–36; as electoral issue, 27
Sihanouk, Prince: approached by Victorian ALP, 97; sought as contact by NLF
fund collectors, 152
Simonds, Archbishop Justin, political position, 128
Sino-Japanese War, generates Australian protest, 102
Snedden, Billy, North Vietnamese travel position, 180
Society for Democratic Action: anticonscription activities, 156; antiestablishment outlook, 156; objectives, 150–51
South Australia censorship record, 177
South Africa: civil libertarian concern over racial policies, 172; as electoral issue,
28; Menzies' approach to Commonwealth membership, 25; object of Australian protests, 102, 103; object of Protestant protest, 123
Soviet Union, public view of as threat, 117
Spender, Sir Percy, as external affairs minister, 25
Student Guerrilla (Queensland) attack on establishment, 156
Students: partisan outlook, 159, 160; as political activists, 152–53; political outlooks, 154–55
Students for a Democratic Society: aid to Hanoi, 156; membership, 153; merger
plans, 157; objectives, 150–51; political outlooks, 155–57
Suez crisis, Menzies' role, 25
Sydney Mobilization Rally. *See* October Mobilization Rally
Sydney Morning Herald, grade of readership, 18
Sydney, University of: conscription and Vietnam student survey, 157–58; political
activist survey, 153; setting for Vietnam Objectors Group, 150

Tasmania, University of: conscription and Vietnam academic survey, 147–48;
conscription and Vietnam student survey, 158
Television: general characteristics, 14–15; public reaction to, 15
Thant, U: cited by peace groups, 108; peace appeal endorsed by academics, 146
Thomas, K. W., intention to visit North Vietnam, 179–80
Tomasetti, Glennis, anti-Vietnam gesture, 148
Trade: Asian, 10–11; Chinese, 68–69

United Nations: Australian role in forming, 8–9; Liberal Reform Group perception of role, 55–56; parliamentary attendance at, 21; proposed by ALP
for Vietnamese settlement, 48
United States: ALP views on alliance, 49–50; ALP views on need to prod in
Vietnam, 44–45; Australian fears of Asian disengagement, 168; L-CP views
on possible Asian disengagement, 166–67; L-CP view on urging to persevere
in Vietnam, 52; October Mobilization Rally members' views on as threat, 177
Universities: applications of conscription violation regulations, 188; applications
of National Forces Protection Act, 183–84; curricula, 17; enrollment, 17;
general characteristics, 142–45; objects of attacks, 175–77
University Vietnam Civil Relief Appeal, 145

Vatican Council, Australian role in, 128
Victoria: censorship record, 177; student protest activity reactions, 176–77
Vietnam: October Mobilization Rally members' views on unification, 117; recipient of Australian foreign aid, 44; voluntary aid to, 135–37, 139
Vietnam Action, organ of Vietnam Action Campaign, 106, 109
Vietnam Action Campaign: objectives, 106; origins, 107
Vietnam Aid Committee, 136

236 *Index*